Simms's Poems

Available from the Simms Initiatives and the University of South Carolina Press

The Army Correspondence of Colonel John Laurens, ed.
As Good as a Comedy
Beauchampe
Border Beagles
Carl Werner, an Imaginative Story, 2 vols.
The Cassique of Accabee
The Cassique of Kiawah
Castle Dismal
Charlemont
Charleston and Her Satirists, 2 vols.
The Charleston Book, ed.
Confession
Count Julian
The Damsel of Darien, 2 vols.
Donna Florida
Eutaw
Father Abbot
The Forayers
The Geography of South Carolina
The Golden Christmas
Guy Rivers
Helen Halsey
The History of South Carolina
Joscelyn
Katherine Walton
The Letters of William Gilmore Simms, Vol. 1
The Letters of William Gilmore Simms, Vol. 2
The Letters of William Gilmore Simms, Vol. 3
The Letters of William Gilmore Simms, Vol. 4
The Letters of William Gilmore Simms, Vol. 5
The Letters of William Gilmore Simms, Vol. 6 (exp. ed.)
The Life of Captain John Smith
The Life of Chevalier Bayard
The Life of Francis Marion
The Lily and the Totem
Marie de Berniere
Martin Faber and Other Tales, 2 vols.
Mellichampe
Michael Bonham
The Partisan
Pelayo, 2 vols.
Poems, Descriptive, Dramatic, Legendary, and Contemplative, 2 vols.
The Remains of Maynard Davis Richardson
Richard Hurdis, 2 vols.
Sack and Destruction of the City of Columbia
The Scout
Selections from the Letters and Speeches of the Hon. James H. Hammond, ed.
Simms's Poems Areytos
Slavery in America
South Carolina in the Revolutionary War
Southward Ho!
Stories and Tales
A Supplement to the Plays of William Shakespeare
Vasconselos
Views and Reviews in American Literature, History and Fiction, 2 vols.
Voltmeier
War Poetry of the South
The Wigwam and the Cabin
Woodcraft
The Yemassee

Simms's Poems

Areytos or Songs and Ballads of the South with Other Poems

William Gilmore Simms

Critical Introduction by Jason W. Johnson

With a Biographical Overview by David Moltke-Hansen

The University of South Carolina Press

Cloth original published by Redfield, 1860
Paperback published by the University of South Carolina Press
Columbia, South Carolina 29208

www.sc.edu/uscpress

Manufactured in the United States of America

22 21 20 19 18 17 16 15 14 13
10 9 8 7 6 5 4 3 2 1

ISBN 978-1-61117-262-1 (pbk)

Published in cooperation with the Simms Initiatives, a project of the University of South Carolina Libraries with the generous support of the Watson-Brown Foundation, and with additional funding by the John Govan Simms Endowment.

William Gilmore Simms: A Biographical Overview

David Moltke-Hansen

Introduction

Harper's Weekly put it succinctly in its July 2, 1870, issue: "In the death of Mr. Simms, on the 11th of June, at Charleston, the country has lost one more of its time-honored band of authors, and the South the most consistent and devoted of her literary sons" (qtd. In Butterworth and Kibler 125–26). Indeed no mid-nineteenth-century writer and editor did more than William Gilmore Simms to frame white southern self-identity and nationalism, shape southern historical consciousness, or foster the South's participation and recognition in the broader American literary culture. No southern writer enjoyed more contemporary esteem and attention, at least after Edgar Allan Poe moved north. Among American romancers (or writers of prose epics), only New Yorker James Fenimore Cooper was as successful by the 1840s. In those same years, Simms was the South's most influential editor of cultural journals. He also was the region's most prolific cultural journalist and poet, publishing an average of one book review and one poem per week for forty-five years.

Before his death Simms saw his national reputation fall along with the Confederacy he had vigorously supported and with the slave regime that many in the North had come to despise. Nevertheless reprints of most of the twenty titles in the selected edition of his works, first published between 1853 and 1860, appeared up until World War I. Thereafter only *The Yemassee*, an early romance about an Indian war in South Carolina, continued in print. The tide began to turn in the 1950s, when five volumes of Simms's letters appeared and a growing number of his works were issued in new editions. Publication in 1992 of the first literary biography, by John C. Guilds, and establishment of the William Gilmore Simms Society and the *Simms Review* the next year at once reflected and fostered this revived interest. Yet not until the 2011 launch of the digital Simms edition of the South Caroliniana Library of the University of South Carolina did scholars of southern, American, and nineteenth-century culture have the prospect of ready access to all of Simms's separately published works. With the University of South Carolina Press's cooperation, readers also will have access to sixty works in paperback editions by the end of 2014. Simms himself never saw nearly so many of his works in print at one time.

Clearly the decline in the critical standing of, and historical attention to, Simms and his oeuvre in the century after his death has reversed in the years since. The last three decades of the twentieth century saw more published on Simms than the previous hundred years (Butterworth and Kibler 126–200; MLA International). The last decade of the twentieth and first decade of the twenty-first centuries saw more dissertations and theses on him (forty-one) than had appeared in all the years before. This is not to say that Simms is yet given the attention directed to some of his contemporaries. For the first decade of the twenty-first century, the Modern Language Association International Bibliography lists roughly four times as many scholarly publications on James Fenimore Cooper, more than ten times as many on Nathaniel Hawthorne, and sixteen times as many on Edgar Allan Poe. Not surprisingly, therefore, Simms is not yet included in most anthologies of American literature, although he is a subject or a source in an expanding and ever more diverse body of scholarship.

To prepare to read Simms, it is important to see his writings in multiple contexts. He rarely wrote about himself outside of his more personal poems and his letters (some fifteen hundred of the many thousands of which survive). Yet he systematically drew on his background, personal experience, and relationships in his work. He also shaped that work through a progressively developed poetics and philosophy of life, history, and art. He did so in the context of his very broad reading of both contemporary and earlier Western literature and in the midst of multiple professional engagements and responsibilities. The richness and variety of these writings and involvements make Simms a key figure for future understanding of the literary culture, issues, and networks in mid-nineteenth-century America.

Background

Simms's family history reflected the dynamics that fueled the spread southward and westward of the populations, plantation economy, and society of the South Atlantic states. Simms's ancestry also reflected the Scots-Irish and English roots of what became identified as southern culture by the 1830s, a generation after the end of most immigration to the region. Two of Simms's grandparents, William and Elisabeth Sims, were Scots-Irish and migrated to South Carolina from Ulster. One, John Singleton, was an American-born son of putatively English immigrants, who had come to South Carolina from Virginia. The fourth, Jane Miller, was daughter of two Scots-Irish and Irish descended people—John Miller, of North and then South Carolina, and Jane Ross. Ross's family also migrated to South Carolina from western Virginia, where members lived cheek by jowl with other Scots-Irish families, who migrated to the Carolinas (White, *Ross*). Simms's father and Uncle James migrated in 1808 from Charleston to Tennessee, then to Mississippi. This was after the bankruptcy of the elder William's business and the deaths of his wife and their other two sons. Following the last of these losses, the elder Simms's hair turned white in a week. To his anguished eyes, Charleston appeared "a place of tombs" (qtd. in Guilds 6, 12).

For the son, however, Charleston was home—so much so that he refused to leave his maternal grandmother and move to Mississippi when his uncle came to get him in 1816. Then the fifth largest and by far the wealthiest city, as well as one of the greatest ports, in America, Charleston was at the peak of its influence (Moltke-Hansen, "Expansion" 25–31; Rogers). Cotton culture on the sea islands to the south, begun in 1790, and rice culture in impounded lowcountry tidal marshes meant that the port was filled not only with sailors of many lands and languages, but also with enslaved people of many African and Creole cultures and speech ways (slaves continued to be imported legally in large numbers until 1808). This street life made vivid the transnational nature of plantation agriculture and the fact that the developing region's dramatically expanding borders "were not just geographic; they also were human, historical, and intellectual" (Moltke-Hansen, "Southern" 19).

Even more important for the future author, the expanding region's borders and nature were taking imaginative shape. The West of the senior William Gilmore Simms and the first Creek War in which he fought, the Revolutionary War of the young Simms's maternal grandfather, the backcountry of many related Scots-Irish settlers, all these became grist for a lonely, energetic boy, who spent as much time with books as he could (Simms, *Letters* 1:161). The possibilities of such settings, incidents, and characters were not confined to history alone. Simms reported that he "used to glow and shiver in turn over 'The Pilgrim's Progress,'" while "Moses' adventures in 'The Vicar of Wakefield' threw [him] into paroxysms of laughter" (Hayne 261–62). Sir Walter Scott's Border and medieval romances and James Fenimore Cooper's Leatherstocking tales also deeply colored his imagination (Simms, *Views* 1:248, and Moltke-Hansen, "Southern" 6–15). As affecting were the ghost stories and Revolutionary War tales of his grandmother and the verses sent, and tales told, by his father.

These diverse tales became reasons to explore—in books, but also on the ground. As a boy, Simms ranged through the city and along the banks of the Ashley River, which fed into Charleston Harbor. He did so in search of scenes of colonial and Revolutionary battles and incidents (*Letters* 1:lxii). He first heard his uncle's and father's many Irish and frontier stories when they visited in Charleston in 1816 and 1818, respectively. He heard more on his trips to Mississippi during the winter of 1824 through the spring of 1825 and again in 1826. The first trip took him through Georgia and Alabama, where he saw elements of the Creek and Cherokee nations. At the time, Simms later reported, he was a boy "cumbered with fragmentary materials of thought, . . . choked by the tangled vines of erroneous speculation, and haunted by passions, which, like so many wolves, lurked, in ready waiting, for their unsuspecting prey" (*Social* 6). When he first got to Mississippi, traveling partly by stage, partly by riverboat, and partly by horse, Simms learned that his father had just come back from "a trip of three hundred miles into the heart of the Indian country" (Trent 15). Later father and son "rode together on horseback to various settlements on the frontier of Alabama and Mississippi" (Guilds 10–11, 17–18). Simms recalled as well "having traveled 150 miles beyond the Mississippi" (Shillingsburg, "Literary Grist" 120). The next year he returned to the Southwest by ship. "During this [second] trip he carried a 'note book.'" There he jotted episodes, encounters, stories heard, characters seen, and descriptions of the landscapes unfolding around him. He also wrote "at least sixteen poems" (Kibler, "First"; Shillingsburg, "Literary Grist" 123).

Simms took a third western trip five years later, writing letters back to the newspaper that by then he was editing (*Letters* 1:10–38). Together these three trips provided materials for his writings over more than forty years. "The first . . . produced mainly short fiction; the second inspired much poetry; . . . the first and third . . . yielded three novels written in the 1830s" (Shillingsburg, "Literary Grist" 119). This was, in part, because of the trips' timing. Sixteen years after the first trip, Simms told students at the University of Alabama that in the interval their world had changed from a howling wilderness into a place of growing civilization (Simms, *Social* 5–6). Had he not gone when he did, he would have been too late to see the frontier. Later travels took him many other places and also provided much grist for his writing. Never again, however, did he experience the frontier firsthand. Furthermore, on these later trips Simms was a practiced professional writer, no longer that boy haunted by passions.

Personal Life

After the ten-year-old boy's momentous refusal to leave Charleston, his grandmother sent Simms for two years to the grammar school taught on the campus and by the faculty of the nearly moribund College of Charleston. By then he already was "versifying the events of the war [of 1812]," just concluded, publishing "doggerel" in the local papers, and learning to read in several languages (*Letters* 1:285). His trip west a decade later helped him decide to pursue both literature and a career in law, but back in Charleston—this despite his father's urging that he stay in Mississippi. Upon his return home, he began to read law and also launched a literary weekly, the *Album*, which ran for a year. He became engaged as well to Anna Malcolm Giles, daughter of a grocer and former state coroner.

A year later the young couple married. This was six months before Simms was admitted to the South Carolina bar, on his twenty-first birthday, not long before he was appointed as a city magistrate. Although living up the Ashley River in the more healthful, less expensive village of Summerville, Simms kept a law office in the city. Shortly after using his maternal inheritance to buy the *City Gazette* at the end of 1829 and moving down to Charleston Neck, just north of the city limits where he had lived as a boy, Simms lost both his father and his maternal grandmother. He also found himself attacked because of his Unionist stance in the Nullification crisis resulting from South Carolina's rejection of a federal tariff. Then, in early 1832, Simms's wife died. Soon after, he took his four-year-old daughter back to Summerville to live and determined to sell his newspaper and leave the state for a literary life in the North.

Fueling his ambition was the correspondence Simms had begun several years earlier with an accountant whom he had published in his *City Gazette* but not yet met—Scots immigrant James Lawson. At the time Lawson, seven years Simms's senior, edited a New York City newspaper and, in addition to writing plays and poetry, was a friend (and, later, informal literary agent) to a wide circle (McHaney, "An Early"). Simms's trip north in the summer of 1832 saw the two begin a lifelong friendship, cemented as they squired ladies about and interacted with Lawson's literary circle. In subsequent years Simms multiplied the number of his friendships, in both the North and the South, making them in some measure a replacement for the family that he had lost. Lawson remained the closest of his northern friends, while James Henry Hammond, a future governor and U.S. senator, became his closest friend in South Carolina.

Late in 1833, after his Summerville house burned, Simms wrote Lawson to say that he was enamored of "a certain fair one" (*Letters* 1:73). Seventeen-year-old Chevillette Eliza Roach was the daughter of "a literary-minded aristocrat of English descent" with two plantations on the banks of the Edisto River in Barnwell District (later County) (Guilds 70). The courtship was protracted, as Simms felt it necessary first to clear debts that friends had bought up on his behalf. He also was determined "to marry no woman" before he was "perfectly independent of her resources, and her friends" (*Letters* 1:78). Therefore he did not propose until the spring of 1836. The nuptials took place seven months later, and as a result, Simms came to call the four thousand acres of Woodlands Plantation, with its seventy slaves, home. It was twenty years, however, before he took over management of the plantation and, then, only in the wake of his father-in-law's final sickness and death. Five years after that, he lost his wife, the mother of fourteen of his fifteen children. Nine of the children Chevillette bore him had already died, devastating Simms repeatedly. Five were still living (three sons and two daughters), as was Simms's daughter by his first marriage, who helped raise the youngest of her siblings. Those remaining children—even Gilly, who fought in the Confederate army—all outlived their father. Gilly and a brother-in-law ran Woodlands after the war, when Simms, though dying of cancer, was earning what he could by writing again for publications in the North and editing one or another South Carolina newspaper.

Career

The trip north in 1832 did not result in Simms moving there. Except during the Civil War, however, he returned almost every year. This was because the contacts he made, and the exposure to literary culture that he enjoyed, helped him define his future as an author. Earlier he had written fiction and criticism as well as journalism, filling the pages of several short-lived cultural journals and his newspaper, but between the ages of nine and twenty-six Simms had focused his literary efforts primarily on poetry. Beginning with his first book of verse in 1825, he had published five small volumes in Charleston. A couple had received positive notice in New York, and in the fall of 1832, J. & J. Harper issued the sixth anonymously from there, *Atalantis: A Story of the Sea.* Coming back the following summer, Simms had in hand for the Harpers a gothic novella, *Martin Faber,* and after his return south, he also would send the manuscript of his first two-volume border romance, *Guy Rivers: A Tale of Georgia.*

The reception of these and the romances and short stories that followed quickly made Simms one of the nation's most successful fictionists. He continued to issue poetry as well—roughly a collection every three years over the thirty-seven years that he worked as a professional author. But this output was dwarfed by the fiction—on average a title every year (counting several serialized works but not counting the many revised editions). Then there were the two dozen separately published orations, histories, and biographies as well as edited collections of documents and dramas and a geography of South Carolina. Add to these the revised editions and the further printings and issues of his own works and it appears that Simms saw a title coming off the presses at the rate of one every three months or so. Making that figure all the more astounding is the fact that, during more than a dozen of those years (the early-to-mid 1840s, the late 1840s-to-early 1850s, and the mid-to-late 1860s), he also was editing a cultural journal or newspaper. Furthermore he contributed reams of reviews and poems, hundreds of op-ed pieces and columns, and dozens of short stories and public addresses, which were never collected and published in volume form.

His career mapped an arc. It ascended meteorically in the 1830s and peaked in the early-to-mid 1840s, before beginning to descend. One reason was the popularity of the historical fiction that Simms began to write. When he left behind the law, his first newspaper, and the Nullification controversy, as well as his sadness, historical fiction was all the rage. Sir Walter Scott had fueled the craze, beginning with the publication of his first Border romance in 1814. He died in September 1832. Seventeen years Simms's senior, James Fenimore Cooper, the closest America had to a Scott at the time, was at the peak of his reputation and success, having started publishing his romances in 1820. Thus the way had been prepared for a writer of Simms's historical imagination and preoccupations. Within five years of his first trip north, moreover, Lawson's (and now his) circle became loosely affiliated with a nationalistic and Democratic group, self-styled Young America, this after Young Italy and similar ethnic, nationalist, European, cultural and political movements (Moltke-Hansen, "Southern"). Edgar Allan Poe and other members gave Simms's first fictions positive, if not uncritical, attention.

By the end of the 1830s, paradoxically, Simms, like Cooper, found his success attracting unauthorized editions of his works because Britain and America did not have an international copyright agreement. Further, in the wake of the panic of 1837, Americans bought fewer books. Simms's response was to diversify his portfolio. He turned to biography and history, including his hugely successful *Life of Francis Marion* (1844). He also returned to the editor's chair, overseeing one and then another cultural journal. These were unlike the ones he had edited in the 1820s: they included contributions by numerous authors, not just those from Charleston, but from the region and also the North. The ambition motivating the journals was to connect and promote Charleston intellectually. Consequently the journals more closely resembled metropolitan quarterly reviews in their offerings.

The mid-1840s saw Simms involved in politics, even serving a term in the South Carolina legislature. By the middle of the Mexican-American War in 1847, he had concluded that the South needed to become an independent nation. Thereafter, although he maintained ties with many in the Young America circle, he no longer promoted his writings as fostering Americanism in literature (*Views*). Instead he increasingly emphasized the ways in which his three romance series—the colonial, the Revolutionary, and the border—were making tangible and meaningful the origins and development of the future southern nation and the sad but inevitable consequences for Native Americans (Watson, *From Nationalism*; compare Nakamura).

Sectional politics colored more and more of Simms's perceptions, speeches, and private communications. The rising tide of abolitionism had him aghast. It also fed his growing sense that his position in American letters was slipping. He returned to editing, and his poetry, which was more often explicitly about the South, became increasingly patriotic in tone. Although his first biographer, William Peterfield Trent, insisted that Simms's declining standing reflected the change in literary fashion from historical romances to realistic novels, Simms in fact wrote more and more as a social realist in the 1850s (Wimsatt, "Realism").

The Civil War consumed Simms. As he wrote Lawson, "Literature, especially poetry, is effectually overwhelmed by the drums, & the cavalry, and the shouting" (*Letters* 4:369–70). He did manage to editorialize often and to rework and finish things long on his desk, including poems, a novel, and a dramatic treatment of Benedict Arnold, the northern traitor in the Revolutionary War. Then, in the wake of the Confederacy's loss and the failure of his vision for the South, he found himself recording the loss in a new newspaper, dealing with the trauma in his poetry, and becoming more existential and psychological in his fictional treatments. Simms's old New York friends tried to help. He did edit and see through publication a volume of Confederate war poetry. Yet it is a measure of his reduced stature that the several new romances he published appeared only in serial form. In part this may have been because he was in a sense competing with himself. Publishers were beginning to reprint volumes out of the selected edition of his writings. Many of Simms's works were available in book form, just not new works.

Associations

As the *Letters* testify, Simms had complex, overlapping networks of friends and colleagues. As a boy and young man, he received the friendship, patronage, and commendation of a variety of well-placed people in Charleston, including Charles Rivers Carroll. It was Carroll with whom he read law, to whom he dedicated his first romance, and after whom he named a son. Both men were Unionists during the Nullification controversy. So were Hugh Swinton Legare (later U.S. attorney general) and the considerably older William Drayton, as well as lawyer and editor Richard Yeadon and Greenville, South Carolina, newspaper editor Benjamin Franklin Perry. Also considerably older was James Wright Simmons, who had joined with Simms to launch the *Southern Literary Gazette* in 1828, when Simms was twenty-two. Through him Simms had direct contact with such British literary figures as Leigh Hunt and Byron (Kibler, *Poetry* 15).

The next group of influential friends and collaborators that Simms acquired were members of the Lawson circle and included such figures as Edwin

Forrest, the Shakespearean actor, and Evert Duyckinck, who published several of Simms's volumes in Wiley and Putnam's series Library of American Books, which he edited. Among the many others were poets and editors William Cullen Bryant and Fitz-Greene Halleck. Simms also made nonliterary friends in New York and Philadelphia, such as John Jacob Bockee and William Hawkins Ferris, the cashier at the U.S. Treasury office in New York who, after the war, helped Simms, Henry Timrod (poet laureate of the Confederacy), and others.

As a Barnwell planter, Simms met a widening circle of South Carolina's leaders and literati. For instance his acquaintance with James Henry Hammond began in the late 1830s and deepened into a friendship in the early 1840s. It was in the early 1840s, too, when he again was editing cultural journals, that Simms became friends with many southern writers. He regarded several of them, including Virginians George Frederick Holmes, Edmund Ruffin, and Nathaniel Beverley Tucker as members, together with Hammond and himself, in a "sacred circle." Uniting the circle were members' devotion to the South and a shared sense of the marginal status and critical importance of the life of the mind in a largely rural and unintellectual region (Faust, *Sacred*). Others of Simms's wide connections in the region did not interact as much with each other, but Simms long corresponded with Maryland novelist and lawyer John Pendleton Kennedy, Irish-born Georgia poet Richard Henry Wilde, Alabama lawyer and writer Alexander Beaufort Meek, and Louisiana historian and assistant attorney general Charles Gayarré, among others. By the 1850s, when Simms once more returned to editing a cultural journal, many of the writers whom he recruited were members of a younger generation. Poets Paul Hamilton Hayne and Henry Timrod were two. Often they and a half dozen others of Simms's and their generations met in John Russell's Charleston Book Shop and adjourned to dinner at Simms's Smith Street home, "dubbed 'The Wigwam'" (*Letters* 1:cxxxvi). Shortly before his death fifteen or so years later, Simms wrote Hayne, "I am rapidly passing from the stage, where you young men are to succeed me" (*Letters* 5:287).

Thought

The welter of Simms's works disguises unities and dynamics of the thought underlying them. From early on Simms was convinced that art ennobles or transforms, as well as gives voice to individuals and societies; therefore it must be cultivated assiduously. Without the potential for high artistic attainment, he insisted, societies are not ready for the independence and regard of free peoples. This is where Simms the historian joined Simms the poet. Societies develop, he argued (using the stadialism of the Scottish historical school), from imitation through self-assertion to achievement and also from savagery through strife to settled agricultural communities and, ultimately, to a hierarchical civilization supporting a rich artistic life. It was the job of the artist to help envision the goal, inspire the pursuit, and inform the process. That process was at once progressive and dialectical. Order, without dynamism, stifled development, as did the obverse—the dominance by ungoverned impulses or uncontrolled license. This was true in the individual, but also in societies as a whole. War was necessary for civilization, but its success was measured in the securities of the home, the center of cultural production and reproduction.

Whether in the public or in the domestic arena, "the true governor, as [Thomas] Carlyle call[ed] him—the king man—" guided rather than impeded the forces of change and progress (Simms, "Guizot's" 122). There were few such men with the capacity to lead. The same was true of nations. Neither all people nor all peoples were equal in either capacity or attainment. That was why Native Americans were overrun and Africans had been enslaved by European peoples in the New World. Indeed, Simms argued, "slavery in all ages has been found the greatest and most admirable agent of Civilization," giving education and examples to less evolved peoples (*Letters* 3:174). The degree to which a people had evolved mattered. That was why, he held, Americans had won independence from the most powerful empire in the world. They had done so through their Revolution, led by an elite that felt correctly its time had come (Simms, "Ellet's" 328). By mid-1847 that also was Simms's judgment for the South: the region had evolved enough to become independent (*Letters* 2:332). The hope inspired and then failed him and the people he sought to lead.

While not all men could rise to the highest rank, they all had the same responsibility at home. There the father was patriarch, protector, and head, while the mother was nurturer, moral instructor, and heart. There, too, children's characters and minds were formed by age twelve ("Ellet's"). Children's upbringing was critical to citizenship, and it was through her sons and the support of her husband, father, and brothers that a woman shaped the public sphere. The culture and character instilled in the child expressed and informed not just the household, but the larger society—the people.

"The history of peoples and their embodiments in institutions, states, and artistic productions—these were the great subjects" in Simms's view (Moltke-Hansen, "Southern" 120). Yet "poets were the only class of philosophers who had recognized" this until his own day, when at last "we now read human histories. We now ask after the affections as well as the ceremonies of society" ("Ellet's" 319–20). Peoples or races—that is, ethnic groups—were not unchanging any more than were their politics and their cultures. They either advanced or were overrun by history. Further, new peoples emerged, and old identities were submerged. The Spanish conquistadors were the creation of centuries of conflict with the Moors: their motivation was the glory of conquest, not the routine of trade or the plow. On the other hand, the English settlements in North America reflected the impulse to transform the wilderness into verdant farms and build society (*Views* 64, 178–85; *Social* 8). The same impulse drove Americans westward in Simms's own day and gave Americans their Manifest Destiny.

To explore these facts of the South's settlement and its place in international conflicts, Simms wrote all together, between 1833 and 1863, two romances set in eighth-century Spain, two set during the Spanish exploration and conquest of the Americas and two during the later English colonization of South Carolina, seven set during the American Revolution, and—depending on how one counts—perhaps eight set on the borders of the nineteenth-century South. After the war he published one more Revolutionary romance and two more that, like it, were set beyond the boundaries of civilization. He also left two unfinished romances, also set beyond society's normal reach. These late works, however, no longer had as their framing justification the cultivation of the South's future and civilization.

White southerners had their independence foreclosed by the war. In his last works, therefore, Simms found himself exploring the psychological, philosophical, and historical impulses that led to the Confederacy's demise and what, in the aftermath, it meant to be a good man and to build for the future, however impoverished. On the first score, he argued that the impulse to idealism behind abolitionism ignored historical realities, becoming inhuman in its consequences. On the latter score, he affirmed responsibility for one's dependents and the virtues of stoicism, as well as a continued commitment to the beauty and truth of art and the impulses to the cultivated life and fields. Therefore, in the face of the burning of his Woodlands home and library in February 1865—during Sherman's march and in the midst of desperate circumstances—he insisted that home, or the ideals and past characterizing its potential, still was at the center of true civilization, but only if elevated by art (*Sense* 8, 17). It was wrong to measure civilization by the getting, spending, and mad dashing, or material progress and utilitarianism, characteristic of both a capitalistic North and also many southerners. These traits he often had attacked even before the war, insisting that "the work of the Imagination, which is the Genius of a race, is only begun when its material progress is supposed to be complete" (*Poetry* 12).

Writings

Simms expressed many of his ideas most personally in letters and most cogently in essays, speeches, and occasional introductions to his books. But he illustrated them most fully in his fiction and poetry. By the time he arrived in New

York in 1832, he had formed many of the core ideals and beliefs that would shape his work. His application of them, however, modified his understanding over time. Growing as a writer and growing in knowledge and experience, he also grew as a thinker.

In his hierarchy of values, poetry came first. It was a prophetic calling as well as evocative of the deeply felt (or, sometimes, the fleeting) and thus testimony to the perdurance and transcendence of the beautiful and the human spirit. Yet, as Simms often ruefully reflected, prose spoke to many more people. That was a principal reason why he turned to writing prose epics or romances. He gave his most concerted consideration of poetry's value and roles in three lectures in Charleston in 1854. Over the prior three years he had given portions of them in Augusta, Georgia, Washington, D.C., and Richmond and Petersburg, Virginia. Entitled *Poetry and the Practical,* they did not see print until 1996, as Simms never found the time to expand them as he wanted. On the other hand, his last address on the same themes, *The Sense of the Beautiful,* was issued soon after he delivered it, also in Charleston.

Many of his important reviews have not yet been gathered, but Simms collected some in 1845–46, and *Views and Reviews in American Literature, History and Fiction* came out in 1846 and 1847 in two "series." Beginning with a consideration of "Americanism" in literature, the first series explored the themes and periods of American history for treatment by the novelist. Simms argued there, and in forewords to several of his romances, that fiction rendered the past more truthfully, interestingly, and tellingly than histories and biographies could because fiction—like poetry—required imagination to look beyond what is not known or expressed. The second series examined additional American writers and what distinguished them, for instance, in their humor.

Despite their early success, Simms's romances, novellas, and stories provoked mixed reviews. Poe eventually concluded that Simms had become "the best novelist which this country has, on the whole, produced" but also insisted that "he should never have written 'The Partisan,' nor 'The Yemassee.'" This was in a review of *Confession.* That novel, like the gothic *Martin Faber,* demonstrated, Poe contended, that Simms's "genius [did] not lie in the outward so much as in the inner world." Yet he nevertheless wrote of Simms's short-story collection *The Wigwam and the Cabin* that "in invention, in vigor, in movement, in the power of exciting interest, and in the artistical management of his themes, he has surpassed, we think, any of his countrymen." Other critics, especially in the genteel and Whiggish Knickerbocker circle, joined Poe in condemning what they considered to be the excessively graphic and vulgar qualities of many characters and scenes, and Simms's prolixity and sententiousness, in his romances (Butterworth and Kibler 64, 50).

The violent realism and earthiness of the romances did not result in realistic novels. Although Simms received early praise for his characterizations (particularly of women), he used the romance formula, with its stereotypic heroes and heroines, predictable themes, and conventional polarities. People were on quests or had lost their way or were fighting long odds or were carrying forward the banner of (and modeling) civilization or were mired in the slough of despond or were resisting all the claims of civilized society and behavior or were pursuing love interests. Deceitfulness, selfishness, and greed opposed honor, high-mindedness, and honesty against the backdrop of the South's development from the earliest days of Spanish exploration to the westward movement in Simms's own youth.

It was only gradually that Simms married the psychological acuity of some of his portraits of the interior struggles of his gothic characters and fiction to the historical romance. Helping him think through how to do so were the biographies he wrote in the mid-1840s, but also the incidents on which he focused particular fictions, such as the murder in *Beauchampe; or, The Kentucky Tragedy* (1842). However incomplete the blending of realism and romanticism or of stereotypical and socially individuated renderings through the 1840s, by the 1850s Simms fundamentally had made the transition to social realism in such works as *Woodcraft* and *The Cassique of Kiawah.* Indeed some scholars have considered *Woodcraft* the first realistic novel in America (Bakker; Wimsatt, "Realism").

In some sense disguising the transition is the fact that Simms also increasingly wrote as a humorist and, in so doing, often rendered his late narratives fabulistically, when not writing social comedy or stories of manners. This dimension of Simms's work was largely hidden, however, until the 1974 publication of *Stories and Tales,* volume 5 in the Centennial Simms edition. There, for the first time, readers had access in print to "Bald-Head Bill Bauldy." There, too, for the first time one could read together that story, "Legend of the Hunter's Camp," and "How Sharp Snaffles Got His Capital and Wife," which was published posthumously in *Harper's Magazine* in October 1870. These and other stories and tales made it clear that Simms was a fecund contributor to southern and American humor.

Humor let Simms take up issues that he could not otherwise address in print and still expect to be well received. He did so both during and after the war. The war also pushed Simms past the emerging fashion of social realism. Having destroyed the familiar, the preoccupation of much realistic fiction, the war made the liminal central (Shillingsburg, "Cub"). While his romances and tales had often explored life on the edge or in extreme circumstances, whether in war or on the frontier or on the verge of madness or in fanciful realms, it had done so against a backdrop of, and with the goal of affirming, social norms and development. In the war's wake that goal seemed absurd. Mythologized memories of a healthy past might nurture a sense of the beautiful but could not help one deal with the present. Thus Simms's conclusion, in a March 1869 letter to Paul Hamilton Hayne: "Let us bury the Past lest it buries us!" (*Letters* 5:214). Fifteen months later he lay dead in the 13 Society Street, Charleston, home of his oldest daughter, with the shell holes in the walls of the bedroom he had shared with several children.

Posthumous Reputation

The twenty years after Simms's death saw him often respectfully treated, first in obituaries, later in memoirs and columns, and also in literary dictionaries and encyclopedias. Yet Charles Richardson's 1887 *American Literature: 1607–1885* proved a harbinger of a shift: Simms, Richardson observed, was "more respected than read," having "won considerable note because he was so sectional" and then having "lost it because he was not sectional enough," although he showed "silly contempt for his Northern betters" (qtd. in Butterworth and Kibler 130). Five years later Trent's biography of Simms appeared. It was the first full-length, scholarly treatment. Its central thesis was that Simms's environment frustrated his abilities: the South was inimical to art and the life of the mind, and Charleston high society's hauteur marginalized Simms despite his talent and character. Trent's second thesis was that Simms's commitment to the romance and his romanticism meant that his works had become largely unreadable in an age of literary realism. Although Vernon Parrington and later scholars recognized Simms's impulses to realism, the two theses long shaped Simms criticism and, indeed, also helped frame study of antebellum southern literature and intellectual life (Parrington 119–30).

A Virginian born in 1862, Trent was a progressive who wanted a New South radically different from the old. He saw his pioneering study of Simms as an opportunity to criticize what the Civil War had made untenable. From his perspective the Old South was not the expanding and rapidly developing environment, with a deep history, that Simms portrayed, but a place where slavery stultified and stunted the growth and progress displayed by the North. Southern—especially South Carolinian—writers occasionally challenged Trent's agenda and conclusions, but those critiques had little impact. Not until after publication of the Simms letters in the 1950s did scholars begin to consider the author in the historical and contemporary contexts that he had rendered in his poetry and fiction. And not until after the centennial of his death did a growing number of scholars, having concluded that southern intellectual history was not an oxymoron, begin to study in detail the culture in which Simms participated and to which he contributed so voluminously and variously.

Some of these scholars also have had agendas: they have wanted to see Simms included in the American literary canon, for instance, or they have wanted to defend the heritage that in their view Trent, and so many others, inappropriately belittled or ignorantly dismissed. More fruitfully, other scholars have begun to reframe the understanding of nineteenth-century American intellectual life by stripping away preconceptions that characterized earlier evaluations of Simms and his contemporaries. They are closely examining the historical record and transatlantic and other contemporary contexts and developments in the process. Although the pursuit of canonical status in a post-canonical age seems quixotic at this point, the explosion of the canon is leading to more varied fare being offered and may, therefore, mean that Simms, once his work is widely available, will be more often anthologized as well as studied. Defensiveness about Simms and the antebellum South may warm the hearts of like-minded people, just as critics of the Old South have been encouraged by shared presuppositions and disdain. Yet dueling cultural ideologies do not advance comity and may only reinforce mutual incomprehensions. Continued, deep research in original sources and the theoretical reframing that Atlantic history, the history of the book, and other perspectives offer—these approaches promise most for further study of Simms, his works, and his world.

Works Cited

For amplified readings by and on Simms and on his world, go to http://simms.library.sc.edu/bibliography.php.

Bakker, Jan. "Simms on the Literary Frontier; or, So Long Miss Ravenel and Hello Captain Porgy: *Woodcraft* Is the First 'Realistic' Novel in America." In *William Gilmore Simms and the American Frontier,* edited by John Caldwell Guilds and Caroline Collins, 64–78. Athens: University of Georgia Press, 1997.

Butterworth, Keen, and James E. Kibler Jr. *William Gilmore Simms: A Definitive Guide.* Boston: G. K. Hall, 1980.

Faust, Drew Gilpin. *A Sacred Circle: The Dilemma of the Intellectual in the Old South, 1840–1860.* Baltimore: Johns Hopkins University Press, 1977.

Guilds, John C. *Simms: A Literary Life.* Fayetteville: University of Arkansas Press, 1992.

Hayne, Paul Hamilton. "Ante-Bellum Charleston." *Southern Bivouac* 1 (October 1885): 257–68.

Kibler, James E. "The First Simms Letters: 'Letters from the West' (1826)." *Southern Literary Journal* 19 (Spring 1987): 81–91.

———. *The Poetry of William Gilmore Simms: An Introduction and Bibliography.* Columbia: Southern Studies Program, University of South Carolina, 1979.

McHaney, Thomas L. "An Early 19th-Century Literary Agent: James Lawson of New York." *Publications of the Bibliographical Society of America* 64 (Spring 1970): 177–92.

Moltke-Hansen, David. "The Expansion of Intellectual Life: A Prospectus." In *Intellectual Life in Antebellum Charleston,* edited by Michael O'Brien and David Moltke-Hansen, 3–44. Knoxville: University of Tennessee Press, 1986.

———. "Southern Literary Horizons in Young America: Imaginative Development of a Regional Geography." *Studies in the Literary Imagination* 42, no. 1 (2009): 1–31.

Nakamura, Masahiro. *Visions of Order in William Gilmore Simms: Southern Conservatism and the Other American Romance.* Columbia: University of South Carolina Press, 2009.

Parrington, Vernon L. *The Romantic Revolution in America, 1800–1860.* Vol. 2 of *Main Currents in American Thought.* New York: Harcourt, Brace and Company, 1927.

Rogers, George C., Jr. *Charleston in the Age of the Pinckneys.* Columbia: University South Carolina Press, 1980.

Shillingsburg, Miriam J. "The Cub of the Panther: A New Frontier." In *William Gilmore Simms and the American Frontier,* edited by John Caldwell Guilds and Caroline Collins, 221–36. Athens: University of Georgia Press, 1997.

———. "Literary Grist: Simms's Trips to Mississippi." *Southern Quarterly* 41, no. 2 (2003): 119–34.

Simms, William Gilmore. *Atalantis: A Story of the Sea: In Three Parts.* New York: J. & J. Harper, 1832.

———. *Beauchampe; or, The Kentucky Tragedy.* 2 vols. Philadelphia: Lea and Blanchard, 1842.

———. *The Cassique of Kiawah: A Colonial Romance.* New York: Redfield, 1859.

———. *Confession; or, The Blind Heart. A Domestic Story.* 2 vols. Philadelphia: Lea and Blanchard, 1841.

———. "Ellet's 'Women of the Revolution.'" *Southern Quarterly Review,* n.s. 1 (July 1850): 314–54.

———. "Guizot's Democracy in France." *Southern Quarterly Review* 15, no.29 (1849): 114–65.

———. *Guy Rivers: A Tale of Georgia.* 2 vols. New York: Harper & Brothers, 1834.

———. *The Letters of William Gilmore Simms.* Edited by Mary C. Simms Oliphant, Alfred Taylor Odell, and T. C. Duncan. 6 vols. Columbia: University of South Carolina Press, 1952–82.

———. *The Life of Francis Marion.* New York: Henry G. Langley, 1844.

———. *Martin Faber, the Story of a Criminal; and Other Tales.* 2 vols. New York: Harper & Brothers, 1837.

———. *Poetry and the Practical.* Edited by James E. Kibler. Fayetteville: University of Arkansas Press, 1996.

———. *The Sense of the Beautiful: An Address . . . before the Charleston County Agricultural and Horticultural Association, May 3, 1870.* Charleston: Charleston County Agricultural and Horticultural Association, 1870.

———. *The Social Principle: The Source of National Permanence. An Oration, Delivered before the Erosophic Society of the University of Alabama . . . December 13, 1842*. Tuscaloosa: Erosophic Society, University of Alabama, 1843.
———. *Stories and Tales*. Vol. 5 of *The Writings of William Gilmore Simms*. Centennial edition; introductions, explanatory notes, and texts established by John Caldwell Guilds. Columbia: University of South Carolina Press, 1974.
———. *Views and Reviews in American Literature, History and Fiction*. 2 vols. New York: Wiley and Putnam, 1845 (1846).
———. *The Wigwam and the Cabin*. 2 vols. New York: Wiley and Putnam, 1845–46.
———. *Woodcraft, or Hawks about the Dovecote: A Story of the South, at the Close of the Revolution*. New York: Redfield, 1854.
Trent, William Peterfield. *William Gilmore Simms*. Boston: Houghton, Mifflin, 1892.
Wakelyn, Jon L. *The Politics of a Literary Man: William Gilmore Simms*. Westport, Conn.: Greenwood Press, 1973.
Watson, Charles S. *From Nationalism to Secessionism: The Changing Fiction of William Gilmore Simms*. Westport, Conn.: Greenwood Press, 1993.
White, William B., Jr. *The Ross-Chesnut-Sutton Family of South Carolina*. Franklin, N.C.: Privately printed, 2002.
Wimsatt, Mary Ann. "Realism and Romance in Simms's Midcentury Fiction." *Southern Literary Journal* 12, no. 2 (1980): 29–48.

Critical Introduction

SIMMS'S POEMS: AREYTOS OR SONGS AND BALLADS OF THE SOUTH WITH OTHER POEMS

Jason W. Johnson

William Gilmore Simms once referred to *Simms's Poems: Areytos or Songs and Ballads of the South with Other Poems* (1860) as "a volume containing a selection from my fugitive pieces, song & sonnet, the growings of thirty years" (*Letters* 4: 193). His description is appropriate. The 416 page volume – second in length only to the 700-plus page *Poems: Descriptive, Dramatic, Legendary, and Contemplative* (1853) – is a selection of poems, many of which had been published in newspapers and literary journals but never in a collection. These "growings of thirty years" come from every period, and represent well the arc of Simms's career, from the fledgling pieces of a novice to the more nuanced and sophisticated experiments of a wiser and more world-weary poet.

Simms framed these "fugitive pieces" with a title he had used once before, *Areytos; or, Songs of the South.* Though these two volumes bear the same title, the 1860 collection should not be mistaken for merely a second edition of the 1846 collection. More than a few poems from the 1846 volume appear in the 1860 collection (e.g., "My Forest Harp" and "Maid of Congaree"), but many others do not. "The Texian Hunter" and "The Land of the Pine," for example, were published in the first *Areytos* and in the second volume of *Poems*; neither was selected for the 1860 *Areytos*. Presumably, Simms used the title again not to indicate definitely a second edition but because a number of poems in the 1860 volume were "songs of the South." While these aspects of the collection problematize a view of it as simply a second edition, one could argue that it is a continuation of a project begun almost fifteen years earlier, a sequel meant to be read, or at least compiled, with the first collection in mind.

In both volumes Simms explained his choice of such an unusual title. In the dedication of the 1860 volume, he discussed the origin of the word "areytos":

> I need not say to you that the word "Areyto," or "Arieto" is borrowed from the aboriginal language of the island of Cuba. There, at the firs coming of Columbus, the gentle race in possession of the soil, inspired by the smiling and blue skies which overarched them, the delicate languors of the atmos-

> phere they breathed, the delicate fruits and flowers by which they were encompassed—with blooms and beauties scarcely equaled and seldom subject to change—had their songs of tenderness, of love, of passion, and enthusiasm, to which they gave the name of Areytos. This word, so very musical, belonging thus exclusively to our hemisphere, seems to me deserving of preservation and preference in our literature. It is quite as worthy of use as that of *lay, ballad, canzone,* or *sircente,* and as sweet and significant as any in the poetical dialects of OC and OU. The Provençal troubadour had none more appropriate, for such a collection, in all his melodious vocabulary. (v, original emphasis)

According to him, then, "areyto" is another word for "song" or "songs of tenderness, of love, of passion, and enthusiasm." The poems in his final collection certainly run this particular gamut of subjects.

But Simms could have used another title to convey the same meaning, as he did decades before in *Early Lays* (1827). His real reason for choosing the title was that the origin was not European but specific to the New World, "belonging thus exclusively to our hemisphere." He here continued the work he began with "Americanism in Literature" (1845), in which he complained that American "writers think after European models, draw their stimulus and provocation from European books, fashion themselves to European tastes, and look chiefly to the awards of European criticism" (7). By using a word coined in the New World in a non-European language, Simms informed the reader that the poems or "areytos" that followed would not be imitations of European models, but American in character. He defended the "areyto" by explaining that it was "quite as worthy of use" as any European name such as "*lay, ballad, canzone,* or *sircente.*" In short, Simms's productions, while they might acknowledge their own European origins, were essentially American.

Background[1]

Poems: Descriptive, Dramatic, Legendary and Contemplative (1853) is Simms's most important collection, if not his best. When critics discuss Simms's poems — which, sad to say, is not often — they usually confine their comments to those pieces the poet selected for the two-volume *Poems*. There are a few good reasons. First, the majority of Simms's best work was selected for *Poems*. Second, because the collection surveys over two decades of Simms's output, it is perhaps the most representative of any volume published before or after 1853, with the obvious exception of James E. Kibler's annotated edition of Simms's selected poems. Such a retrospective selection is convenient for the scholar looking to understand the poet's evolving aesthetic as well as to gain some insight into Simms's taste in his own poetry. Third, *Poems* and Kibler's *Selected Poems of William Gilmore Simms* are the only extensive editions of the poetry. Therefore, if a scholar does discuss a piece not in *Poems*, chances are that he or she is using Kibler's edition.[2]

In a letter to Evert Augustus Duyckinck, Simms expressed the desire to add to *Poems*: "I am anxious to put forth my complete poetical and dramatic writings in 3 volumes" (*Letters* 5: 90-91). Unfortunately, for Simms scholars, the poet was unable to achieve his aim. Because such a complete edition was never brought to fruition, his last selected poems, *Areytos*, becomes that much more important to Simmsians seeking to better understand the arc of Simms's career.

Exactly when Simms first thought to gather a new poetry selection is uncertain, but he initially discussed the possibility on 18 June 1858 in a letter to J.T. Fields of the Boston publishing firm Ticknor and Fields:

> I am thinking of a new collection of 'Southern Passages', & 'Areytos', & should greatly like an edition in blue and gold. When the poetical epoch comes round again, and the public feels a return of its periodical *furore* in behalf of verse, advise me of your readiness to avail yourself of the spasm. (*Letters* 4: 67)

Apparently, Ticknor and Fields did not predict such a "poetical epoch" any time soon, as they never published the proposed volume. Simms spent the next two years assembling and revising the manuscript before submitting it to Justus Redfield, who agreed to publish it. Sometime during the summer of 1860, Simms went to New York to foster the book through the press. He believed he would finish the publication process by the first week of September (*Letters* 4: 238), but as Kibler points out, he "had received at least some of the proofs by Sept. 28, 1860" (*Introduction* 103).

Until this point, Simms had faced problems most authors encounter when publishing a book. But in addition to these common problems, Simms was beginning to contend with more than a little reluctance from his publisher. He reported the first sign of trouble to James Lawson in November:

> He, Redfield, wrote me that now was not the time for publication. In other words he was not in a condition to publish. But there would be a sale of the small edition I proposed, say 250 copies:—as I stated R & J. [Russell and Jones] had alone agreed for 100, or 200, and I wished 50 myself, to give away, resolving that the Publisher should not exercise the right exclusively of giving copies, & meaning to give them to such only as were worthy, and willing to read poetry. (*Letters* 4: 261)

Not only did Redfield not do a run of the book under the firm's own name, but the publisher did not pay for the stereotyping, leaving the cost to the author. Redfield owed Simms "over 600 dollars" in royalties (*Letters* 4: 269), and it was with this balance that the author paid for the stereotyping. In the same letter to Lawson, Simms wrote with obvious frustration, "What a commentary upon the way I am treated by all these men that after the book is stereotyped, there is no publisher among them." The change in plans meant that there would be further delays. The volume was finally released in December 1860, but its market was limited to Charleston.

Simms's troubles did not end after the small run had been released. Sometime before March 17, the author learned that a number of copies of *Areytos* had been destroyed by fire. In disbelief, Simms wrote to Lawson asking, "Are you sure that my books *were* burned"? Simms then reflected on the perpetual presence of fire in his life, both personal and literary:

> It seems to be my luck to be always in danger of fire. My plates destroyed by fire in Harper's vaults; my House destroyed by fire; my books in Widdleton's hands by fire; my books (Areytos) in Redfield's hands destroyed by fire. What the d—l does it mean? Here is a chapter of mischances, all in my case, which should hardly occur in the case of any three other persons. (*Letters* 4: 350)

Apparently Simms had his doubts that this particular fire had occurred: "I fancy this fire is sometimes a false fire and an invention. See if Redfield approves of this faith in fire: If he believes in Widdleton's fire" (*Letters* 4: 350). Kibler argues that Simms's incredulity as to the fate of the copies is understandable and that he "had a right to question if Redfield was withholding the copies under the guise of their being burned," considering how the publisher had mistreated him only months before (*Introduction* 104).

Exactly why Redfield dealt so badly with Simms is not immediately clear. After all, as Guilds points out, Simms was the New York firm's "mainstay Southern author" (*Life* 278). Guilds and Kibler argue that the reasons for such mistreatment were financial and political. Guilds contends that, "as sectional animosity grew, particularly after the secession of South Carolina, the New York publisher exploited the situation" by "withholding royalties" from Simms (278). Kibler writes that "the whole affair is revelatory of the quiet manner in which Northern business interest took advantage of a difficult situation" (*Introduction* 104). That is, Redfield realized that he could use the growing tension between North and South to save money at Simms's expense. This line of reasoning works if we are only concerned with explaining Redfield's refusal to pay Simms the $600 in royalties owed him, but it does not explain why the publisher printed the book for another imprint yet did not market the text in New York. After all, he had often published more-or-less simultaneously, with Simms's Charleston publishers, apparently printing the copies for both houses.

Though Redfield's printing and marketing decisions were in part financially motivated, the firm was probably not "trying to take advantage of a difficult situation"; rather, it was trying to avoid placing itself in a difficult situation by distancing itself from *Areytos*. As the title indicates, many of the poems were "Songs and Ballads of the South." Perhaps Redfield thought that poems about the South would not sell well in the North in a time of such regional tension. In fact, he surmised that "now was not the *time* for publication," meaning perhaps that the book's subject matter would impede sales. Also, Redfield might have believed that the northern reading public would be unforgiving of a New York publisher who allied himself with the South and with a writer who had been such an outspoken anti-abolitionist. Not only might he lose money on *Areytos*, but he might also lose across the board. Had the volume been proposed a decade earlier, the New York firm probably would have published it under the Redfield name. But the combination of the collection's southern subject matter, the author's proslavery stance, and the political climate of the time made the venture far too risky, especially given Redfield's precarious financial circumstances, which led to his bankruptcy within months.

Because of the collection's limited market and lack of popularity, *Areytos* never went to a second printing, much less a second edition. Consequently, Simms's final collection did not see the light of day again until the spring of 2012 when the Simms Initiatives digitized it and made a facsimile available and full-text searchable on the Initiatives website. For the first time in its 152 year history, therefore, *Areytos* is accessible to anyone in the world with internet capability, not simply to the residents of and travelers to the Simms holdings at the South Caroliniana Library in Columbia, South Carolina.

Characteristics

In so many ways *Areytos* serves as an excellent model of a collection of selected poems, particularly if a selection is supposed to represent the concerns and obsessions of the poet. A reader unfamiliar with Simms's poetry could become aware of the poet's concerns and obsessions simply by reading *Areytos*. Thus, in terms of both form and content, Simms successfully assembled a volume that accurately portrayed the recurring preoccupations of a long career.

His interest in poetic form is evident from the title of the collection. By focusing on the sonic quality of the aboriginal word "areyto," which he called "so very musical" (dedication in *Areytos* v), Simms directed the reader to pay close attention to the sonic qualities of the entire volume, as well as to the author's use of form to create a non-European American literature.[3] Consider Simms's experiments with the sonnet. While he followed the "European models" to the letter from time to time, he regularly – in fact, usually – deviated from the legitimate format and created his own.[4] Most of the sonnets in *Areytos* followed the latter trend. His innovations often mixed two different sonnet forms, such as the rhyme schemes of the Italian and English traditions. He also quite regularly departed even further by inventing a rhyme scheme out of whole cloth. Of course, Simms did not isolate his experiment to one form. Several poems in *Areytos* that bear the title "ballad" do not approximate in any way the ballad stanza one would find in *Percy's Reliques of Ancient English Poetry* or Sir Walter Scott's *Minstrelsy of the Scottish Border*. A number of "ballads" are written in non-ballad meters (iambic pentameter, for example) and rely on elaborate rhyme schemes that we might associate with the troubadour tradition Simms mentioned in the dedication.

Just as often as he tinkered and revised existing traditions, Simms created his own forms, stanzas, and rhyme schemes that have no European predecessor, or any precedent for that matter. Take, for example, "Come, While the Evening Sets Sweet and Clear," a stanza of Simms's own invention which runs $abab_4cc_2d_4ee_2dff_4$. These experiments with poetic form are one of the more distinctive characteristics of the collection. Unfortunately, in a number of poems, such experiments are the only redeeming quality. The best poems in *Areytos* and they are numerous, rather are perfect syntheses of form and content.

Not only did Simms provide a variety of poetic forms, but he wrote about a wide range of topics. As Kibler has noted, "The world of Simms is indeed expansive; the scope of his art can in no sense be labeled narrow. In fact, a good case could be made for his being the most richly diverse of all our American poets, old or new" ("Introduction" xix). Though lacking the expansiveness of *Poems*, *Areytos* is "richly diverse" nonetheless. A number of subjects appear briefly in the collection. Religion, for example, is only discussed directly occasionally but is represented well in "The Bride of Christ," a poem not critical of Christianity but of the Church (i.e., the manmade institution of Christianity).

A few of the poems are little more than versified advice, as in the case of "Strike! – As Said the Anvil" (58). The speaker tells a young man, "Speed to the work! – we'll all have time for sleeping, / When we have shuffled off these mortal coils" (58).[5] The poem – which echoes the cliché, "Strike while the iron is hot" – reminds us that only "seventy years [are] allotted to the best," so we must not procrastinate but fulfill our purpose now (58). The transience of this life is also dealt with in "Now, When the Spring Is Over" (62); unlike the previous poem, though, the speaker does not offer advice, but simply states that all is fleeting and that nothing lasts and that the young will soon grow old and die.

A number of other minor subjects and themes crop up, but most of the poems fall into only a few categories. One of the more prominent subjects in the collection is love. Most of these poems, however, lack the depth of much of Simms's best work. Repeated readings of these pieces generally are not necessary, as most of them suffer from transparency and univocality. "Serenader Implores His Mistress to Come Forth" (229) and "Why Meet Me with Aspect So Chilling?" (17) are good examples of the kind of love poems Simms selected for *Areytos*. Not all of such poems are quite so superficial. Consider, for example, "Now Weave Your Spells, Young Maiden," in which Simms alluded to "Sir Patrick Spens":

> Now weave your spells, young maiden—
>   Love's sweet and mystic charms;
> For the old moon now comes laden
>   With the young moon in her arms. (181)

The last two lines echo closely two lines from the Scottish popular ballad:

> I saw the new moon late yestreen
>   With the old moon in her arms;
> And if we go to sea, master,
>   I fear we'll come to harm. (Child no. 58)

By appropriating lines from a tragic ballad, Simms indicated that the spell cast by the maiden will have tragic results. A reader must be familiar with "Sir Patrick Spens" in order to fully understand the poem. Such an allusion adds depth to the piece and necessitates several readings, characteristics not shared by most of the love poems in the selection.

While Simms's love poems tend to be shallow, the majority of the poems concerning nature have a depth and sophistication one might expect to find in the mature work of Wordsworth and Coleridge. As Kibler points out, Simms "writes of nature and of nature's manifold roles as teacher, source of inspiration, restorer of a tired spirit, spiritual guide, aid to reflection, nurturer, and symbol of immortality" ("Introduction" xxiv). In *Areytos*, Simms discussed all of nature's "manifold roles." The "Chimney Cricket" (173-179) is an example of nature as teacher and spiritual guide. According to the speaker, it is the cricket's job to "[t]each your young ones truthful seeing, / And conduct them to the beauty / That lies sure in homely duty!" (177). In "The Mountain Winds" (65-70), Simms celebrated the beauty of Mount Tyron, and framef the mountain, and nature, as teacher, as nurturer, as spiritual guide, as symbol of immortality, and as restorer: "and the exquisite repose / Of nature, from the striving world releases, / Taught me forgetfulness of mortal throes, / Life's toils, and all the cares that wait on human woes" (65). In all of his nature poems, nature is a source of inspiration and an aid to reflection.

Simms thus expressed his own ideas of Romanticism, a philosophy he learned from the British Romantic poets. He did not conceal his influences, but instead "[made] his debts explicit," often echoing poems by poets such as Wordsworth and Coleridge (Brennan 78). In "My Forest Harp," Simms used the title to allude to Coleridge's "The Eolian Harp." As Matthew C. Brennan has noted, "Simms's use of the wind image draws especially on the associations of renewal and of imaginative power" (90). In poems such as "My Forest Harp," in which the "wind image" signifies such renewal, Simms implicitly acknowledged Coleridge, who more than any of his British contemporaries, used the motif to great effect. A reader well versed in Coleridge would certainly trace Simms's image back to the author of "The Eolian Harp." Not only did Simms borrow images from his British forbears, but on occasion he quoted their work directly, as he did in "Chimney Cricket," when he called the insect "Thou best philosopher" (176), a direct quote from Wordsworth's "Intimations" ode (l. 110).

Even though these themes play an important role in the collection, they are overshadowed by the "Poems and Ballads of the South," for which the book is named. The bulk of these poems were written several years before the publication of the 1860 *Areytos*. A number celebrate southern landscapes; an example is "Oh, the Sweet South!," which describes the landscape and its maternal relationship with the poet (9). But the majority of these poems are patriotic pieces, some to the point of xenophobia. First published in 1856, "Elegiac.—It Is the Cause," for example, is a warning to southerners in general and to South Carolinians in particular to be mindful of foreign power. The foreign power Simms described was not England or Mexico, but the northern United States and the federal government. His poems about the Mexican-American War appeared in the late 1840s. His poems that address England as the enemy are about the American Revolution or the War of 1812.

Overall, the poems about these earlier conflicts give specific details that indicate the subject of the text. "Elegiac," on the other hand, offers no such clues. Simms's contemporaries would not have needed any, as a political and moral divide between North and South was well under way. Simms characterized "the Cause" (a word he capitalized throughout) as a crusade, writing that the South "...needs some noble martyr, / To bear his breast, and perish for his kind!" (63). The word "kind" suggests a xenophobia that had become common in both regions. The poem is a call to arms, an admonition to a people who have grown too comfortable and, as a result, are unaware of "the Destinies that wait" (63).

There are other poems like this one, but most of them are not as effective because they rely too often on abstract language rather than on images, a characteristic that makes "Elegiac" such a provocative piece. The better southern patriotic pieces in *Areytos* are instead about the Mexican-American War. Most of the poems in this vein are placed near the end of the volume in a sequence about the exploits of the Palmetto Regiment, called by Simms "our gallant little regiment" (*Areytos*, dedication v). The poems in this sequence are an encomium on South Carolina's contribution to the nation's victory in the conflict with Mexico.

The series begins at the end of the war with "Ode.—Welcome, Thrice Welcome," which, according to Simms, "was written to welcome the return of the remnant of the Palmetto Regiment from Mexico" (381). The ode both celebrates their return and laments the loss of so many men. Following the ode, Simms related chronologically the movements and losses of the regiment, beginning with their organization before departure in "Carolinians, Who Inherit" (384) and continuing with "The March to Alvarado," which details the loss of soldiers on the march to Mexico. Simms detailed the regiment's desire to join the fight in "We've a Right from Ancient Valor" (391). But not all of the poems are about the regiment as a single entity. In fact, a few are elegies for individuals who died and those at home who bore the loss. "The Widow of the Warrior" (394), for example, describes a woman's grief over the loss of her soldier husband. Simms did not simply discuss the war and the army in terms of battles and casualties *en masse* but reminded us of the personal aspect of war. Such a nuanced and sophisticated depiction is lacking in Simms's other patriotic poems, which often suffer from a didacticism that borders on propaganda.

The majority of the regiment poems were first published in *Lays of the Palmetto: A Tribute to the South Carolina Regiment, in the War with Mexico* (1848). As Simms explained in the dedication to *Areytos*, "Most of [the poems in *Lays of the Palmetto*] were written at the moment when the event which they seek to honor first reached our ears" (v). These poems were not reflections but what Simms called in the advertisement to *Lays* "almost improvisations, outpourings of a full heart" (3).

Even though the regiment poems are not secessionist or xenophobic, Simms must have been aware when he selected them for *Areytos* that the public might very well read them with rising regional tension in mind. In a letter — the letter in which he relayed Redfield's decision not to issue the book — Simms discussed the timing of the book's release: "This is the very time for that vol. in the South, a large portion of the material being patriotic" (*Letters* 4: 261). Whether or not Simms included the lays in *Areytos* because of the growing regional tension, he clearly saw the necessity of such patriotic verse, which he hoped would galvanize and encourage his southern readers in uncertain times.

Reception, Then and Now

Despite the book's subject matter, it did not fare well with the southern reading public. In an attempt to justify the volume's relative failure, Simms explained to Lawson that "...people here breathe nothing but war, & read none but military books now" (*Letters* 4: 326). That *Areytos* only achieved marginal commercial success cannot be blamed on negative reviews, but rather on a public that usually might be interested in a volume like Simms's but that at the time had other tastes and concerns. Yet reviewers, both northern and southern, had not lost their interest in Simms's verse, as is evidenced by their positive reception of *Areytos*. Not surprisingly, northern critics and their southern counterparts saw the collection quite differently.

The critic for the *Charleston Mercury* (22 December 1860) praised the book without qualification but only took interest in the southern patriotic verse. In this particular instance, *Areytos* was used for a larger political purpose, as is evidenced by the placement of the review. On the same page appeared an article titled "E Pluribus Unum, in which the anonymous author wrote:

> The most impressive feature in the action of South Carolina is the concentrated unanimity of her people. Having long, carefully and deliberately considered her position in the Federal Union, and arrived at her conclusion, her people have come up to the work of her independence from vassalage and ruin under Northern rule. (n.p.)

Such vitriolic, stirring language was compounded by a piece on "The Demonstration Last Night" in which the author reported:

> A very imposing procession marched last night through our principal streets with flags and several bands of music. The Washington Artillery, the Zonaves, the Palmetto Riflemen, the Cadet Riflemen, the Carolina Light Infantry, the Union Light Infantry, the German Fire Company, the Minute Men and the citizens generally, participated.

These two articles and the patriotic speeches that follow all suggest that Simms's poetry was being drafted in service to the Cause. While Simms would have been happier had his southern reviewers discussed in more detail the complexities and nuances of the book, he must have approved of their conscription of the patriotic verse. The review ignored entirely all other aspects of *Areytos* in order to rally its readers around the Palmetto flag.

The *Southern Literary Messenger* likewise discussed the southern verse, writing that "Mr. Simms's muse is a patriotic goddess" (157). Of the patriotic verse, the anonymous reviewer paid particular attention to "Make Gay the Spear with Flowers" and "The Ballad of Old Hickorie." Of the former poem he stated, "[it] breathes a spirit of strategic defence, with stirring appeals to be prompt in action, nor let an opportunity slip, which may be mourned for when it cannot be recalled" (157). Of the latter, he wrote:

> "The Ballad of Old Hickorie" hurries you along with it irresistibly as you read, producing the effect of lively martial music, to which your feet must keep time, whether your will go along or not, and you presently find yourself marching whether you will or not. (ibid.)

Unlike the *Mercury* reviewer though, the critic for the *Messenger* penned a more comprehensive appraisal, taking into account not only the patriotic verse, but poems in other veins as well. For example, he quoted "The Lost Pleiad" extensively and praised Simms's handling of the theme of "[t]he obliteration of a world from the Universe" (ibid.). Not only did the reviewer praise individual poems but he spoke well of the book in general:

> Throughout a great portion of the songs in this volume there is a vein of exquisite sadness, which is apt to be the tone of all poetry which is not intensely young; of poetry which has had its boyishness, its huge credulity, its positiveness as to the heroism in man and the angelism in woman rudely chipped, rubbed, scraped off, by observant criticism, and daily contact with a world anything but the creation of a boy-poet. (158)

The critic's balanced treatment suggests that the *Messenger* did not see Simms's volume primarily in service to the Cause, but judged it as a work of literature, not propaganda.

Northern reviewers were not critical of the patriotic verse; in fact, they did not discuss those poems at all. In the book notices for March 1861, Louis Godey praised the volume, focusing on the poet's formal gifts: ""The lyre of Mr. Sims [*sic*] is one whose tones must always command approval. Classical without coldness, the poetic utterances in this present volume are such as will add to their author's already high reputation" (275). The reviewer for *Harper's* likewise praised the poet and his poems. While acknowledging Simms's "eminent position"

> in American literature depends on his merits as a novelist rather than on his poetical productions, the latter, which are here collected in a volume, evince

the genuine feeling of the poet, and powers both of imagination and expression of no common order. (411)

Even when critical of the poet and his craft, as he was of Simms's versification, which he described as "unequal," he praised his handling of form as being "vigorous and spirited" (ibid.). Notice here that the reviewer did not frame Simms as a southern, but as an American, poet. In this regard, the *Harper's* review is more than fair.

Two points are worth considering about the North's response to *Areytos*. First, if these two reviews are any indication of northern reception the book, then Redfield's apparent concerns were clearly unfounded. Kibler is right when he points out the attacks leveled at Simms by the northern press (101). But, while northern newspapers may have been critical of Simms's failed 1856 lecture tour in the North, as well as of his anti-abolitionist attacks on Harriet Martineau, they obviously approved of his poetry. Such approval suggests a complex response to a complex human being.

Unfortunately for Simms, the critical attention to *Areytos* was brief, if generally favorable. Of course, the volume has received some attention by scholars more recently, but by and large it has been consigned to oblivion. There are three notable exceptions. The first scholarly consideration of the volume is Kibler's brief discussion in *The Poetry of William Gilmore Simms: An Introduction and Bibliography*, a seminal account of the book's origins and publication background. Any understanding of *Areytos* must begin with Kibler's entry. Guilds wrote the second treatment of the volume in *Simms: A Literary Life*. Like Kibler, Guilds offers a history of the book's conception, publication and reception (277-278). Matthew C. Brennan, in *The Poet's Holy Craft: William Gilmore Simms and Romantic Verse Tradition*, offers an invaluable discussion of Simms's revision strategies in *Areytos*. Like Kibler (*Introduction* 102), Brennan concludes, after consideration of Simms's letters about *Areytos*, that the poet did not find revision as distasteful as has been supposed (50).

While no one has done a thorough analysis of the volume as a whole, a few of the poems in *Areytos* have received substantial attention from Kibler and Brennan. In *The Selected Poems of William Gilmore Simms*, Kibler offers thorough notes on poems selected from the 1860 collection, such as "Chimney Cricket" (397-398n) and "The Slain Eagle (Saluda" (340-341n). His notes on these poems and many others from *Areytos* often go beyond historical and personal context into insightful analysis. In *The Poet's Holy Craft*, Brennan discusses a number of the poems from Simms's last volume of poetry. For example, he considers Simms's "Lamia.—the Beautiful Sin" in comparison with Keats's "Lamia," pointing out that "Simms's speaker despite his 'pall'd and palsied soul' successfully flees and ends his narrative in a distinctly un-Keatsian but conventionally Victorian way: He blesses 'the good God for the granted grace'" (39). Brennan performs a number of other deft interpretations, but his discussion of "Lamia" is his most valuable contribution.

Kibler, Guilds, and Brennan have laid the groundwork for a reading of *Areytos*, but there is still much to be done if we are to understand the collection's overall affect. Thus far, the individual poems that have been culled from the book have not been read within the context of the volume. The very nature of the work, as a selected poems, lends itself to such a strategy, but a reading of *Areytos* as a single text would yield interesting results. How does one poem play off an adjacent poem? How does this poem relate to another of the same subject? Is there a continuous narrative that runs from the beginning to the end of the volume or do the poems run at cross purposes? That is, do poems contradict each other or do they serve to support one another and in so doing generate a unified set of themes? Who are the notable influences on Simms in this book? How does form play a role, not simply in individual pieces, but in the collection as a whole? Are the same formal strategies used throughout and, if so, why? Does a particular meter recur in the text and, if so, why? The list of questions could go on and on. An attempt to answer just a few of them would serve to complicate an already complicated oeuvre and an even more complicated poet. Now that *Areytos* is available in print again, there is no reason why these inquiries cannot commence.

Notes

1. The publication history offered here would not be possible without Kibler's researches in *The Poetry of William Gilmore Simms: An Introduction and Bibliography.*

2. Other resources have been available to the Simms scholar. *The Simms Reader: Selections from the Writings of William Gilmore Simms* edited by John Caldwell Guilds and *An Early and Strong Sympathy: The Indian Writings of William Gilmore Simms* edited by Guilds and Charles Hudson offer a sampling of the poetry, but with a few notable exceptions (for example, "The Mountain Tramp" in *An Early and Strong Sympathy*), the selections can be found in Kibler's edition.

3. For a more detailed discussion on the ways in which Simms uses form to establish a distinctive, non-derivative American literature, see my article, "'Dazzling Outlawries of the Imagination': William Gilmore Simms and the 'Americanism' of the Sonnet."

4. The most comprehensive study of Simms's sonnets is Brennan's *The Poet's Holy Craft: William Gilmore Simms and Romantic Verse Tradition.* In Chapter Three, "The Romantic Sonnet," Brennan offers several examples of Simms's formal innovations of the sonnet. Brennan also provides two helpful appendices in which he lists a number of rhyme schemes Simms used in his experiments in the sonnet tradition (141-143).

5. As there are no line numbers in this particular edition of *Areytos*, the citations refer to page numbers. Quotes from the texts of other poets such are cited by line number unless otherwise indicated.

Works Cited

Brennan, Matthew C. *The Poet's Holy Craft: William Gilmore Simms and Romantic Verse Tradition*. Columbia: U of South Carolina P, 2010.

Child, Francis James, ed. *The English and Scottish Popular Ballads*. 5 vols. 1882-98. New York: Cooper Square Publishers, 1965.

Coleridge, Samuel Taylor. *Samuel Taylor Coleridge: The Major Works*. Oxford: Oxford UP, 2009.

Godey, Louis. Rev. of *Simms's Poems Areytos or Songs and Ballads of the South with Other Poems* by William Gilmore Simms. *Godey's* LXII Mar. 1861: 275.

Guilds, John Caldwell. *Simms: A Literary Life*. Fayetteville: U of Arkansas P, 1992.

Johnson, Jason W. "'Dazzling Outlawries of the Imagination': William Gilmore Simms and the 'Americanism' of the Sonnet." *Simms Review* 14.2 (2006): 5-13.

Kibler, James Everett, ed. "Introduction." *Selected Poems of William Gilmore Simms: Twentieth Anniversary Edition*. Columbia, SC: U of South Carolina P, 2010. xvii-xxvii.

——. *The Poetry of William Gilmore Simms: An Introduction and Bibliography*. Columbia, SC: *Southern Studies*, 1979.

Rev. of *Simms's Poems Areytos or Songs and Ballads of the South with Other Poems* by William Gilmore Simms. *Charleston Mercury* Dec. 22, 1860.

Rev. of *Simms's Poems Areytos or Songs and Ballads of the South with Other Poems* by William Gilmore Simms. *Harper's* XXII Feb. 1861: 411.

Rev. of *Simms's Poems Areytos or Songs and Ballads of the South with Other Poems* by William Gilmore Simms. *Southern Literary Messenger* XXXII Feb. 1860: 156-159.

Simms, William Gilmore. "Americanism in Literature." Holman. 7-29.

——. *Areytos: Or Songs of the South*. Charleston: John Russell, 1846.

——. *An Early and Strong Sympathy: The Indian Writings of William Gilmore Simms*. Ed. John Caldwell Guilds and Charles Hudson. Columbia, SC: U of South Carolina P, 2003.

——. *Lays of the Palmetto: A Tribute to the South Carolina Regiment, in the War with Mexico*. Charleston: John Russell, 1848.

——. *The Letters of William Gilmore Simms*. Ed. Mary C. Simms Oliphant, Alfred Taylor Odell, and T. C. Duncan Eaves. 6 vols. Columbia: U of South Carolina P, 1952-82.

——. *Simms's Poems Aerytos or Songs and Ballads of the South with Other Poems*. Charleston: Russell & Jones, 1860.

——. *Poems Descriptive, Dramatic, Legendary and Contemplative*. 2 vols. New York: Redfield, 1853.

——. *Views and Reviews in American Literature, History and Fiction*. Ed. C. Hugh Holman. Cambridge, Mass: The Belknap P of Harvard UP, 1962.

Wordsworth, William. *William Wordsworth: The Major Works: Including the Prelude*. Oxford: Oxford UP, 2008.

SIMMS'S POEMS

AREYTOS

OR

SONGS AND BALLADS OF THE SOUTH

WITH OTHER POEMS

By W. GILMORE SIMMS, ESQ

AUTHOR OF "THE YEMASSEE," "THE CASSIQUE OF KIAWAH," "THE PARTISAN," "EUTAW" "THE FORAYERS," ETC

CHARLESTON, S. C.:

RUSSELL & JONES

1860.

TO

PROFESSOR JAMES W. MILES,

OF SOUTH CAROLINA.

You, my dear Miles, are in some degree responsible for this collection, and I feel justified accordingly in using your name for this inscription. But for your encouragement, which seems to give a sanction to the entreaties of others, I should probably have been slow to persuade myself that these productions—the occasional effusions of some thirty years—the asides of fancy and feeling from the more deliberate labors of my profession—would be likely to commend themselves to public favor. You have thought otherwise, and have thus ministered to that paternal love which had not the courage to destroy its errant offspring, and still takes the fugitives to his heart, as if they had not been, for so many long seasons, the very waifs and strays of letters—wanderers, almost outlawed, rarely acknowledged, of his early affections. To you they are generally better known than to most other persons. Hitherto unclaimed, except in few instances, they have been suffered to make their way as they could. through periodicals and papers, and not unfrequently have I found them, with the original earmarks obliterated, bearing the brands of other parties, and so making friends, in a sort of gipsy progress, which I propose, by this collection, to arrest. I have sometimes found it necessary to reclothe them in fresh habiliments; to restore them to their full proportions; refine them of their crudities, and so attune their speaking as to fit them, as well as I can, for the acquaintance of better classes of society. The children, in large proportion, of my youth and early manhood, I confess to a degree of fondness for them, which will not permit me to be indifferent to their costume, their conduct, and their success in life. They declare for the fancies, the emotions, the passions, and affections of periods which were most precious to me; when the passions were all honest, and ere the affections were rendered cold by the varied experiences of a most capricious manhood. They are representatives, not simply of my own moods, thoughts, and feelings, but are memorials of the changing phases of so many several periods in my life; hardly one of them being without its peculiar individual association, and capable, even now, after longest lapses of time, of being referred, by memory, to the particular occasion which called for its utterance. Many of the songs and sonnets, the epigrams and smaller pieces, are absolute improvisations, as will perhaps be sufficiently apparent to the least critical reader. A fair proportion were deliberate attempts in art, but made originally at a period when the art of the author was yet in its infancy, and for these it needed the more mature revision of a far later period. Perhaps a severer revision would commend other pieces more gratefully to the public ear; but I have felt, but too frequently, that it would be a task equally ungrateful and difficult to apply the *labor limæ* to productions which are never so grateful as when they declare for the spontaneous emotion, the sudden flight of fancy, or the voluntaries of sentiment and passion. We must take such performances as so many short bird-flights—so many little momentary effusions of the songstress, suddenly awaking in the wood, with chirp, or cry, or carol.

You will note that, though largely mingled with the moral and didactic, with the dramatic as well as the essayical elements, I have yet given to the collection a purely lyrical title, as the lyrical so much more numerously preponderates over all other forms in the book.

I need not say to you that the word "Areyto," or "Arieto" is borrowed from the aboriginal language of the island of Cuba. There, at the first coming of Columbus, the gentle race in possession of the soil, inspired by the smiling and blue skies which overarched them, the delicate languors of the atmosphere they breathed, the delicious fruits and flowers by which they were encompassed — with blooms and beauties scarcely equalled and seldom subject to change—had their songs of tenderness, of love, passion, and enthusiasm, to which they gave the name of Areytos. This word, so very musical, belonging thus exclusively to our hemisphere, seems to me deserving of preservation and preference in our literature. It is quite as worthy of use as that of *lay*, *ballad*, *canzone*, or *sirvente*, and as sweet and significant as any in the poetical dialects of Oc and Ou. The Provençal troubadour had none more appropriate, for such a collection, in all his melodious vocabulary.

The "Lays of the Palmetto," which, with a few exceptions, I here republish, were, as you will readily see, and perhaps know, the merest improvisations—the simple outgushings of awakened feeling; the outpourings of a full heart, and a passionate fancy, as we were called upon to follow, day by day, the steps of our gallant little regiment in Mexico. Most of these were written at the moment when the event which they seek to honor first reached our ears.

You will perceive that I have given a new rescension of my Poem called "The Lost Pleiad," in which I have sought to render unique a production which, even in its original crude condition, as published in my nineteenth year, was fortunate enough to meet with no small share of critical and popular approval. It needed, not only that I should elaborate the original verse, but develop fully the first leading ideas of the poem.

I know not, my dear Miles, that I need say more in reference to this collection. Much of what I have already said has been designed rather for my readers than yourself. Our communion, night by night, has been too frequent—our intercourse too free—to require that much should be said between us, by way of explanation, even upon graver matters. You will readily see that it had become necessary with me to get rid of these fugitives by some process. I must destroy or publish. I must set my house in order; and, whether I survive for other and better labors, or fold my robes about me for a long sleep, it had become essential that they should be put out of my way. I must clear my decks, whether for action or repose.

Enough, my dear MILES, that I entreat you, in the language of the little *preludium* which follows, to remember how long a term of life has been covered by these pieces—how occasional was their utterance—how far back they stretch—to a period when the thought was immature, the youth ardent; when the fancy, forever on the wing, was naturally but little willing to give ear to the scruples of the sedater and severer judgment. But, of all these things we have discoursed already, in those protracted sessions of thought and speculation, when, either in your studio or mine, we sate together, night after night, looking out upon night and stars, and brooding over those deep, sad, grand mysteries, which affect, quite as earnestly, the dwellers beneath, as those above the moon; "reasoning high"—in the language of MILTON, and with, possibly, as little profit as did his dethroned angels—

> "Of Providence, Foreknowledge, Will, and Fate,
> Fix'd fate, free will, foreknowledge absolute,
> And found no end, in wandering mazes lost."

If these pieces, and this inscription, shall recall gratefully to you those many sad, sweet hours, I shall be content to be, as I have ever been,

Your friend,

W. G. S.

WOODLANDS, *June* 1, 1860.

FIRST FRUITS.—A PRELUDE.

[1846.]

THESE are the flowers of my poetic youth,
In their first fragrance; when a summer bloom
Bore fruitage for the Fancy and the Heart,
Which made each seeming, as each certainty,
A very jewel in the bosom of Life—
Made Life itself a measureless empery,
Where the glad hours, most happy in their waste,
Were but as rolling and sonorous wheels
To the triumphal chariot of a State,
Equal in pomps and freedoms; whose career—
A regal progress in its pageantry—
All flowers and song—processions of glad flight—
Had never the cares of grandeur in its march,
Nor set a watch and sentinel on Time!—
So many days for coursing o'er the heights—
So many nights for raptures in the shade—
All hours, at best employ, on sunny wings,
Ranging each day o'er new-discovered realms;
With regions for fresh enterprise so vast,
That, with the wing outspread, grew never a doubt
Of the new worlds for conquest!
Fancy brought
Aladdin's lamp and ring, which, with a touch,
Summoned a thousand slaves of the Orient,
To spread the banquet. At my whispered will,
On carpet of the Genii was I borne

Into the Caliph's gardens; where I lay
Listening the legends of Scheherezade;
While, mingling with the showers of falling spray,
From numerous fountains silvered by the moon,
I drank in love from the fond bulbul's notes,
Appealing to the rose!
With every dawn,
With new-wing'd vigor from delicious sleep,
I went forth to the hills a conqueror;
And won, by pathways inaccessible,
My entrance to the æron of the eagle;
A conqueror like himself, with wing and eye
Searching all provinces of deeps and air!

Nor less a conqueror, though at set of sun—
The fire of flight subdued to Lydian measures—
Down in the valley, with a dewy eye,
A tremulous speech, the tenderest voice of song,
I made obeisances, with folded wing,
In apprehensive homage at a shrine,
Where the sweet Priestess, as forgetful too,
Lost in her own felicities of conquest,
Grew won while winning.

It was thus I sang,
Fond as triumphant, in the glad caprice
Of ever alert emotions—pride and pleasure—
Even as the bird, with voices of the dawn,
Born of the beauty in unclouded skies,
And virgin forests; never with a doubt,
That fancy would find wings for each fresh flight;
Untroubled with prognostics of the thought,
Such as fling shadows o'er the disk of day,
And hush all birds to silence!

Mine were strains
That, with no purpose, found free overflow
From a confiding and a grateful heart,
That did not question sun, or skies, or time;
Never put Rapture on the rack of doubt;
And deem'd the apparent glory in the sight,
As true as were those fancies of the soul
That found all beautiful, and never fear'd
The fraud in Beauty!

But I must not now
Proclaim my disappointments. Not o'er these
Boy-tokens should I make complaint of griefs,
That made my flowers of manhood lose their hues,
Withering each leaf of fragrance. I would skip
The later sad experience of mine years;
And on the track of happier memories trace
The fiery progress of that flight in youth,
Which, flinging Time beneath his chariot wheels,
Sped unremorseful o'er his neck, nor feared
His terrible spectre, in that form of care,
That hath his being in our scorn of Time!

My record must be that of Youth alone,
Its happy satisfactions, and gay flights,
And generous raptures! There I shrine apart
The golden sun-bright memories of the dawn,
As one close locks the chamber of his youth,
Sacred to sweet communion with the past,
When Youth has gone forever; bearing with it
The joys which made it wingéd, and the hopes
That welcomed manhood ever to a feast;
Nor show'd him, as he quaff'd of gay delights,
The spectre of the Future at each chair!

Here should he dream, and in recovery,
Through memory, of the dear but lost possessions,
Forget the griefs that chide the present hour,
Nor feel the doubt that hangs upon his years—
The fraudulent in Fortune—and the loss
Of all that glad boy-promise which inform'd
Each sense with beauty, and made confident
Each thought in rapture.

It was thus I sang
Untutor'd, unattempting aught of pride,
In those blest days of boyhood, when the thought
Was twinn'd with Fancy, and the redolent Feeling
Ran over with delight. The impulsive soul,
Thus, in its very idlesse, found a voice,
Whose flight, capricious, wanton, as the breeze,
Sported along the ocean sands, while Night
With starry harmonies, of sphere to sphere,
Made echo to the profligate melodist,
And sang him back—as birds that in the grove
Make glad refrain to some gay chorister,
Who never once, as on he sings and soars,
Dreams of the sort of dawn that morning brings—
Nor idly sings, though ignorant of fate!

Thus did I sport and sing along the shores,
Thus spread my wing in heedless happy flight;
Unfearing the great deep, and, recklessly,
As any child, from the fond mother's arms,
Gone errant, and along the precipice,
Catching at purple blossoms o'er the steep.

Oh! censure not the song if immature,
Nor chide the thought, which, in our riper years,
Fades to a fancy! All heart-histories

Are records of illusions; not less precious,
Because they vanish with the growing day!

They had the happiest uses for the heart,
Even while they vanish'd; had their sweets to soothe,
Shed even while flying; temper'd rugged souls
So that they grew to tenderness; subdued,
To sacrifice of self, the vulgar self
With all its greed; and, though in flight they left
The sad, the dusk, in place of purple hours,
Yet left them sweetened with a dewy fondness,
That hallow'd what they left no longer bright.
So the gay thoughtless melodies which tell,
Of the boy-fancies, and the generous dawn—
How sweet the dream was, passing—shall beguile
Fresh fancies; and to other hearts that dream,
Commend themselves as true! They shall be true,
To such as love and dream, and have no purpose
Of the far-reaching policies that make
The head too wise for the heart's happiness—
The ambition too successful with the world,
To be at peace with Heaven.
They shall be echoes
To virgin fancies—voices that declare
For trembling hearts that dare not speak their troubles,
In very raptures dumb.
Oh! hearts shall follow—
Pure, young, fond hearts, that, by the sea-beat shore,
Or hanging o'er the perilous heights at eve,
Like happy children glad of their escape,
Shall find fit echoes to the errant music
That looses their own tongues, and shows the secret,
And where it harbors, in their own dumb hearts.

CONTENTS.

AREYTOS, OR SONGS AND BALLADS.

SONNETS.

EPIGRAMS.

MISCELLANEOUS—MORAL, AND IMAGINATIVE.

LAYS OF THE PALMETTO.

AREYTOS.

MY FOREST HARP.

I.

My forest harp! though late I threw thee,
  In passion's madness from my grasp,
Yet now with better thoughts I woo thee,
  And once again thy strings I clasp:
And though I left thee long forsaken,
  Trust me the grief was mine alone;
The strings about my heart were shaken,
  But thine were true in every tone!

II.

Oh! fond as true; since now the sadness,
  That better speaks the heart subdued,
Usurps thy former notes of gladness,
  And suits our forest solitude;—
I better love thy strains of wailing
  Than livelier tones of joy and youth—
That mournful plaint, those murmurs failing,
  That speak of wo, and speak in truth.

III.

What though the world may frown upon thee,
  And scorn the song that can not soar?
Thou wilt not heed the crowds that shun thee,
  If I but love thy strains the more!
With thee, within the forest hidden,
  I summon gentlest spirits nigh;
And some that seek our groves unbidden,
  Yield song for song, and sigh for sigh.

IV.

Fair forms that live in realms of sadness,
  These hallow, as they hear, thy strain,
And, truer far than things of gladness,
  Requite the love that others feign!
No fleeting pledge is theirs of feeling,
  For death has sealed the vows they make,
And still their plaints their love revealing,
  Soothe all the pangs they yet partake!

COME, WHILE THE EVENING SETS SWEET AND CLEAR.

I.

Come, while the evening sets sweet and clear,
  And the winds are hush'd and the air is balm,
Sing me a Cuban Areyto, dear,
  Of the vine, the orange, and bending palm:
        Paint me the scene,
        The sweet serene,

Of that clime of bliss ere the Spaniard came—
When the simple child
Of the clime ran wild,
Nor needed the fig-leaf to hide his shame;
Sing, while the sunset is mild and clear,
Sing me a Cuban Areyto, dear!

II.

Paint me the gentle slope of hills,
Cover'd with vintage down to the sea;
Show me the flash of the limpid rills,
As they leapt from the thickets, bright and free:
Let me feel the gush,
The happy flush,
That love on the innocent heart bestows;
The clime as at first,
Ere the Spanish thirst
And brutal avarice crushed with blows!
Sing me a simple Areyto, dear,
Of the ancient beauty that harbor'd there!

III.

Oh! how glad was the human life
That once they knew in that Eden clime:
Never a passion that grew to strife,
Never a feeling that led to crime;
With the dance and song
They hurried along,
Till, like children at play, they sank to rest,
Dreaming of play
Some other day,
With still a new song for blessing and bless'd.
Ah! could'st thou feel it and sing it, dear,
As sang the gay children who gambol'd there!

IV.

Paint me the groups, as they wandered away,
  Plucking the fruits from the shrub and tree,
While the Patriarch sate where the shadows lay,
  As now I sit and listen to thee:
        And wanton'd the breeze
        O'er the summer seas,
And the sun set gleaming in purple and gold,
        While the song went free
        O'er the placid sea,
As, chasing each other, the billows roll'd,
  And broke on the ear with a voice of cheer,
  Such as I'd have thy Areyto, dear.

V.

Ah! what have we lost, and what have we won,
  By the change from the savage to social state?
We have blighted the fruits, we have mock'd the sun,
  In our growth to a greater and grander fate;
        We have great increase,
        But we have no peace;
We have pride and wealth and a mighty name;
        But the innocent play
        Of that virgin day
Is vanish'd, that never knew pride or shame!
  Oh, sing me a Cuban Areyto, dear,
  When love had no feeling of shame or fear?

OH, THE SWEET SOUTH!

I.

OH, the sweet South! the sunny, sunny South!
  Land of true feeling, land forever mine!
I drink the kisses of her rosy mouth,
  And my heart swells as with a draught of wine;
She brings me blessings of maternal love;
  I have her smile which hallows all my toil;
Her voice persuades, her generous smiles approve,
  She sings me from the sky and from the soil!
Oh! by her lonely pines, that wave and sigh—
  Oh! by her myriad flowers, that bloom and fade—
By all the thousand beauties of her sky,
  And the sweet solace of her forest shade,
      She's mine—she's ever mine—
      Nor will I aught resign
  Of what she gives me, mortal or divine:
      Will sooner part
      With life, hope, heart—
  Will die—before I fly!

II.

Oh! love is her's—such love as ever glows
  In souls where leaps affection's living tide;
She is all fondness to her friends—to foes
  She glows a thing of passion, strength, and pride;
She feels no tremors when the danger's nigh,
  But the fight over, and the victory won,
How, with strange fondness, turns her loving eye,
  In tearful welcome, on each gallant son!

Oh! by her virtues of the cherish'd past—
By all her hopes of what the future brings—
I glory that my lot with her is cast,
And my soul flushes, and exultant sings:
She's mine—she's ever mine—
For her will I resign
All precious things—all placed upon her shrine;
Will freely part
With life, hope, heart—
Will die—do aught but fly!

WITH AN UNPRESUMING FACE.

I.

With an unpresuming face,
And a manner soft and shy,
Love imperial steals apace,
When you little dream him nigh;
You may note his searching glance,
In the absent-seeming eye:
You may trace him in the trance
Of a young idolatry.

II.

There are spirits yet to win,
There are bosoms still to try,
And he deems it not a sin
To extend his sovereignty;
With a spell of wilder power
Than the mortal kings may ply,
He will scale the haughty tower,
Though it rugged be and high!

III.

For he arms him with a spark
  From a young and artless eye,
And he strikes the lofty mark
  Which would other force defy;
And the lofty tower goes down
  In the conflagration high,
And the chieftain leads he on
  In a long captivity!

IV.

In the wildest storm he soars,
  He is safe in every sky;
And he wins the farthest shores,
  With a wing of victory;
Sleepless still, he speeds apace,
  When you little deem him nigh,
And achieves the hardest race
  That his errant wing may try!

V.

He's the Prince, the Prince of Power,
  And we bow to him alone;
He's the Lord of Tent and Tower,
  Of the Cottage and the Throne;
Peer and Peasant, Clime and Hour,
  All alike to him are known,
And we yield him up the flower,
  And the fruit, of every zone.

MAKE GAY THE SPEAR WITH FLOWERS.

I.

Make gay the spear with flowers,
And soothe the shout with song,
Conceal in pomps the proof of powers
That yet should needs be strong:
And, to the foe
Before us, show
The rosiest treasures of the spring;
Nor let the wreath
Betray, beneath,
The serpent with his deadliest sting!

II.

I know 'twere far more grateful
To brave, and not beguile—
Confront the foe so hateful,
And smite where now we smile:
Daunt soul and ear
With shout of fear—
Take vengeance to the work of Hate—
With trumpet cry
Denounce, defy,
And drag the foe to fields of Fate!

III.

But when a people falters,
Too fond of ease for strife,
Nor heeds, though round its altars
Crawls venom seeking life;

When sons no more
The fields explore
Where fought the sires who made them free,
And fame is sold
For state or gold,
While lusts are strangling liberty:

IV.

When trusted talent barters
Its virtuous might for place,
And men, who should be martyrs,
Smile sleekly on disgrace—
Content to toil
For vulgar spoil—
To sell for self their people's fame,
And, with a lie,
To deify
The power that fills the land with shame:

V.

Oh then how vain to waken
The bugle blasts of strife;
The sleep may not be shaken,
Though still it palsies life;
We can but weep
That reign of sleep,
Of lust, and self, that mocks the past—
But watch and wait
The hour when Fate
Shall rouse us with her trumpet blast!

VI.

Yet watch and wait in armor,
With weapon sharp'd, and soul
Steeled 'gainst each glozing charmer,
That now hath such control!
While brave men moan
O'er virtues gone,
They are not gone—will rouse once more:
But nurse the Power,
The Man, the Hour,
Will come, even as they came of yore!

VII.

But crown the spear with flowers,
And soothe the shout with song,
Conceal in pomps the proof of powers
That yet must needs be strong:
And, to the foe
Before us, show
The rosiest treasures of the spring;
Nor let the wreath
Betray, beneath,
The serpent with his deadliest sting!

EPIGRAM.—DEATH IS HERE.

Death is here!—Death is there!
Death, we know, is everywhere!
But, if still the eye be clear,
And the spirit keep its sphere,
Nothing doubting, free from fear,
Death is neither here nor there!

EYES, EYES, YE HAVE LED ME TO RUIN!

I.

Eyes, eyes, ye have led me to ruin,
  Yet still ye are lovely, and still I adore!
Lips, lips, ye have been my undoing,
  Yet still would I feed on your sweet evermore:
Ye are fatal to fame, and I give up ambition,
  Content but to breathe in the balm ye impart—
To sigh away life in a dreamy condition,
  Forgetting the soul in the calls of the heart!

II.

Eyes, eyes, ye behold without feeling,
  The ruin ye make, and the ills ye have done!
Lips, lips, in the smile o'er ye stealing,
  I see but the sense of the triumph ye've won:
No tender emotion subdues the expression,
  Which vanity wears o'er a conquest complete;
No tear, starting forth at the mournful confession,
  Consoles the poor victim that sighs at your feet!

III.

Why, why, so cruelly sinning
  'Gainst all that is lovely in beauty and youth?
Eyes, why so beautiful—lips, why so winning,
  If still so denying to passion and truth?
Know'st thou not, proud one, that proud gifts in woman,
  Are precious alone while they kindle with heart?
And the moment that beauty forgets to be human,
  All the beautiful gifts of the woman depart?

DUSK, AND WITH HESPER!

I.

DUSK, and with Hesper,
South wind, thou wakest!
With wooing and whisper,
Green leaves thou shakest!
In the hush of the sunset hour,
In the blush of the virgin flower,
In the bright sun-flush, in the soft shower,
Sweet South, thou wakest!

II.

Glide to me soothing,
South, at awaking!
I have had all my youth in
Joys of thy making;
Thou hast taught me Love's sigh in
Thy breath, at day's dying,
Hope's murmured reply in
Thy midnight awaking!

III.

Whisper me fondly,
Forest and lawn in;
Leave me not lonely,
Sunset or dawning;
Come when billows at sunset
Flash with glad onset,
And when fingers of dawn set
Fresh blossoms the lawn in!

WHY MEET ME WITH ASPECT SO CHILLING?

I.

Why meet me with aspect so chilling,
  As if our last squabble were aught
But love, making piquant the willing,
  By a breeze from good policy caught?
Were there nothing but sunshine between us,
  No gusts sudden ruffling our sky,
I'd seek a more changeable Venus,
  And bid your tame beauties "good-by!"
          Yes, I would!
  Bid all your tame beauties "good-by!"

II.

Your eyes are quite precious when smiling,
  Yet nothing it vexes me when,
In a miff, they give over their wiling,
  And show me some foul weather then!
But be cloudy or clear, only time it
  So that storm shall not rule through the year;
And be quick in your changes of climate,
  Whenever you're called on "to clear!"
          Yes, be quick!
  You must shift as the wind does, my dear!

DOST THOU THAT NIGHT REMEMBER?

I.

Dost thou that night remember,
When silently we sped,
The broad blue bay around us,
The blue sky overhead;
The world of stars down-shining,
With each a smile to cheer—
To pierce the loving heart with love,
And wing each fancy there;
Soft zephyrs darting from the deep
In moment-gushes forth,
As if, that instant, from the wave
Each little wing had birth;
The dark mutes bending forward,
Oars plangent in the wave,
That, with our rapt hearts chiming,
Such tender echoes gave;
The stately pines that brooded close
Beside the ocean's brim,
And, dark in foliage, massed behind,
The forest still and grim;
That lonely camp-fire shining out
Upon the headland far,
And, through a rifted realm of cloud,
One little golden star?
Oh! of that holy night, blue heaven and lonely sea,
Keep the sweet memory as a dream—a sad, sweet dream of me!

II.

We sate together lonely,
  But with such loneliness
As love can soothe—love only—
  With silent tenderness:
My right hand grasped the rudder,
  The left was scarcely mine—
'Twas next my heart, but clasp'd by thee,
  It felt each beat of thine;
Then throbb'd the instant passion,
  Then breathed the instant bliss,
Then both hearts swell'd, and both lips met
  In one long loving kiss!
We knew not then of night or sky,
  The billows round our prow,
The Past, the Future, dark or bright,
  We knew but of the Now!
Nor that the slaves were near us,
  Nor did we hear the oars,
As, with their equal stroke, they sent
  The billows to the shores;
Nor, till the boatmen's chorus burst—
  A rude and mournful strain,
The echo of their simple hearts—
  Came we to earth again:
Came we to consciousness of all, that night upon the sea,
That vast of bliss that Life even yet had stored for thee and me!

III.

No more, no more, though feeling
  Still lives in either breast,
Must we recall that happy hour
  Which, mad'ning, made us bless'd—

That hour of bliss which made us both
 Forgetful of the Fate
That mock'd us with a single hour,
 To leave us desolate!
Why were we sent together,
 With hearts so knit to one?
Why had we thoughts, dreams, feelings,
 In such sweet unison?
What hope had we to cherish,
 When thou, already doom'd,
Had but a life for sacrifice,
 A heart already tomb'd?
We knew it both!—yet in that hour,
 With thy hand caught in mine,
That one star, through the rifted cloud,
 Shone forth with fatal sign:
Made us forget that Fate, or Man,
 Was hostile to our bliss—
Made sinful that embrace, and sad
 That first, fond, fatal kiss!
Oh! not less sweet for all the sin, that precious hour with thee,
That wild, weird night, when first we went o'er Coosaw's lonely sea!

IV.

Dim shores and moaning waters,
 That, on that hallowéd night
Beheld her face of troubled joy,
 All pallid mid the bright:
Saw us, in that delirious bliss,
 The first that ever taught
How precious was a mortal kiss
 To Passion and to Thought:

Heard those fond murmurs, half a speech
And half a sigh, that broke,
As from the ecstatic dream of joy
We both together woke!
Oh! keep the memory on your waves,
Your shores, your headlands dark:
So shall ye sway o'er future souls,
In other wandering bark;
And of that glorious form, all soul,
Dark eye, and pale white brow,
Still let the spell be on ye all,
As when ye heard our vow—
As when they won the fond young heart
They could not then requite,
And made, for all his life and thought,
A memory of that night!
So shall ye bear my memories—hers—though far apart we be,
Keeping Love's record well for us—for her—for her and me!

OUR COUNTRY IS A GALLANT BARK!

I.

Our country is a gallant bark,
And gallant seamen man her;
The eagle's spirit makes her flight,
The eagle's wing her banner!
Where heaven unveils its cloudless blue,
Where winds and waves can bear her,
Her thunders speak to hostile realms,
That, hating, still must fear her!

II.

From thirty empires link'd in one
  She takes her strength and glory,
And makes a progress, 'neath the sun,
  That glows, a sunlike story;
In peace she grasps the pride of war,
  In war, her purpose fondly,
Is still to save from cloud the star
  That shines for Freedom only!

III.

And thus with giant might endowed,
  No giant will degrades her;
Of power and wisdom justly proud,
  No injured realm upbraids her;
She heeds no mock of foes who hate,
  But steers with progress steady,
For those who hail with cheers, elate,
  For those with curses, ready!

IV.

O gallant bark! IF EVER THUS
  THY COURSE IN RIGHT PURSUING,
No hostile hate can rear the rock,
  Or wave, to work thy ruin!
The seas shall own thy progress wide,
  The realms of earth thy glory,
And, in his daily march of pride,
  The sun shall write thy story!

TWO SPIRITS, BEARING TORCHES.

Two spirits, bearing torches,
  Stand by each living gate;
One sad and silent marches,
  As willing still to wait:
The other, lightly moving
  And beautiful to see,
Seems ever bent on roving,
  With eager wing and free.

The silent spirit chills us—
  We loathe that he should wait:
The lively spirit thrills us
  With passions all elate;
We dream not he will leave us,
  We never think how soon;
And never vex or grieve us
  Until he's wholly gone.

Ah! when he flies, how changes
  Our mood for him who waits!
He chills not, though he ranges,
  Still silent, at our gates;
Resign'd, if not in gladness,
  We join him on his flight,
Through realms of doubt and sadness,
  As if he bore to light.

Love's torch, thus lifted brightly,
  Flames golden in our sky—
We never think how lightly,
  Or suddenly, he'll fly;

But earth at length he spurneth—
  Death only grasps the torch:
Down then the bright flame turneth,
  And darkens all the porch.

He bears the torch inverted
  The other bore on high:
Love seeking Love departed,
  Then satisfied to die.
And, through the gloomy portal,
  The widowed heart pursues—
Now taught that Love, the mortal,
  To Love immortal woos.

SONNET.—SWEET LADY, IN THE NAME OF ONE!

Sweet lady, in the name of one no more,
Both of us loved, and neither shall forget,
Make me thy brother, though our hearts before,
Perchance, have never in communion met!
Give me thy gentle memories, though there be
Betwixt our forms some thousand miles of sea,
Wild tract and tangled forest! Let me still,
Whate'er the joy that cheers me, or the thrill
That tortures, and from which I may not flee,
Hold a sweet, sacred place within thy breast!
In this my spirit shall be more than blest;
And in my prayers—if haply prayer of mine
Be not a wrong unto a soul like thine—
There shall be blessings from the skies for thee!

BESIDE THE SEA.

I.

Beside the Sea, beside the Sea,
Where the breezes are blowing fresh and free,
And the waves with regular swell subside
From the beaten beach, with the shrinking tide;
And waves grow purple in evening's light,
And the stars steal out before the night;
Where the peace is sure, and the soul, in play,
Forgets how care had come with the day:
Oh there! Oh there!
With the one, o'er all, who is dear to me,
How sweet is the zephyr!—how soft the sea!

II.

But not *on* the sea—the restless sea,
That can never a moment constant be—
Where the zephyr itself can rouse to rage,
And moonlight and starlight fail to 'suage:
Where, mocking the fond heart's loving prayer,
The ocean smothers the young and fair—
Sweeps over the goodly ship, and spoils
The treasure that grew from a thousand toils:
Not there! Not there!
But beside the sea, in its gentle guise,
Let me gaze, at dusk, in the loved one's eyes!

III.

A cottage for me, by the summer sea,
With evergreen coppice and mighty tree,
And a glorious lawn of the tufted green
Stretching down where the white sands spread between;

And, if it so please, with a pile of rock
To fling up the spray at each billowy shock;
While the waves, with a loving moan entreat
The zephyr to wander on wingéd feet:
Oh there! Oh there!
With the one, o'er all, who can feel with me,
How sweet is the breeze, and how soft the sea!

HAYNE.—LET THE DEATH-BELL TOLL.

I.

Let the death-bell toll for the parting soul—
It has paid for the pomp at a fearful price;
Spread gloom o'er the walls of your stately halls,
And deck your homes with each drear device:
For the city lies strangled by hostile power,
And the tyrant's foot is on temple and tower;
Yet one brave heart, in that desolate hour,
Now makes himself ready for sacrifice!

II.

And the toll of the bell shall answer well,
As it lifts his soul o'er the tyrant's aim;
And well he knows, that the hate of foes
Shall win from his people a deathless name;
He sees the black coffin his couch beside,*

---

* Hayne's coffin was thrust into his cell the night before his execution—a wanton cruelty, without excuse. It was covered with black crape, but trimmed with a white fringe, to ridicule, as was supposed, the united colors of America and France.

But the hangman cowers at his glance of pride—*
While he walks his cell with a sovereign stride,
Since he feels that the morrow shall bring him fame.

III.

With the morrow is Fame, but a death of shame—
A mortal agony first, and then
A glad release to the realms of peace,
And a memory living 'mongst loving men!
He hath led to the battle a noble band,
Hath fought the good fight for his father-land;
He hath won, he hath lost; but his battle brand
Shall flash in the eyes of his foes again:

IV.

There are hands that shall wield, in the tented field,
The weapon so sacred in Freedom's sight;
And souls that shall rise, ere the martyr dies,
And pledge to his manés a deathless plight:
Never, while hostile foot shall tread
The soil where the sire hath fought and bled,
To sheathe the good weapon whose flash hath shed,
For the cause of his people, a glorious light!

V.

There are friends who come in the hour of his doom—
Of doom and of gloom—and they have no fear:
But they cower with their grief for the noble chief,
Who answers their pleadings with words of cheer!
To the boy at his side he says: "My son,
Be true to your country!—for though but one,

* The hangman was unknown: he attended at the place of execution masked and muffled.

You are one of a thousand, and realms are won
  Where a single great son shall in arms appear!"*

VI.

And the death-bells toll for the parting soul,
  And he walks 'mid the ranks of the marshall'd foe,
And he smiles as he sees that the balconies,
  And windows, have none who would see the show.
There is silence deep in each mansion proud,
Dread as deep, with no moaning loud,
But the citizen feels as the deathly shroud
  Were wrapping himself in a common woe!†

VII.

Lo! the British are here, and the Hessians there,‡
  And they form the square round the scaffold high,
And the martyr comes, to the sound of drums,
  And will show, by his death, how the brave should die;
He utters his prayer, that his God will spare,
But none to the Tyrant that's sovereign there;
And with brow erect, and soul above fear,
  He dies for his country's liberty.

---

* See the Biographer for the literal speech of Hayne to his son. The calm dignity of his demeanor, equally free from fear and ostentation, is evinced throughout his whole deportment.

† The houses of the citizens were all carefully shut up during the time occupied in the procession and execution; and none but the British, Hessians, and the more malignant of the Tories—who were also mostly Europeans—were to be seen. Hayne walked to the place of execution, attended by Dr. Ramsay (who carried the umbrella over his head), and a few other friends.

‡ The military escort consisted of three hundred men. The place of execution was just without the city lines, near *Radcliffe's Garden*, nearly in front, and within a stone's throw of the present Orphan House building. The troops formed a hollow square around the scaffold, the British troops occupying the front and rear, the Hessians on the right and left.

THE MOUNTAIN PROSPECT.

I.

'Tis glorious all! Here Nature weds
Her mightiest forms to haughtiest heads,
And o'er each brow a halo spreads!

Here, throned within her thunder peaks,
Against the sky she leans her cheeks,
And mocks the lightning as it wreaks

Its wrath upon her sovereign towers;
Clad in her simplest robe of flowers,
And all unmoved, through saddest hours!

Here, lavish of her beauties still,
She bids her blooms the valleys fill,
And o'er her rock she pours her rill:

Relieves, with swelling steeps, the plain,
Smooths rocky height to vale again,
And through it sends a silvery vein,

That lies like serpent crouch'd in coil,
Now silent winds, as seeking spoil—
Now stretch'd at length, as if from toil!

II.

Anon, her murmur takes the ear,
Beyond the mountain ledge, that sheer,
Colossal stands, a silent Fear!

And o'er it foaming, silvery white,
The cataract leaps, a sheeted sprite,
Singing a chaunt of fierce delight—

As if of Freedom!—as it goes,
From conquering conflict to repose,
In meadows where each wild flower blows.

III.

Thus, from the embrace of Terror, glide
The forms of Beauty, side by side,
And crown with Love the heights of Pride!

Thus, hallowing all the gloom, they grow
To Deities of grace; and glow,
Wrapt on their heights, with living Bow,

That, from the sun, through bluest skies,
Still catches all their gorgeous dyes,
And soothes the sad to human eyes!

The foaming torrent leaps through groves
That might have gladden'd Sadi's loves;
Then meek o'er quiet valley roves,

As if, by spells of Love subdued,
It straight forgot each mountain feud;
Content, no longer wild and rude,

To drink in odors from the vale,
And 'quite the flowers with pretty tale
Of mountain griefs—the angry wail

O'er hostile crags, and stubborn bounds
Of rock, that watery force confounds,
And desperate leap that still astounds!

IV.

Ah! wandering lone—away from men,
To see great height and gloomy glen,
And pierce the skies with thoughtful ken—

To feel the eager soul upspring,
Buoyant, as born for rivalling
The mountain eagle's mighty wing—

Track the great billowy range of height,
That rolls in surge, with scalps of white,
'Till vision stops itself in flight—

Make pictures with the mind and eye,
Of Titan wall and arching sky,
And watch their phantoms flit and fly:

Like things that revel in the shade,
When, as of old, the gods array'd
The woods, and fawns and satyrs play'd:

Or, 'neath the giant summits, brood
Upon the Christian God—the mood
That fashion'd worlds and call'd them good:—

That made them fruitful to the thought,
And show'd how wonders might be wrought
By will and majesty untaught;

And gaze beyond, to realms that seem
The abode of mystery and dream;
With ever and anon a gleam

To cheer the doubt and light the dark,
Illume, though still with moment spark—
The dove still issuing from the ark!—

Beyond, where, seeking heavenly groves,
Eternal chase, and fruitful loves,
The Red man's simple fancy roves:

Where still—once leapt the precipice—
The gulph where erring step shall miss—
He wins the realm of perfect bliss!—

His fancy not more vain than ours,
Though born of feebler aims and powers—
Both fancies seeking peaceful bowers!

V.

Ah! thus to dream, o'er cliff and height,
Great range of sea, with ships in sight,
The sun thrown back from sails of white;

Green fields below, that still persuade
The happy song of bird or maid,
And Astrea smiling in the shade;

And thousand charms with these, that tell
Of nymph and dryad, brook and dell,
Each hallowed with a crowning spell:

The common earth, meanwhile—the towers,
As well as vales—all prankt with flowers,
That sing and laugh away the hours;

The glad young waters, leaping free,
Still catching rainbows as they flee
And bound, through beams, eternally;—

With none beside, the bliss to share,
The soul to answer, and to hear,
When, in my joy, I murmur, "There!

"How beautiful!"—To feel no breast
Exulting with mine own to rest
In crags above the eagle's nest;

And watch with me the wondrous show,
The gorgeous vision, passing slow,
Through blue above and green below!—

VI.

This robs from charm in earth and skies!
We ask to see with kindred eyes:
And rapture's self demands replies—

Echoes from genial founts—a voice
That, fashion'd by our spirit's choice,
Sings out, when we would say, "Rejoice!"

VII.

Would I might summon one to see,
And drink the vision in with me—
One dear one, dear exceedingly!

To whose young heart mine own might say,
"This is a God-appointed day,
And all the world is out at play;

"And we will cunningly devise
To see these sports of earth and skies,
Each looking through the other's eyes."

SONNET.—OH! PRECIOUS IS THE FLOWER!

OH! precious is the flower that Passion brings
 To his first shrine of beauty, when the heart
Runs over with devotion, and no art
 Checks the free gush of the wild lay he sings:
But the rapt eye and the impetuous thought
 Declare the pure affection; and a speech,
 Such as the ever-tuned affections teach,
Delivers love's best confidence unbought;
And all is glory in the o'er-arching sky,
 And all is beauty in the uplifting earth,
 And, from the wood, and o'er the wave, a mirth,
Such as lures hope with immortality,
Declares that all the loved ones are at hand,
With still the turtle's voice the loudest in the land!

"VOLANS VIDEO."

I.

GIVE Fancy freedom, freedom to-night!
 Let her soar up in the face of the stars!
What's the soul-virtue, if never, in flight,
 We fling off our sense of the earth with its bars?
The spirit that clings to its fetters of clay,
 Whose eyes never lift in the prayer for a wing,
Hath no pinion of soul which shall bear it away
  To that realm of delight,
  Which is born of the flight,
 Where the very soul-soaring compels it to sing!

II.

It needs but the prayer for the wing, and we rise!
  We have shaken the earth-clogs away from our feet;
Already we taste the cool breath of the skies,
  And the music deliciously wooing and sweet!
See, as we soar, how the provinces spread,
  How the bright vistas persuade us to roam
Oh! friends, 'tis the sky, the blue sky overhead,
      And the realms that he finds,
      In his flight with the winds,
  That make for the soul of the poet her home.

III.

Freed from the fetter, a captive no more,
  With the glad spirit upsoaring, the eye
Takes in the moony realm, ocean and shore,
  Mountain and billow, in cope of the sky!
Lo! the bird crossing the face of the moon!
  How the great vans waver darkly and bright!
He speeds—the crag-ærie will welcome him soon;
      See where the grim steep,
      Hanging over the deep,
  Bathes its forehead of blackness in smiles of the night!

IV.

And, hark! the wild scream from below—
  The eagle's fierce cry of delight!
And see, on the peak of the mount, in the glow
  Of the moon, where his mate is in sight!
She flings off her young from the steep:
  They flutter—are falling—but the sire,
While each feather of his wing rattles loud in its sweep,
      Darts beneath, and they cling,
      Upon shoulder and wing,
  While he rushes up in pride to his spire.

V.

Even he shall not mate us in flight,
  Though a type of the noblest in air;
We aspire to a realm of a braver delight
  Than the lark or the eagle may share:
We've the passport of soul to a clime
  Where the will finds the wing, and the eye,
Touch'd by thought and by fancy with visions sublime,
      No element copes,
      Creates as it opes,
  And wills for itself where to fly!

VI.

Away and aloft, with a bolder aim,
  We swim 'mid the eyes of the milky way;
And we gaze upon beauties with earthly name,
  That never yet sank 'neath an earthly sway!
There, the central group of the Pleiades,
  That never lost sister, as here you see,
Float together serenely on silver seas,
      And woo with a smile,
      Whose meanest wile
  Were a bliss to our mortal destinies.

VII.

Ah! why should we wander yet farther on,
  Since here the Elysium spreads around?
We have but to cherish the fields we've won,
  And the lost Eden again is found.
What a glorious landscape woos us now!
  The plains lie open; the mountains blue
Conduct us on to one snow white brow,
      Where the cataract breaks
      Into silvery lakes,
  That wander away the whole valley through!—

VIII.

And the glory that smiles o'er the landscape gleams
With a brightness such as no sun may show,
Yet we gaze undazzled, as when in our dreams
We hail the great orb in his noonday glow;
While a sky spreads o'er us more pure and clear
Than ever on mortal vision shone,
And we pierce with our souls a nobler sphere—
Whose music is light,
Whose being is flight,
And we float in a sea of fragrance on!

IX.

There swells the blue of a thousand hills;
Together the grand and the soft unite;
And the harmony streams from a thousand rills,
That lapse away from each heaving height;
And lo! where an ocean spreads below,
With wingéd forms on a silvery shore,
That dart and glow, as they laugh and go,
And shed, as they rise,
The light from eyes
That smile with love as they sing and soar!

X.

Now drink your fill, and to memory plead
For the sweetest lore that she ever knew;
See the group that beckons to yonder mead,
With eyes that win, and with smiles that woo!
Hath their happy flight to the better sphere
Made the change so great to your mortal ken,
That ye know not the forms that were once so dear
And can not trace,
In each glorious face,
The charms so precious 'mongst mortal men?

XI.

Lo! the sweet sister, so pale and fair,
  With eyes so blue and cheeks so wan;
Whose hapless dying, the livelong year,
  Gave a sad relief when ye felt her gone:
No death now darkens those lustrous eyes,
  No sorrow now wans that virgin face,
But a wondrous youth in her beauty lies,
    And the bliss that speaks
    In those soul-lit cheeks,
Shows an angel life with an angel grace.

XII.

And note ye the joyous bride that stands,
  Blessing, beside her, and woos us nigh!
How sweetly she waves her snow-white hands,
  And oh! the sweet passion that lights her eye!
Ah! weep—yes, weep! but with joyful tears,
  As at bliss new born in a stricken heart;
The night is gone that was full of fears,
    And, on other shores,
    The soul restores
  What the mortal Terror hath torn apart.

XIII.

This is the vale of the Perfect Peace,
  And how glorious all is the blessed show!
From pleasure to pleasure, with fresh increase,
  In every change, may the inmates go;
They have but to will, and the landscape gleams
  With living treasures of love-delight;
Such as in glimpses they show us in dreams,
    To soothe the woe
    Of our life below,
And win our thoughts to a loftier flight.

XIV.

And the glorious power of soul here lies,
  In this very virtue of will, to call
Into quick presence, from out the skies,
  Each germ of joy, and with shape enthrall;
To summon, from realms in the airy space,
  Of beauty, and bliss, and love, the charms,
To weave the air into shapes of grace,
        Bid the tree shoot,
        Command the fruit,
  And crown the whole landscape with happy forms.

XV.

See, as we gaze, how, with lifted hands,
  And a potent will that need never speak,
They raise around them the bloomy lands,
  And the rocks shoot up to a snowy peak;
And along their slopes, how the crimson flowers
  Gem the green sward as with laughing eyes,
While, on the great summit, a temple tow'rs,
        Where the Perfect Art,
        In a wondrous mart,
  Each image of beauty and love supplies!

XVI.

And lo! from the temple streams a tide
  Of noble and beautiful forms, that grow,
As down, o'er the sunny slopes, they glide,
  Into beings we've known and that still we know;
There stands the manly and white-hair'd sire,
  And there is the loving mother who bore;
How perfect now in their soul attire!
        Unbent with years,
        Untroubled with fears,
  And bless'd by the tears, which they shed no more;

XVII.

And they wave us their blessing, and bid us see
  The glorious clime that their wings have won;
But, alas! our feet are no longer free,
  And all in vain would we wander on:
This is the bound of our mortal flight,
  And a mighty spell in the barrier air,
Checks the wild gush of that warm delight
      Which would bound to gain
      The glorious plain,
  And wander away with the loved ones there.

XVIII.

But a moment's glimpse, and the plain is void:
  They are gone—the beautiful, bright ones, all;
All the grand phantoms of art destroy'd,
  Sudden, as cloudy palaces fall,
When the architect sun forbears to gild,
  And turns away with a moody brow!
Vainly would Fancy the realm rebuild,
      And pierce the screen
      That falls between,
  And shuts the whole scéne from our vision now.

XIX.

Alas! that the earth should still be near—
  That Fancy's limit should now be won!
We have had but a glimpse of the wondrous sphere,
  Which dulls the glory of mortal sun!
And to forfeit all, and to feel the wing
  Clipt in its flight to the spirit's home;
To sink once more where the birds that sing,
      But mock the gains
      Of those grander strains,
  That lift the soul when it seeks to roam!

XX.

And yet, the one glimpse in that happy flight,
  Of the wondrous powers of soul set free,
Shall lift the heart with a long delight,
  In this dream of its immortality!
And what if the promise of earth be low?
  With the soul-promise that flight declares,
We spurn its bonds, with a Hope whose glow
      Shall gild the wing,
      In each upward spring
That carries us out of this Vale of Tears.

XXI.

The Valley of Perfect Peace is ours,
  With all its fruits, and its sweet serene,
If the will to soar bring the soul its powers,
  And through earth's vapors the light be seen.
It is but to soar, and with soaring, see;
  The mount of vision is quickly won,
If we set the soul-pinion with fancy free,
      And shake off the clod
      Of that earthly God,
Who makes his sole realm 'neath a mortal sun:

XXII.

If we break, with a wing, through that narrow ring
  Which binds the base realm of each lowly aim,
And rend from the soul, that earthy control
  Which crushes from spirit its seraph flame;
And rise to the lore, which, taught of yore,
  Moved the eager Thought to an upward flight,
And purged the vision, for realms elysian,
      Where, to use the wing,
      Is to see—to sing,
And the very flight is a birth of light!

SONNET.—METHINKS, YOUNG SHEPHERD, YOU HAVE DREAMED!

Methinks, young shepherd, you have dreamed all this!
  Our fancies are most frolicsome, and oft
  They bear the thought on erring wing aloft,
Where, 'scaped from reason, it is lost in bliss.
Beshrew me, but it is a pleasant spot
  For fairies to make merry on, until
  The steeple's clock, from yonder gray-browed hill,
Doth warn them from their vagrant sports, I wot!
Yet, till the dawning, they may brush the dew,
And it may be, methinks, in daylight too,
Albeit we see them not: the glare of day
May take, perchance, their feebler fires away—
As the stars fade when the full moon is fair,
And yet we know they still are twiring there.

THE BALLAD OF OLD HICKORIE.

Oh! dreary and cold was the sullen night,
When the bands of Old England, famous in fight,
Drew near, in the pride of their martial might,
  And the pomp of their ocean chivalrie!

Never they fear'd the meagre array
Of the hunter tribes that stood in their way,
Like the snake in his coil, or the wolf at bay,
  On the mighty banks of the Mechachebe!

They came as a confident martial race,
Bold in their strength, and lofty of place,
Never once dreaming of dread disgrace
  At the hands of that rustic infantrie!

And they sang, as they came, a proud insolent song
Of Beauty and Booty, the triumph of Wrong,
Such as, of yore, made them daring and strong,
  In their progress of lust over land and sea!

Great were the Captains that led them on,
Famous in fields where crowns are won,
And trained by the genius of Wellington,
  To pluck from the Fates the red victorie!

Oh! glorious then was the grand array
Of shining steel and of plumage gay,
While the martial instruments evermore play,
  With blare of the Saracen minstrelsie!

There were thousands on thousands, doughty and tall,
In solid phalanx, with regular fall
Of timéd steps, as they one and all
  Strode over the banks of the Mechachebe!

And, great white clouds, like the wings of fame,
Their mighty squadrons of shipping came,
Ready to belch, in bolt and flame,
  Their vengeance and hate on the fair citie!

And the cannon roar'd the approaching war,
As the lion roars his coming afar,
Shaking the nations with terrible jar,
  And making their timid tribes to flee!

And the plains they shook with the mighty tread,
And over their march hung a cloud of red,
And under their iron feet, dying or dead,
  Shrank the green children of industrie!

Oh! that mighty host, what power shall stand?
So terribly arm'd, with such great command?
Where is the arm, in this forest land,
  To brave them, and make them backward flee?

What groups of a rustic race are these,
From the piney woods, from the prairie seas,
With nothing of pomp to appall or please,
  And none of the banners of chivalrie?

How shall their simple weapons tell,
In the conflict fierce with a foe so fell?
And whose is the name of might to spell,
  Till their courage shall mount like a raging sea?

Oh! simple and few are that forest race,
But well they know how the foe to face:
They have grappled the panther in wild embrace,
  And torn off his hide in his agonie!

And they follow a chief, whose eagle look
The eye of a master could never brook;
Whose soul with no feeling of fear ever shook—
  And they lovingly call him Old Hickorie!

He carries a staff of a wondrous might,
As potent in season of peace as in fight;
It only needs he should wave it in sight,
  To win, or to conquer, the victorie!

Oh! Packenham boasts of a mighty name,
But let him beware, lest he come to shame,
When he meets with that eye of an eagle flame,
  And feels that staff of Old Hickorie!

But the pride of Britain will never hear,
'Till the danger rings on the heart as ear:
'Tis the riving bolt that shall make her fear,
  And curb her cruel rapacitie!

And her hosts stride on in their grand array,
While her martial bands of her conquests play—
Of the beauty and booty, the fruits of the fray,
  That make the charms of her victorie!

And they heed but little that rustic band,
That silently gathers to guard the land,
Or the eye of that Lord of the Dread Command,
  With his knotted staff of old hickorie!

How, with souls of strength, and with hearts of hate,
Like tigers in jungle, they watch and wait,
Ready to spring, with the talons of fate,
  To grapple with England's chivalrie!

Oh! the gallant hearts that are beating high,
Elate with the rapturous battle cry:
The night shall see them all stiffening lie,
  With never the spirit to fight or flee!

Short grows the terrible space between,
And the ranks rush on to the fearful scene,
And with lips close set, and a deadly mien,
  They leap to the bath of blood fearlesslie!

And the cannon roars, and the column sinks;
The stream of the Mechachebe drinks
The purple torrent—its turbid brinks,
  From the curdling rivers of carnage flee!

But ever the Briton presseth on,—
For the veteran troops of Duke Wellington,
Trained in the struggle where crowns are won,
  Must perish or pluck the red victorie!

And the column it springs, where the column falls,
And it mocks with a cheer the hurtling balls,
And rising in stirrup, brave Packenham calls:
  "To the conquest, my merrie men, follow me!"

But, even as he rusheth to reach the prize,
The forest chief opens his eagle eyes,
And he bids his young wolves from the jungle rise,
  And he throws out his staff of old hickorie!

Oh! terrible then was the sudden shout,
That rang at the waving, the field throughout,
And horrid the clash of that battle-bout,
  That followed the glance of his eagle e'e!

And Packenham drinks of the gore and the sand;
And thousands beside, of his gallant band,
Lie stretch'd in death, at the wave of that hand,
  That bore the staff of old hickorie!

The soldiers of Wellington strew the plain;
They rally their broken hosts in vain;
And the wounded howl, while over the slain
  The terrified fugitives tramp and flee!

But for ages long shall the people tell
Of him that so wielded the powerful spell,
That hickorie staff, and the stroke so fell,
  That he gave by the waters of Mechachebe!

And ever, should other foes arise,
Then the people shall warm with old memories
Of that mighty staff, and those eagle eyes,
  And the fearless soul of Old Hickorie!

SONNET.—I'VE ROUSED THE KENNEL!

I'VE roused the kennel! They are at my heels,
The whole cur rabble—the promiscuous pack—
Sneak, Skunk, and Scurril, dogs of low degree,
Who think my shadow much too large for me!
One growls, one yelps, another squeaks or squeals—
Well, with such venom, that in teeth they lack;
A stick or stone would send them howling back—
But where the profit? 'Twere but loss of time!
And he who hath his goal in sight—such goal
As rouses all that's God-like in the soul—
Who sees his temple, with its towers sublime,
High, in the distance, with great dome and arch,
Looking fond welcome, urging him to march—
Hath little need to chafe in heart or mind,
Well pleased to leave the little dogs behind!

BALLAD.—THE JEWELL'D BREAST OF NIGHT.

I.

THE jewell'd breast of night
  Swells calm beyond the breeze,
While, like a bird, we take our flight
  O'er wild and lonely seas!
Yet many a prayer is given,
  To ward the tempest's wrath;
And hearts, laid bare to Heaven,
  (Dear hearts! sweet hearts!)
Send blessings on our path!

II.

One home I know unsleeping—
  One dear, sweet cottage home!
Ah! there one heart is weeping
  Within a silent room!
Her fancies follow fast my flight;
  She strains her eyes throughout the dark,
And shuddering, fears, in storm and night,
  (Sweet heart! fond heart!)
That wild seas wreck my barque!

III.

Ah, me! how still we doubt
  Even of the hope possess'd:
As ruby lips will perk and pout,
  Though pleased to be caressed!
I sudden doubt, if weeping now,
  That loved one watches sad and lone;
A jealous fancy racks my brow—
  (Frail heart! false heart!)
Am I forgot as soon as gone?

IV.

We vex our hearts with idle fears:
  For, ah! too well we know how soon
The smile will chase away the tears—
  To loving memories such a boon—
And thus we doubt if they are sad,
  The distant dear ones whom we fly;
We fancy that each face is glad,
  (Vain hearts! false hearts!)
With thoughtless joy in every eye;

V.

That through the gay saloon they rove,
  While mirth and music glad the sense—
Hear other lips in speech of love,
  To other hearts make recompense;
That, circled by a stranger's arms,
  The faithless loved one, shaming both,
To other words of pleading warms,
  (Frail heart! false heart!)
And all forgets her plighted troth!

VI.

Let *me* not doubt the maid *I* leave;
  Yet, ah! what hours of true delight
Would I to fortune now forgive,
  To know she sorrows through the night:
Hears rising winds with rising tears,
  Watches each cloud-wreath through the day;
And in her chamber, pale with fears,
  (Sweet heart! dear heart!)
Weeps the slow, weary night away!

WHEN I MET THEE, CORA LEE.

I.

When I met thee, Cora Lee,
Thou wast surely unto me,
What the star is to the midnight—what the blossom to the tree;
In thy face, so soft and fair,
Was the dawn and morning air;
And the sunset in thy hair
Was a glory, Cora Lee!

II.

Thine were eyes, my Cora Lee,
Which it dazzled mine to see,
But still won, with all their dazzle—won me ever after thee;
And I follow'd with a pace
That but shamed thy maiden grace,
Though with backward-looking face,
Thou still won'st me, Cora Lee!

III.

But no more, on land or sea,
Shall my footsteps follow thee:
My star of midnight's gone, and my blossom of the tree;
And thy face of morning fair,
And thy grace of flight and air,
And the sunset in thy hair,
They are gone, forever gone, Cora Lee!

IF FROM MY HEART I TEAR THEE.

I.

If from my heart I tear thee,
Thou fasten'st on my sight;
And when I most forswear thee,
Then most thou look'st delight;
Yet when I turn to woo thee,
'Tis then thou mock'st my heart:
Thou flout'st when I pursue thee,
Yet woo'st when I depart!

II.

I seek, in others' smiling,
For loves that warm to mine:
Alas! when most beguiling,
Then most they look like thine;
Even brighter beauties only
Remind me of thy charms,
And my heart is then most lonely,
With another in mine arms.

III.

If love to me denying,
Why still to memory cling?
If thus resolved on flying,
Why still look back and sing?
What profits thee to capture,
Yet still refuse to chain;
Forbear the very rapture
That consecrates the reign?

DEATH, BUT NEVER DISHONOR!

I.

DEATH, but never Dishonor!
  If Freedom we now must resign,
Be the fields where our fathers first won her,
  Her burial-place and her shrine!
There let us marshal our powers,
  Sworn to our ancestors' fame,
And if victory may not be ours,
  At least we shall sink without shame.

II.

Sons have forgotten their mothers,
  Traitors with foes are allied,
And those we have cherished as brothers,
  Shrink in dismay from our side;
Realms that still share in our danger,
  Tremble to share in the strife—
Yield up the field to the stranger,
  Liberty selling for life!

III.

Never for us thy foul story,
  Unless from the past you may tear
Every record that tells of the glory
  Of the sires whose weapons we wear!
The birthright of place which they gave us,
  Is naught to their birthright of fame;
Foes may crush, but they shall not enslave us!
  Hate may conquer, but never shall shame!

SONNET.—METHINKS THERE IS NO BLINDNESS.

Methinks there is no blindness such as this:
  To know not, though the treasure near us lies,
  Love's treasure, first and dearest, which the skies
Vouchsafed when earth had lost all right to bliss—
The treasure of a true heart: which to roof
  Lowly, brings life; and when, all fortune spent,
Cheers with devotion and the sweetest proof,
  So that the sufferer freshens with content;
And, in the desolation at his door,
  Sees but the sweet security of all
  Which, lost to hapless Adam at the fall,
Eden regained, had left possession poor!
Yet daily, in our blindness, we rush on,
Though hearts around us cry, imploring to be won.

SHALL ALL, THEN, BE FORGOTTEN?

I.

Shall all, then, be forgotten,
  As if we never knew
Of the whispering dusk, the starlight,
  The dim valley, night and dew?
Of the doubt that grew to madness;
  Of the bliss akin to fright;
And the dreaming, so like madness,
  Love's convulsion and delight?

II.

Can it be that hearts so kindred
  Should be sunder'd now, and lone?
That the keen, fond sense of rapture
  Of those moments, should be gone?
Shall we part, yet feel no anguish?
  Meet, yet know no more the thrill,
That hath made our mutual bosoms
  At once passionate and chill?

III.

Ah! what of life's illusions,
  When even Love a traitor grows,
And the flame that burn'd like Ætna
  Shall be changed to Arctic snows?
When thine eye, that ever kindled
  As it rose to meet mine own,
Can bear, unmoved, the glances
  That still seek for thee alone?

IV.

Go! what to me thy fortune?
  It was faith in thee I sought!
Go! what to me thy beauty,
  If it mocks each loving thought?
'Twas a wingéd soul I worship'd,
  Not a vain caprice, whose breath,
In its cold and cruel changes,
  Could make Love a thing of death!

WELL, LET THEM SING THEIR HEROES.

I.

Well, let them sing their heroes' deeds of fame,
  Their belted warriors, great in souls of might;
We, too, have gallant chiefs we joy to name,
  Glorious in soul, and fearless in the fight!
There's not a spot in all this land of ours,
  From Ashley's wave to Apalachia's steep,
Though smiling now in green, and gay with flowers,
  That has not seen their charging squadrons sweep:
    That has not heard the cry
    Peal through the blood-red sky—
A cry of death and terror to the foe:
    That has not felt the strife
    For liberty and life,
The wild alarm, the gallant charge, sharp shot and fatal blow!

II.

And if the Peace that blossoms through our land,
  The boon of Valor, won from matchless Hate,
Be once again by foreign legions bann'd,
  And all be terror that was triumph late;
Then shall the spirit of old days awaken,
  And through our plains the glorious cry shall speed,
The share thrown by, the sword again be taken,
  And pluméd War bestride his battle steed:
    The soul of Sumter then,
    Shall stir each hill and glen,
And Marion rouse the swamp and range the plain;
    Brave Moultrie by the deep,
    Fling off his ancient sleep,
And, from his mountain heights, old Pickens dart again.

AH! HEARTS THAT LATE WERE BEATING.

I.

Ah! hearts that late were beating
  With joyous music's flow,
To brighter regions fleeting,
  Do ye forget us now?
You're free: but is the rapture
  That fills ye as ye soar,
Oblivion of the dear ones
  That weep ye evermore?

II.

We follow, in our fancies,
  The happy flight ye take;
We pray that your's be rapture,
  Whatever clime ye seek:
That joyous seasons greet ye,
  And dear ones, gone before,
Stand waiting, wing'd, to meet ye,
  And teach ye how to soar!

III.

Ye can not, sure, forget us,
  Whose true affections yet,
Are striving, fond as ever,
  And never can forget?
Ye see us where we wander,
  Ye hear us, as we cry;
Ah! wherefore not, to cheer us,
  With blessing, hover nigh?

ELEGIAC.—DEAR WANDERER.

I.

Dear wanderer from thy boyhood's hearth,
  To homes that made thee native there,
Thou hadst a blessed gift at birth,
  To make thee welcome everywhere!
Alas! that love, who welcomed fond,
  Should not possess the power to save;
Denied to keep—all power beyond—
  To watch thy couch—to deck thy grave!

II.

'Twere vain to say that thou wast dear,
  Where truth and love and virtue shone;
More vain, if we could keep thee here,
  To say thou hadst not from us gone!
What love, and art, and watch could do,
  Were done for thee—alas, in vain!
With sinking hearts, we could but view,
  Not soothe, not stay, nor share thy pain!

III.

So calm and placid, sweet and clear,
  Thine eyes' last gentle meanings shone,
We knew some higher, happier sphere
  Had surely claimed thee for its own:
Yet felt those sorrows fill each breast,
  That still our selfish loss deplore,
And grieved to see the being bless'd
  That ever bless'd our hearts before!

STRIKE!—AS SAID THE ANVIL.

I.

STRIKE!—as said the anvil to the hammer—
  Strike! and never let your iron cool;
Up head, my boy! speak bravely!—do not stammer,
  Lest all the world should write you down a fool!
We have no time allowed for shilly-shally,
  But seventy years allotted to the best:
Down with the rock, tear up the fertile valley,
  Work out your purpose—leave to God the rest!

II.

You have a purpose—should have—then begin it
  An earnest working purpose is a power,
Which, if you straightway seize upon the minute,
  Will make its progress surer every hour.
Build up your fortunes by it—lay them deeply—
  Make your foundations sure!—then, day by day,
Raise up your walls—a fortress—never cheaply—
  Good purposes demand a large outlay!

III.

Strength, faith, devotion, toil, and resolution!—
  These make your capital—these freely spend:
Once sure of your design, the execution
  Needs all that you can give it, to the end.
Oh, boy!—man!—what a world is in the keeping
  Of him who nobly aims and bravely toils!
Speed to the work!—we'll all have time for sleeping,
  When we have shuffled off these mortal coils.

NIGHT SCENE.—HOW STILL IS NATURE NOW!

I.

How still is Nature now,
 How quiet all her sleep!
The dews are on her brow,
 And all her dreams are deep;
Closed darkly is her eye,
 Her breathings soft and low,
As if the spirit, once so high,
In challenge of the earth and sky,
 Would cease to flow.
And out on the black waste of ocean,
 We hear no commotion:
And the billows that lazily break on the shore
 Have a life, but no roar:
And the winds, that were chafing all day with the waves,
 Are subdued into slaves,
That crouch, and but murmur and wait,
As the night, trailing cloud robes, marches on in her state!

II.

Above the expanse of dark,
 That forms her sombre pall,
One star, with glowing spark,
 Looks loving out o'er all;
There spreads a tract of fleece,
 White, in the dusky west:
Like some fair Isle of Peace,
That, when the tempests cease,
 Smiles out on ocean's breast!

And we dream, as we gaze, of old fancies,
Found in ancient romances:
Of strange dwarfish races, of delicate graces,
That peopled such places—
To be seen when the sun was at setting,
On the sands pirouetting;
And who sped, on the star-beam, from islet to sea,
With frolicsome pinion, fantastic as free!

III.

A murmur from the sea,
A faint and dying strain,
Takes, as the night-winds flee,
Their parting moan again;
And the twin voices link
Their pinions for the shore,
Flutter with plaining on its brink,
Then on the sands subside, and sink
To sleep once more!
And they bury white heads in black pillows,
Those great rolling billows;
And the vast world of sea, in her bosom,
Doth lovingly close 'em;
While her murmur of lullaby, soft as the mother's,
Their deep sobbing smothers;
And the white fleecy isle, that we look'd on erewhile
In the west, passes east, and broods o'er with a smile.

IV.

Westward, two rivers wind,
Sweetly yielding to the deep;
In one embrace they find
The silvery sway of sleep:

And, from the embosomed bay,
  Ascends a spell, whose chain
Subdues their murmurous play
Of sounds, which melt away,
  As echoes from the plain;
And the skiff that late glided rejoicing,
    With lute-music and mellowest voicing
Now feels the same magic dominion,
    And floats, but with folded-up pinion;
The peace of the sky and the ocean
    Hath hush'd even rapture's emotion,
And the hearts that were stirr'd at each musical word,
Now sleep on their wings as a satisfied bird.

ASK ME NO MORE FOR SONG.

Ask me no more for song, dear maid,
  A mournful lyre like mine,
That can not now one heart persuade,
  Would do no grace to thine;
The song to win such youthful ear,
  Should breathe that matin tone,
Which, born of Love's own blesséd sphere,
  Makes every sphere its own.

Once, not in vain, the lip that speaks
  Had bid my numbers flow;
While throbbing veins, and flushing cheeks,
  Had told what none should know!
Had we but met in earlier days,
  Thou had'st not asked in vain:
Nor I, beneath thy beauty's blaze,
  Refused to wear its chain!

NOW, WHEN THE SPRING IS OVER.

I.

Now, when the spring is over,
  Now, when the summer's gone,
Why play the thoughtless lover,
  With winter hurrying on?
Love needs a time of flowers,
  And a lovelier sky than this;
Oh! 'tis in our youthful hours,
  That Passion may dream of bliss!

II.

When the sun waxes cold in heaven,
  And the bleak winds sweep the plain,
And the green from the tree is riven,
  And down falls the sleety rain:
When the eye no longer kindles
  With the glow in a loving breast,
And the joy to a memory dwindles,
  And we dream that we once were bless'd:

III.

Oh! then, how idle the fancy,
  To summon, by spells of art,
Or by any necromancy,
  The youth that once fill'd the heart!
We only know that 'tis over,
  The season of youth and spring,
And Love, that summer rover,
  May sadly fold up his wing.

ELEGIAC.—IT IS THE CAUSE.

It is the Cause—it is the Cause ennobles
  Each mortal pang and bleeding sacrifice;
And when our sky is full of fiery troubles,
  Then Freedom has its penalty—and price!

The lusts that subjugate a pampered people,
  And blind them to the Destinies that wait,
Need fiery bolts to shatter the high steeple,
  And startle men to consciousness of Fate!

We dance—we sing—unheeding of the hour,
  And where it hurries us: and mock the skies,
That fail, in timely shows of wrath and power,
  To warn the vain, in season, to be wise!

That ready argument, in fields of barter,
  That prompts, in base Expediency, to find
Escape from peril, needs some noble martyr,
  To bare his breast, and perish for his kind!

What less shall rouse us from this sad condition
  Of drowse and dream and dance, our fears that hush:
Teaching that safety lies in base submission,
  And he, the Foe, WILL spare, when he MAY crush?

Oh! we are ready for the scourge and halter,
  Unless, dear God! with startled souls, we swear,
By this young victim, bleeding at the altar,
  To buckle armor on, and seize the spear!

And shall we question of the danger brewing,
  Each barrier trampled down, or torn away?
Doubt of the doom, with still the foe pursuing,
  With scorn and hate and venom, day by day?

When his wild Priesthood, Moloch in profession,
  The weapon consecrates, and bids him smite:
Cries "DEUS VULT!"—and goads each hungry passion,
  Till Lust persuades itself that Crime is Right?

Oh! we had sires, that long ago had taken
  The bow and spear, and, hurrying to the breach,
The fiery bolt had sped, the falchion shaken,
  And taught the foe the lesson he would teach!

Alas! we have forsworn each great example:
  We crouch in cold stagnation: mouse for spoils
And fancy life, itself, a boon most ample,
  Consumed in petty strifes and slavish toils!

And we have weapons only for a brother—
  A syren song beguiles us from the foe;
Our hate for HIM, we sing to sleep, or smother,
  But strike down those who strike for us the blow!

O noble youth! O friend of gentlest 'havior!—
  So young, so generous—it had been our pride,
If, as thy people's champion—ay, their savior!—
  First in the glorious struggle, thou hadst died!

But thus!—and yet, thou shalt not vainly perish!
  Thy blood shall wash anew each ancient shrine;
Our drooping tree of Freedom feed and cherish!—
  Yet would it had been any blood but thine!

THE MOUNTAIN WINDS.

I sate upon the lofty Tryon's* brow,
While yet the sun was struggling up the east;
Broad was the realm around, and fair below
The plains, with summer fruits and flowers increas'd.
The soul and eye were at perpetual feast
On beauty; and the exquisite repose
Of nature, from the striving world released,
Taught me forgetfulness of mortal throes,
Life's toils, and all the cares that wait on human woes.

Never was day more cloudless in the sky—
Never the earth more beautiful in view:
Rose-crowned, the mountain summits gather'd high,
And the green forests shared the purple hue;
Midway, the little pyramids, all blue,
Stood robed for ceremonial, as the sun
Rose gradual in his grandeur, till he grew
Their god, and sovereign elevation won,
Lighting the loftiest towers as at a service done.

Nor was the service silent: for the choir
Of mountain winds took up the solemn sense
Of that great advent of the central fire,
And pour'd rejoicing as in recompense;
One hardly knew their place of birth, or whence
Their coming; but, through gorges of the hills,
Swift stealing, yet scarce breathing, they went thence
To gather on the plain—which straightway thrills
With mightiest strain, that soon the whole vast empire fills.

---

* Mount Tryon, a lofty summit, looking from North, into South Carolina.

From gloomy caverns of the Cherokee—
  From gorges of Saluda—from the groves
Of laurel, stretching far as eye may see,
  In valleys of Tselica—from great coves
  Of Tensas, where the untamed panther roves;
The joyous and exulting winds troop forth,
  Singing the mountain strain that freedom loves—
A wild but generous song of eagle birth,
That summons, far and near, the choral strains of earth.

They come from height and plain—from mount and sea:
  They gather in their strength, and, from below,
Sweep upwards to the heights—an empire free,
  Marching with pomp and music—a great show
  Triumphal—like an ocean in its flow,
Glorious in roar and billow, as it breaks
  O'er earth's base barriers: first, ascending slow,
The mighty march its stately progress takes,
But, rushing with its rise, its roar the mountain shakes!

O winds! that have o'erswept the viewless waste
  Where nature dwells in verdure—where the wild,
Not barren, though a wilderness, is graced
  With flowers more sweet than e'er in garden smiled;
  Or, in strange mood, by northern snows beguiled,
Have swept the *mer de glace*, nor felt the cold—
  Unfold to me, as to a yearning child
That longs for marvels—in its longings bold,
The story of your flight—the experience yet untold.

The world is yours, for ever, generous winds!
  Ye have won all its avenues; have swept
Where Nature in her stern dominion binds
  The waters in ice-fetters; nor have crept,
  Though the sad sun himself in heaven hath slept,

O'ercome with chills of apathy; and thence
  Have brought the doom to flowers, that, unbewept,
Do not all perish! Yet 'twould recompense
Your wrong, to share with us your strange intelligence.

The cultured and the wild, the height, the plain,
  Ancient and present seasons, all are yours!
Ye have heard Israel's monarch harp complain—
  Have swept old Homer's lyre on Hellas' shores—
  Hearkened while Dante's savage soul deplores,
And Milton moans his blindness in your ears—
  Yours only! Oh! how boundless are your stores
Of treasured legends: yield them to my prayers!
Make fruitful all the thought to rove through perishing
    years!

Methinks, as now your billows from below
  Roll upwards, and with generous embrace
Swell round me, that I hear a murmuring flow
  Of song, which might be story: and I trace
  The faint, far progress—men, and time, and place,
Commercing in relation fit—till start
  The actors into action: art with grace
Appealing to the kindred in our art,
Till all grows life and light, for fancy and the heart.

I climb the mighty pyramids, and scan
  The boundless desert—vacant, vast and wild,
Yet still I see the ancient prints of man!
  Ye sweep away the sand above him piled,
  And pierce his vaults—reveal him as the child
Of an ungoverned passion, fierce and strong,
  Rending his way to power: his nature filed
With savage lusts, that teach a joy in wrong,
While Vengeance broods above, nor spares the usurper
    long.

How, as your murmurs swell upon the sense,
  Grow they to voices, and inform the ear!
The imagination, in its dream intense,
  By natural consequence becomes the seer:
  The vanished ages at its will appear;
The gates of Nimroud open; o'er the plain
  Stream forth the servile myriads, dark and fair,
In fatal pomp, the power is wed to pain,
Sennacherib leads the host, and piles the fields with slain.

And Judah, as a captive in his hands,
  Droops to his dungeon. The sad wife and maid
Go to their lowly toils in stranger lands;
  Their silent harps among the willows laid,
  Resound not, though by the fierce conqueror bade
Repeat the glorious God-rejoicing strains
  That ever, morn and eve, glad tribute paid
To the great giver of their happy gains,
Ere guilty deeds had changed their raptures into pains.

Their mournful harps ye swept with trailing wings,
  To unseen spirits; with a power to cheer,
The sorrowful chaunt re-opened sacred springs
  Of love and worship; the consoling tear,
  Though salt, had yet its sweetness, and made clear
Jehovah's promise of that coming hour,
  Howe'er remote, the dawn of happier year,
When, in the fullness of his wakening power,
The widowed bride should wear, once more, the bridal
      flower.

Thus, on your wings ye bear to unknown times
  The empire's conquering shout, the captive's song;
Your voices are the voices of all climes!—
  All ages—great and base—the weak, the strong—
  Their cry of grief or rapture, prayer or wrong,

Move with your choral pinions. Ages die,
  But still their accents rise and linger long,
Even as the light from stars that fleck the sky
Will strain through space, though they no longer burn on
    high.

I list ye, and these valleys teem with life;
  The desert puts on verdure; cities soar
Beneath the mountain; and the glorious strife
  Of purpose and performance, evermore
  Resounds from human haunts; the generous lore
Recalls the beautiful when earth was young;
  Legions of glorious aspects ye restore—
Shades of those mighty minstrels who have sung
When Nature was a child, and Art first found her tongue.

I travel with ye o'er each sacred spot,
  Made holy by the march of mightiest men:
Here was the altar-place; this mystic grot
  Harbored a muse; within yon wooded glen,
  Pan marshalled all his satyrs; here, again,
Gathered the little phalanx of the free,
  Prepared to welcome the last struggle then,
For shrines and temples dear to liberty,
The gift of shadowy sires that watched the strife to see.

Where the glad nation, lapsed in summer bliss,
  Forgot her vigilance—where the conquering race
Stood forth, and bridged with death the precipice
  That kept them from the bright luxurious place,
  Ye lead me still, till meeting, face to face,
I gaze upon the past o'er walls of time—
  Each circumstance of power, and pride, and grace
Unveiled with realms of each delicious clime,
  Where glory wraps her pall around the hills sublime!

What empires ye unfold to me, blest airs,
  That travel o'er all wastes of time and earth;
Those mighty shadows, when the strife was theirs,
  Have felt your pinions, and, with sense of mirth,
  Thrown wide their bosoms, feeling a new birth
In your cool breathings; in the storm of fight
  Ye swept the plain, and to the soul of worth
Brought cheer, in echoing answers of great might,
From other godlike souls that strove for home and right.

Oh! sing to me for ever, from your heights—
  Roll from your deep abysses the proud strain
That teaches power, and tells of wild delights,
  Of a sad grandeur, half allied to pain!
  Oh, billowy anthems, upward swell again,
With all your awful voices, that unite
  The ages with their gods—a shadowy train,
That trail great robes of purple on the sight,
And, in the maturing soul, look down with eyes of might!

THE WINTER FLOWER.

I

When winter comes with icy mien,
  To silver o'er this little brook,
Upon its banks thy form is seen,
    By all forsook.

II.

No shrub then lingers on the plain,
  To feed the warm and watchful gaze;
Nor sprig of grass the fields retain,
    Nor blade of maize.

III.

Far as the searching eye may bend,
  O'er gentle slope and bedded vale,
The barren, cheerless plains extend,
      Thou tell'st their tale.

IV.

Thou, of the autumn train the last,
  A mournful truth thy form conveys,
Thou lingering relic of the past,
      And brighter days.

V.

No other flow'r, that late could vie,
  Superior once in bloom to thee,
May now unfold, beneath the sky,
      Its pageantry.

VI.

Struck in the sullen clod too deep,
  Thy roots the wintry winds defy,
And while thy thousand brethren sleep,
      Thou lift'st thine eye.

VII.

What secret spring of life is thine?
  And what art thou, pale flow'r, to gain
Such partial favor, thus to shine
      Last of thy train?

VIII.

Unhurt, when all around are dead,
  Unshrinking, though the blasts arise,
And lifting still thy fearless head,
      In fearful skies?

IX.

Such lot, methinks, can ne'er be blest:
  To feel ourselves in life alone—
A late, and watchful, lingering guest,
    When all are gone!

DESOLATION.—ALL LONELY IS THE DWELLING.

I.

All lonely is the dwelling now,
  Where happy voices rang;
And gone to waste the pleasant bower
  Where still the garlands hang;
And mute and motionless is all,
  Once full of life and speech—
Ah, me! how much of human woe
  Doth this sad ruin teach.

II.

How many hopes have here been crush'd,
  As innocent as dear—
How many smiling eyes been taught
  The language of a tear;
And dreams of early, rich delight,
  Like specks upon the waste,
Have only come to cheat the sight,
  While they defraud the taste!

III.

While thus I stand and look around
  On scenes so lately gay,
And call to mind the happy tones
  I heard but yesterday:

That reverend father's friendly voice,
  That merry maiden's song,
That sank so deep into my heart,
  And warmed it well and long:

IV.

The wild-eyed boys that sprang to meet
  When they beheld me near;
And even the household dog, that crouch'd,
  My sure caress to share;
All gone—the little paling down,
  The grass above the stone,
The shutter broken from its hinge,
  And Ruin there alone:

V.

I can not weep, though sad the sight,
  And sad the thought it brings,
Of what was dear, and what is lost,
  Of sweet familiar things;
The voices at my heart grow dumb,
  And like some dread despair,
They echo in their loneliness
  The silence that is here.

VI.

And grief is lost in great surprise
  That, in my manhood's noon,
I still should love the things so well,
  That pass away so soon.
A flower that kiss'd me in a dream,
  By zephyrs borne along,
Had filled my chamber with its bloom,
  And lulled me with its song;

4

VII.

An unsubstantial joy, the gift
 Of warm and generous youth,
In one delirious moment fill'd
 My yielding heart like truth;
Till, in my fond forgetfulness,
 A shadow and a bird
Brought pictures to my pliant soul,
 The sweetest seen and heard.

VIII.

The shadow and the bird are fled—
 The kind hearts kindliest known,
More sweet and swift than summer flowers,
 Are perished all, and gone;
They came like summer winds at night,
 To win us with a breath,
Then sink, in quietude away,
 To the pale groves of death.

LAMIA—THE BEAUTIFUL SIN.

I.

Oh! the Sin, the Beautiful Sin,
 How it haunted me night and day,
Ever with pleading most sure to win,
 Ever with winning most sure to sway;
So, together, by shore and sea,
 In grove and in city, ever the same,
With that Beautiful Sin I wanton'd free,
 Nor heeded the sin, nor dream'd the shame;
Blinded and madden'd, I never could see,
 Nor fear the sin, nor feel the shame!

II.

And oh! so sweet was that Beautiful Sin,
  I laid myself down by the adder's nest,
Nor heard the hisses that rose within,
  Nor fear'd the rise of each snaky crest;
I slept in the folds of her fatal form,
  Nor dream'd of the vipers that made her breast,
And the pillow was soft, and the clasp was warm,
  And I thought that the beautiful thing was bless'd;
In my heart's madness lay all the charm,
  And I peril'd my soul, and thought it bless'd!

III.

And I wander'd away from the ancient fold,
  So sacred from age and a thousand ties:
For I fancied the ancient and pure were cold,
  And lacking in light of beautiful eyes;
Beautiful eyes still floated before
  The dreamy visions that won mine own,
And they drew me away with a passionate lore
  From all the dear haunts to my childhood known;
From the precious of boyhood away I tore,
  And shook myself free from the early known—

IV.

The innocent places of play—the groves,
  In whose hallowed shelter my childhood grew,
That should have been precious to thousand loves,
  For I felt them pure, and I knew them true;
Alas! in that wild and willful hour,
  As I wander'd off under Passion's sway,
I strove to forget each tree and flower,
  Nor hearken'd the bird as it sang by the way!
'Gainst that Beautiful Sin she had no power,
  And I shut mine ears to her pleading lay!

V.

Oh! how the dear friends of my boyhood strove
  'Gainst the Tempter's glozing, but all in vain;
For my soul was drunk with the deadliest love,
  That wrought like a madness in breast and brain!
How he mock'd at the life, so tame and cold,
  That my comrades lived in their simple sphere;
How he sang of the braver life, so bold,
  That wrestled with Passion and knew no fear:
Drain'd the purple fires, and grew more bold,
  And wrestled with Passion and knew no fear!

VI.

Never was Tempter so subtly arm'd
  With the spells that snare the innocent heart;
How he sang and spoke; with what passion charm'd,
  With ever-fresh fancy, and glozing art!
He suffer'd no brooding thought to rise,
  No memory fond of the Past to plead,
But with ever-new magic for fancy's eyes,
  He won me on to each erring deed;
'Till the earth grew changed, and the very skies
  Were fashion'd in aspect to suit my need.

VII.

So to regions of other delights we came,
  And here, he said, let us haply dwell;
Here the Beautiful Sin, with her eyes of flame,
  Wrapt every sense in a magic spell;
She flung through the air her mystic powers,
  She breathed o'er the forests a subtle sweet,
And the very breath that was breathed from the flowers,
  Had a magic to fetter the soul and feet;
I lapsed in dream for a thousand hours,
  Nor felt the bonds on my soul and feet!

VIII.

'Twas a wild delirium then that I felt,
  Most fatal to thought in that wizard clime;
I lapsed away, as the icebergs melt,
  'Neath the fiery beams of the summer time;
I lapsed away, till the will to strive,
  To seek, resist and achieve, was gone!
I was, of the thousand things alive,
  The very least living in blood and bone:
What need had the brain or the soul to strive,
  When the uses of both were dead and gone?

IX.

And for long, long seasons, that Beautiful Sin
  Was all that I craved in that magic place:
She wrapped me without, and pierced me within,
  And nestled me fond in her close embrace;
She sang me such songs of a passionate bliss,
  That I shut mine eyes the better to hear;
She showed me such charms, that, at every kiss,
  I opened mine eyes, while I shut mine ear:
But, at last, I awaked to the adder's hiss,
  And, beneath the bright flowers, I saw him near!

X.

'Twas the last moment, the perilous hour,
  When all the good spirits that watch o'er men,
So hopeless long, of each holy power,
  Made one fond effort to save me then;
And sudden beside me up-sprang a flower,
  The rarest and brightest to mortal ken—
And a starry cross, in its breast, had power
  To chase from mine eyes all the glamour then:
To blight the false blooms in that fatal bower,
  And show me the nakedness round me then!

XI.

'Twas a terrible waking, and dread the change!
In place of bright skies and a sunny clime,
The place grew sterile and wild and strange,
As suddenly blighted by storm and time;
The flowers all withered, and in their place
Grew nightshade, and hemlock, and weeds of ill;
And she, the so beautiful form of grace,
In her was the change more fearful still:
Instead of fair form and angel face,
Was the demon visage and look to kill!

XII.

The wine cup she bore held a venom'd draught,
That was fatal of poison to soul and heart;
Her smile of love was a deadly shaft,
The very last hope from the soul to part;
Her arms that wound me, so fond and warm,
Were coiling snakes; and her heaving breast,
Once snowy white, with each melting charm,
Were heads of the serpents laid to rest;
And she, herself, wore a snaky form,
And her tresses were adders that made her crest!

XIII.

I fled!—but with pall'd and palsied soul!
With such feeble limbs, for my strength was gone,
I felt I should never reach the goal,
That flitted before as I hurried on;
The goal of refuge, in calmer sphere,
Beyond me lay, and a patch of blue
In the distant sky, show'd a realm as clear
As that was horrid from which I flew;
Yes, still I could see the pure, bright sphere,
Far off, all wooing, and meant to woo.

XIV.

And, even as I fled, the Terrible Sin,
  Her snakes uncoiled, in her rage pursued!
Oh! the horrid hiss, the cruel din,
  Of the rattling scales of that viper brood!
And fainting I sank on the desert plain,
  And had perish'd there; but I sudden heard
The dear sweet song of my home again,
  That pleading lay of the household bird,
The same, as I sped from my native plain,
  That had followed my flight with its pleading word.

XV.

"My mother! my mother!"—'twas then I cried—
  "The ancient home and the simple sphere!
The peace! the peace! worth the world beside!
  Oh! why did I leave ye to perish here?"
'Twas my mother's voice in that bird-song rose,
  And it strengthened my heart, and it bore me on;
And it checked the rush of my eager foes,
  And they howled with rage as they found me gone.
How I sped, as the bird before me rose!
  How I shouted with prayer, when my foes were gone!

XVI.

And mine eyes grew clear, and my heart grew light,
  And my soul grew strong as I fled apace;
And the blue skies warmed to a beautiful bright,
  And the woods grew sweet with an innocent grace;
And the sweet bird flew, before, till I knew
  All the ancient oaks in the well-known place;
And down on the sward my form I threw,
  And blessed the good God for the granted grace:
For the peace restored that my childhood knew,
  And the innocent joy of that ancient place!

THE LOST PLEIAD.

I.

Not in the sky—no longer in the sky,
Where, beautiful as high,
She swayed serene,
The centre of her circle, and its Queen—
Most bright of all her happy sisterhood,
And by all bright ones woo'd!—
Secure of homage from fond eyes, that brood,
Nightly, in spheres below;
Who, looking with deep longing, feel their wings
With each pulsation grow;
Feel, with the yearning for immortal things,
The strength for heavenward flight;
And travel far, with fancy, to delight,
Still upward drawn by the sweet welcoming eyes
That showed them, first, the skies!

II.

Gone from the skies! In vain
We seek her beauty through the ethereal plain,
And the far blue of its mysterious deep!
No more—no more
Shall Ocean, in the mirror of her sleep,
Give back the beauteous image to our gaze!
And, in our sad amaze,
We turn from sky to sea, from sea to shore,
And, as the white caps of the glistering wave
Flash, as with gems cast up from Ocean's cave,
We start, with joyful cry:
We dream the beautiful Queen once more on high,
The bright one of the sky!

Alas! the fond illusion! It is o'er!—
Not even the sovereign Fancy may restore
OUR sovereign to her throne! We must go weep,
That the Bright Watcher may no longer keep
Her sphere, at summons of the adoring eye!

III.

Gone!—gone!
From sky and earth, from mount and sea!
There is a void of Beauty! Never more
Shall rise the chaunt from forest home or shore;
The sweet fond homage of most worshipping eyes,
That swim in sorrow, gazing on the skies,
Where vacancy makes eminent the void!
How lone!—how lone!—how lone!
The bright'st of all the brightest ones destroyed!
The lesser loveliness that still is left,
But shows the greater glory in the Lost!
Of this, the ONE, bereft,
We are as men at sea, by tempests tost,
Looking out vainly for the one true star,
Worth all the host, to teach us where we are!

IV.

Men need their beacons all!
Their stars and guiding lights, to save from thrall;
And, something dearer, shining from above,
To teach them where to look, and how to love!
For we all rove!
We are but children on the Desert! Some
Never reach home!
Others, for yet a thousand years will roam,
Lacking some starry pilot of the sky;
And so they droop along the path, and die
Of a dear blindness, never opening eye!

Thou wast the Eye to many—dear to most;
As central, and the fairest of Heaven's host,
Thou wast their boast!
Oh! did'st thou grow thine own?
Thou wast their thing of worship and of pride—
By their devotion fed, and deified!
Did'st thou forget? and had'st thou to atone?
We know that thou art gone;
Hast left thy sapphire throne;
And, never again to cheer
The Mariner, who holds his course alone
On the Atlantic, through the weary night.
When common stars turn watchers, and do sleep,
Shalt thou appear,
Over all others bright,
With the sweet, loving certainty of light,
Down-shining on the shut eyes of the Deep?

V.

Shall the sky lose
Her glory, and the ungrateful Earth refuse
Her lamentation? Shall the Beauty part
From Nature, and the great void of the heart
Have never a ministry of Love, whose tear
Shall soothe the suffering, and subdue the fear;
Bring precious nurture to the Hope that lies,
Buried and perishing fast, beneath our eyes?
Shall no responsive wail
From the defrauded elements prevail,
When Night is shorn of Beauty, and the Day,
Palsied goes staggering on his sullen way?

VI.

It is not so permitted—so decreed!
At each great loss, the world's great heart must bleed,

Must feel the throes of anguish, and deplore
The vacancy it feels forever more,
And can not, by its prayer,
Or passionate plaint restore:
For the first time, aware
Of that wan spectre, whom we call Despair!
Thus Sorrow broods along the lonely hills,
And wilder griefs go surging through the floods.
How vexed the chiding of the little rills!
How dread the murmur in the mighty woods!
In night and silence each sad fountain fills
Her cistern, and a Spectral Presence broods,
Blackening their waters! Through the unhallowed
Steals a stark, shuddering Fear,
That cowers and crouches ever as it goes,
As dreading ambushed foes,
Without the feet to fly,
The heart to cry!

VII.

See, as the day is spent,
The Arab leaves his tent;
Well hath he conn'd, of stars, the mystic lore:
His studies teach
A mortal Fate in each,
Pledged, at each several birth,
To some lone pilgrim of the benighted earth,
That shows the path and guides him evermore!
So, too, the shepherd on Chaldea's hills,
At evening, home returning with his flocks,
Looks, from his perilous heights, along the rocks,
For the one star whose smiling preference fills
His soul with faith and rapture; glads his gaze
With promise of protection, sweet as sure!
But now, no beauties blaze,

No smile comes sudden with a sweet surprise!
Vainly he strains his eyes
For the soft glory that made clear his ways!
Much doth he marvel, in the saddest maze,
While through the sorrowful vault the Dark distils
Her dews that blight;
Lingers in longing, dreaming yet that Night
Will surely bring the expected and sweet light
So natural to his sight.

VIII.

Nor earth alone,
Nor man! The Sorrow broods
Above the rocks, the plains, the rills, the floods.
Afar! afar!
In realms of Sun and Star!
There, glorious Beings, each upon his throne,
Join in the common moan!
There, where at first she shone,
Radiant among the sisterhood, the wail
Streams nightly on the gale!
Well may they chaunt, in melancholy tone!
How should they dream, until HER fate was known,
That such as they are confiscate to Death?
That Fate and dark Oblivion should prevail,
The Perfect and the Beautiful to mar?
That, like the creature of far lowlier spheres—
The common blooms of earth—
Beings of mortal breath,
As mortal birth—
The seraphs should be blasted, doom'd to fears;
Lose all their rich effulgence, sink in years;
Sudden extinguish'd in some fatal hour;
Flash even in falling, and with meteor rush,
Sweep down their summits, all one glorious gush;

Then the dread Darkness, and the horrid Hush!
And this without one omen to prepare;
Even while the song floats free in pride and power,
And liquid echoes linger in the air,
That shows all peaceful on the eternal heights!
Oh! in the very midst of dear delights,
And dreaming never of such dread mischance,
The heavens aflush with congregate forms and wings
That swim together in twiring maze and dance,
While some superior seraph sits and sings—
Even then, the wild deep wail! From whence? Oh!
where?
There! there!
Over the precipice!
Far down the black abyss!
A flash! a glory, shed from golden plumes,
The Stygian depth illumes—
A moment, and but one!
The gulph's black billows o'er a sister roll,
And a dread shudder shakes each kindred soul,
Down-gazing, in their horror, as they see!
All their concerted springs of harmony
Snapt rudely—all the generous music gone,
And dread and terror now, where joy alone
Made all felicity!
And shall there be no moan?

IX.

Oh! still the strain,
As of fresh sorrows, wailing through the sky,
Repeats the sad refrain—
Soul-chaunting, and soul-wakening melody!
The sister stars, lamenting in their pain,
That one of the selectest ones should die:

Torn from the rest,
When loveliest, happiest, best—
Blessing and blest;
When her own song was sweetest, and her eye
Brightest of all on high!
That such as she should fall
Headlong, in all the beauty of her bright,
From the empyreal grandeur of her height,
Over such precipice,
Down to such drear abyss—
The depths of fathomless night!—
May well be life-long terror to them all!

X.

Alas! the Destiny
Clogs ever the possession with a Fear!
That haunting sense of Insecurity
Makes every treasure of the heart a care!
Even as we cry
"Eureka! Soul, be joyful! It is here!"
The bitter, mocking echo, makes reply,
"Where? Where? Oh! where?"
And the storm sweeps our starbeam from the sky!
Thus, fastened to the bosom of the Bliss,
Clings ever a sad caprice!
We snatch the flower above the precipice,
And fall in snatching. Our free footsteps miss,
While our hands clutch, and, with the treasure won,
We are undone!
In very Rapture, a sharp Terror abides;
Her song-burst carries anguish in its tone—
Like the deep murmur of the swelling tides,
Though full and bright,
No cloud in sight,
The glorious Moon, in smiles, o'er ocean glides!

The Hope most precious is the soonest lost!
The flow'r of Love is first to feel the frost!
Methinks, all beautiful, of earthly things,
First die; and little doth it then console,
To know that it hath put on heavenly wings,
And is already shining in its goal!
We only feel 'tis gone—forever gone,
The blessed thing we've known,
And we are lone! How lone! How very lone!
Ah! like the bright star shooting down the sky,
Was it not loveliest as it fell from high,
And, darkling, left the sphere,
Now cold and drear,
It ever made so beautiful and dear?

SONNET.—LOVE, THE PURIFIER.

Lady, when o'er my heart thy love was cast—
A moon-flush o'er wild waters—thou didst wake
That passion of song within me which must last,
Less for its own frail worth than thy dear sake.
The muse thus hallows fond devotion's prayer,
Though lowly; lifts the worshipper on high
To mounts of song in the Olympian air,
And makes earth pregnant with divinity.
Love thus, itself, converts to excellence,
Clay that was meanest; purges it of dross;
Lights the dull eye with raised intelligence,
And makes a gain to good of evil's loss.
Thus hath that smile of thine uplifted me;
How can the heart be ill thus full of thee?

ASK ME NOT WHITHER.

I.

Ask me not whither!—ask me not whither!
Fly with me, dearest, fly with me thither;
What if no flowers
Garland thy bowers!
What if no bird in thy roof-tree makes song!
Yet a true heart beside thee
Is throbbing to guide thee—
A heart that hath loved and hath sigh'd for thee long!
Oh! few hearts
Are true hearts!
Then fly with the true heart o'er ocean and earth—
Hither or thither—no matter whither—
Who wins the true heart, wins all that's worth!

II.

Be the home lonely, lowly as lonely,
Yet if thine, with the fond heart that offers it only,
What need thy bowers
The vain bloom of flowers,
Fancies that perish in moment of birth?
The true heart brings treasure
To crown beyond measure
The faith whose own flower is priceless in worth!
Oh! few hearts
Are true hearts!
Hast thou found one, yet ask better fortune than this?
Fly with him thither—no matter whither—
The true heart makes barrenness fruitful with bliss!

OH, THE DAYS!

Oh, the days!—oh, the nights!
  Dreams and dalliance, precious hours,
  Of the starlight, of the flowers,
And the thousand dear delights
  We have known in happier bowers!
    When, by life untaught,
    We had never a thought
    Of what life hath brought:
  Storm and frost and showers,
  Killing all the flowers.

We have slept! Oh! the dreams
  That sweetened all that sleeping:
Glorious in their blooms and gleams,
  Giving way to weeping,
  Joy in sorrow steeping.
    Ah! too lately taught,
    By the woes they brought,
    We awake to thought—
  Thought, with memory scheming,
  To destroy all dreaming.

EPIGRAM.—FROM THE SPANISH.

Teresa's eyes so brilliant are, and black,
That your own fail you, at the first attack!
"Black should they be," a suffering victim spoke,
"If but in mourning for the hearts they've broke."

MY MUSE, 'TIS TIME FOR MOVING.

I.

My muse, 'tis time for moving:
  What's here should make us stay?
Thought should be free for roving,
  When Fancy would go play.
Here, Mind but works in shackles,
  With never a cheer of mirth;
Wit, like the fire that crackles
  Upon the pauper's hearth.

II.

We'll break these bonds of custom,
  And feel our wings in flight!
These routine laws, let's burst 'em,
  And make of Thought delight.
It is not Thought, this bondage
  To what is writ and done;
And Genius means brigandage,
  Where unknown spoils are won.

III.

Sweet Fancy, we shall range ill,
  If, bent on noble toils,
We meet not with some angel,
  And wrestle for our spoils.
There broods the Old Tradition,
  A miser on yon height;
Come on, it is our mission,
  To rob his trunks to-night.

IV.

And yon's a secret valley,
  And yon's a mystic grove:
On these, with sudden sally,
  Their hidden wealth we'll prove.
The elves, in these, have treasures,
  Deep buried from the sun;
We'll keep no timid measures,
  When such are to be won.

V.

The spoils of Thought require
  Such courage as will brave
Worn saws of ancient sire,
  Dull maxims of the slave;
And he who hopes to forage
  In realms of Fancy still,
Must arm himself with courage
  To wander where he will.

VI.

The path-ways worn and travell'd,
  He still eschews, and finds
In realms unblazed, ungravell'd,
  New routes for other minds.
He dares—and that's Dominion;
  He soars—and in his flight,
He wins an eagle pinion,
  From every starry height.

SONG BE OURS.

I.

Oh! Song be ours, though flying
  The rapture ever be;
For, wooing and winning and dying
  Are aye the destiny.
Beauties, that now enkindle,
  And glory that now upsprings,
Still, ere the daylight, dwindle
  Into mere mortal things.
Yet, who would scorn the treasure,
  For that in use it flies?
Song be ours, and pleasure,
  Though in very budding it dies!

II.

Zephyrs of light have shaken
  From off their golden wings,
Odors, but lately taken
  From the depth of Sonora's springs.
Tampa's flowers have given
  Sweets, that, even as they fall,
Make us still fancy that Heaven
  Hath somewhere a blessing for all!
Oh! moments wing'd and gilded,
  Ye will all too soon have pass'd:
Souls of Love, be yielded,
  Now, while your raptures last!

III.

Hark! the song ascending,
  Kindles the dreaming heart,
Till, with Love's own phrenzy blending,
  Tears, all of rapture, start!
Oh! never count you the minute,
  As a minute already known,
Till all the joy that's in it
  Is certainly made your own?
He who mid life's young flowers,
  Wrapt in delight like this,
Stops to measure the hours,
  Was never decreed for bliss.

THE BLUE WAVE MOUNTS.

I.

The blue wave mounts our packet's side,
  The breeze blows fresh and free,
And the rippling gleams of the moonlight glide,
  Making pathways through the sea;
And in gushes sweet from the orange groves,
  O'er the longing sense the odors swell;
And, oh! that song—it is surely Love's,
  Breathing fond promise and sad farewell—
Passionate promise of meeting soon,
Sworn by the zephyr, and sea, and moon!

II.

Oh! sweetest of all, in this sweet hour,
  Would mine were yon happy minstrel's art!
Then, with strain of a wild and witching power,
  Would I win away thy heart!—

Would I sing thee a song of love, so true
  To the kindred glories of sky and sea,
That moon, and zephyr, and star should woo,
  In a fond sweet prayer with me;
'Till thy lips should murmur with fond return,
And thy breast with a kindred passion burn!

III.

Oh! could I sing thee what now I feel,
  With voice subdued to this realm of bliss!
Make the moon's tenderness o'er thee steal—
  Waft thee mine with the zephyr's kiss!
Teach thee, through scent of the orange grove,
  How hearts should be loving, and maidens true!
Spell thee to dreams of a faithful love,
  By waters so bright, 'neath a sky so blue!—
Till through zephyr, and sky, and moon, and sea,
Thou would'st share all the passion I feel for thee!

I HAVE HAD DREAMS.

I.

I HAVE had dreams of bowers,
  Far off, beautiful, bright, and blest,
Fill'd with rich fruits and the sweetest flowers,
  That delight, but disturb my rest!
Ever with rapture smiling,
They spread themselves, wooing and wiling,
To very madness beguiling,
  The passions that fill my breast.

II.

Fain would I fly, but I fly not—
  I have no strength to depart:
I would try, but I try not,
  To drive their spells from my heart.
And my hopes of ambition are dying,
And my promise of fortune is flying,
Still on these visions relying,
  I am spell'd by the cruellest art!

III.

Thus the bright serpent lies coiling,
  Watching the forest tree,
While the bird, won down by his wiling,
  Flutters in vain to flee!
Like that fated bird, the lover
Round his danger will hover,
Till fetter'd by Fate, the rover
  Droops sad to his destiny!

TO-MORROW!—OH, TO-MORROW!

I.

To-morrow!—oh, to-morrow!—
  With that fearful word, my heart
Grows to agony, from sorrow—
  With the morrow we must part.
The pleasant dream which made
  Of our doom forgetful long,
Hath deliver'd us, betray'd us,
  And the madness follows wrong.

II.

Oh! deeply, for the error,
  Must our thoughtless hearts atone,
When, from tenderness, in terror,
  We start up to feel alone!
With the stays that bound us shiver'd,
  With the hope that warm'd us fled,
Our summer vessels sever'd,
  And the horrid storm o'er head!

III.

Ah! how blind, how deaf, each bosom,
  To the warning voice that told
How the beauty of Love's blossom,
  Should not shield it from the cold;
How, in Passion's generous error,
  Never heeding human bound,
Love should rear her fruits in terror,
  And no plea for mercy found.

IV.

But in vain the cruel-hearted
  Would our true affection shake:
We may perish, not be parted—
  May be sunder'd, not forsake!
The one solace still is left us,
  In all other things undone:
They have not of Love bereft us,
  And they can not—we are one!

LOW SLEEPS THE BARD.

I.

Low sleeps the Bard, no stone above his rest,
Far in the unbroken forests of the West;
No pilgrim seeks the spot, with generous care,
With flowers the grassy hillock to repair.

II.

But far, in happiest homes, his song is heard,
While gentlest hearts with sweetest woes are stirr'd,
And memories, that embalm the name they keep,
Even while they murmur his, in homage weep.

III.

Well they remember, with rebuking sense,
How great his toils, how small his recompense;
How lone he lived—unhonor'd 'till he died—
A people's scorn in life, in death their pride.

EPIGRAM.—FROM THE SAXON.

THE POOR ROGUE.

Thy business base, yet at thy business base!
Since all thy toils, thy smooth deceit of face,
Prompt lie, low artifice, employment mean,
Keep thee still ragged, wretched, and unclean!

LET THE BUGLE BLOW!

I.

Let the bugle blow along the mountain!
Shrilly blow! shrilly blow!
We must leave each pleasant grove and fountain,
We must go to battle—we must go!
For the storm is raging on the highlands;
It has swept the valleys all below;
And, from fertile plains and sunny islands,
Pours the foe—the bloody, insolent foe!
Let the bugle blow—shrilly blow!
We must meet the foe—the hateful foe!
Blow, then, for battle, fiery battle, blow,
Thou mountain bugle, blow!
Blow! blow!

II.

See, as blows our bugle, how they gather
Bugle blow—shrilly blow!
There rides up the old and grisly father,
And the son is spurring from below!
We must dye in purple this green heather,
We must free the country from the foe,
Though we ride abroad in fearful weather,
And o'er mountain summits clad in snow!
Let the bugle blow—shrilly blow!
Though we perish, we must meet the foe!
Blow for battle, mountain bugle, blow
Let each mountain echo feel ye blow—
Blow! blow!

III.

Let the bugle blow, from wild Autauga,
Bugles blow—shrilly blow!
See the hunters come, of Canasauga,
Rifles ready shotted for the foe:
From far vales of Cumberland they gather,
And from slopes of green Saluda, lo!
Fiery son of speed, and fearless father,
Eager for the grapple with the foe!
Give them joyful welcome, bugle, blow!
Welcome for the champion—and the foe!
Blow for the coming battle, bugle, blow,
A peal of vengeance on the hateful foe!
We must meet and crush him at a blow.
Blow for the fight and triumph, bugle, blow!
Shrilly blow, thou mountain bugle, blow!
Blow! blow!

QUILP'S ASSOCIATES.—FROM THE SAXON.

QUILP'S choice in fellowships and friends—
Behold his levées' countless throngs:
Bad measures—meant for viler ends—
Foul thoughts, and meditated wrongs;
All passions low, all base desires,
And prejudices—monster grown—
Crowd to the saloon of his sires:
Yet Quilp is in his house alone!

OH, NEVER STOP.

I.

Oh, never stop
At the bead on the top,
Drink, deep as desire, till you drain every drop;
The grapes that were crush'd
When this ruddy stream gush'd,
In the very first smiles of the sun-god have blush'd.

There is life-giving sweet in the stream;
See, the purple of Love in each gleam;
Drink to Life! drink to Love!—drink and dream!
And never you stop
At the bead on the top,
Drink, deep as desire, till you drain every drop!

II.

Stay not to sip,
For there's many a slip,
That spills the rich draught, with the cup at the lip:
The juices that rise,
To entreat at your eyes,
Are a gift of the gods to the worthy and wise.

There is life-giving love in the draught,
Which the wisdom of Solomon quaff'd—
Soul kindled, heart sang, and eye laugh'd!
He did not stop
At the bead on the top,
But drank, deep as desire, and grew wise at each drop!

WHY BY THESE FORESTS LINGER?

I.

Why by these forests linger,
  When there the ocean flows,
And still the sun's bright finger
  Rich realm of promise shows?
Here would'st thou struggle vainly,
  Thy better powers denied,
Or used in toils ungainly,
  That only vex thy pride!

II.

Unloved is still the mortal,
  Who, born to lead his kind
To Truth's mysterious portal,
  Yet leaves the race behind.
They follow, but they madden,
  That he should still go first;
And though his gifts may gladden,
  They hate the giver worst!

III.

How gladly—could you show them,
  That he who guides them now,
Stood once, in youth, below them
  Would they rejoice to know!
They'd rather tell how feebly
  His master sway began,
Than now confess, how ably
  He rules the realms of man!

'TWAS A MAID OF CONGAREE.

'Twas a maid of Congaree,
But no Indian maid was she;
Large blue eyes and fair white face,
Spoke her of the Saxon race.
Stately in her step and mien,
She might well have been a queen;
And a queen o'er hearts was she,
By the rolling Congaree!

Subjects many had she there,
All to love and some to fear;
Few to hope. Alas! the day,
When I sank beneath her sway!
Still compelling hearts to feel,
Yet her own as stern as steel;
Tyrant hath she been to me,
That fair maid of Congaree.

Yet, though chief of all my foes,
Would I not that queen depose;
Be her sovran sway complete,
Still with thousands at her feet;
Every hour as bright as this—
Blest, though still denying bliss;
Queen forever, fair and free,
Over hearts, by Congaree!

WELL, THOUGH THOU HAST DENIED ME.

I.

WELL, though thou hast denied me long, with words of scorn or strife,
And sent me forth in exile far, I love thee more than life:
Thy hills, thy vales, thy streams, thy woods, thy skies of softest blue;
And, though thy sons have done me wrong, I feel I love them too.
They can not rob my heart of that sweet solace, where I go,
To love, in Christian mood and mind, the thing that is my foe;
Nor can they take from me the pride, held dearly through the past,
Whate'er my future lot may be, with thine that lot was cast!

II.

Thou hast had me in thine arms, thou hast borne me on thy knee,
Yet hast thou been, my mother land, but a step-dame unto me;
A thousand sons thou hast caress'd, with kindlier deed and tone,
Yet sent me forth, a thing unbless'd, to sink or swim alone.
No loving word to soothe my heart, no hope to cheer my way,
Unmov'd, thou saw'st my feet depart, and still thy smile was gay;
Thou kep'st the revel in thy halls, while sorrow sate in mine,
Nor heard the last, fond, pleading calls my heart sent out to thine!

III.

Yet did I, with thy favorite sons, heir all that gives thee name;
My fathers bravely struck, with thine, for liberty and fame;
Their blood is on thy battle-fields; their toils have served to raise
Those glorious monuments on which their son no more shall gaze;
Their groans, from prison-ship, I hear;—alas! they speak for mine;
Now poured, at midnight, for thine ear, across this waste of brine.
Ah! little did they think to hear, in homes so bravely won,
The doom of exile, dark and drear, for this their only son!

IV.

I see thee on my vision rise, O clime forever dear!
Thy revelry but mocks the pang, in which thou dost not share.
The stranger comes, an honor'd guest; thy proud saloon is bright;
Forms swim in twiring dance and eyes grow glorious in his sight.
A little hour and he forgets—nay, mocks the love that shows
Such homage to the foreign form, of whom it nothing knows;
While at thy knee, thy native sons, unlov'd, uncherish'd, pine,
For, oh! how small the boon of love, so precious as 'tis thine!

V.

But yield them *that*, and they will bound, in danger's path, to dare,
With song and sword, to serve and strike, and all thy woes to share.

How true their hearts, how strong their hands—what deeds
unmeasured done,
To prove their might, assert thy right, and both to render
one!
'Tis but to claim them as thine own, with loving pride and
care,
Accord the smile for service done, and bid them do and dare;
Watch fondly o'er each infant grace, each germ of goodly
pow'r,
And give each noble talent place, and every Muse her flow'r.

VI.

Yet, let me not upbraid thee now, whose pride it still hath
been
To lift thy name, and win thee fame, though nought from thee
I win;
To paint, as I would have thee show, a glorious form and high,
Beyond approach, and worthy all thy sons' idolatry;
Depict the deeds that make thy past a grand romance of
pride;
Show how for thee the patriot strove, and how the hero died;
On what near fields, in trial stern, the breast and blade they
bare,
And make the foreign foeman learn to honor thee in fear!

VII.

How fenced thee against his shaft and hate, and foot to foot in
fight,
Pluck'd from his grasp thy shield of state, and sworded it
with might!
And from the past, with tongue of fire, speak to the present
hour;
Rouse living hearts, with fond desire, to toils of equal power;

Wake patriot love to jealous strife, and patriot will, to aim
At all the arts that win from life, security for fame;
Till, over all, supreme thou stand'st, the world's bright eye, that far,
Wins wond'ring nations to thy feet, their cynosure and star.

VIII.

No more! no more! the passion fond, which makes the heart complain,
Hath birth in something yet beyond, which must not sing in vain:
'Tis love that moans o'er love denied—the privilege to share
That service in a field of pride, which needs to brave and dare.
Even now thy dangers threaten all—thy future as thy past—
The very men who man thy wall, shrink cowering from the blast;
The foe insidious makes his way, with near approach, and arts
That well may rouse the patriot fear in fond and faithful hearts.

IX.

Where are the champions now that stood, the favorites in thy grace?
They traffic with the hostile brood, for pension or for place.
The motes that peopled all thy beams, the flies that suck'd thy flow'rs—
Are these the things to fling thy flag defiant from thy towers?
Call back thy banish'd sons that knew no favor at thy hands;
Go seek them where with strength they strew the wilds of western lands;
And if their love be such as mine—as *theirs*, when bade depart—
There shall not sound one call of thine, in one unwilling heart!

At Sea—1833.

COO! COO! TE WEET TU WHU!

The birds that sing in the leafy spring,
With the light of love on each glancing wing,
  Have lessons to last you the whole year through;
For what is, "Coo! coo! te weet tu whu!"
But, properly rendered, "The wit to woo!"
A wit that brings worship and wisdom too!
  Coo! coo! te weet tu whu—
  The wit to woo—te weet tu whu!

The verb "to love," in the tongue of the dove,
Heard noon and night in the cedar grove,
  Is very soon taught where the heart is true:
For the wit to woo, and the wisdom too,
Lie in the one sweet syllable, "Coo!"
But echo me well, and you learn to woo—
  Coo! coo! te weet tu whu—
  The wit to woo—te weet tu whu!

In every zone is the language known,
But in spring it takes ever the sweetest tone,
A something betwixt a carol and moan;
And if you have only the wit to woo,
You will do it in song as the young birds do,
And maidens will listen the whole year through—
  Coo! coo! te weet tu whu—
  The wit to woo—te weet tu whu!

And never was word, of the forest bird,
Sweeter than that of the maiden heard,
When once to the depths her heart is stirred;

For she hath the proper wit to woo,
And the gift of song to sweeten it, too!
She hath but to coo, and she teaches to woo,
The whole sweet lesson, te weet tu whu—
Coo! coo! the wit to woo—te weet tu whu!

WE SINK OR SWIM TOGETHER.

I.

Now row, my gallant brothers, row,
  Give way with will and sinew;
These seas that rise before our prow,
  Will try the muscle in you!
But what's the fear if hearts be true?
  We've but to pull together—
True hearts and hands, all bent to do,
Will bear us bravely, bear us through,
And save the ship, and save the crew,
  In spite of wind and weather!
Row, brothers, row! row, brothers, row!
  One long strong pull together!

II.

And cheer with courage, as ye row;
  What though the tempest brewing,
Works fate for many a brother now,
  That drives, head on, to ruin?
'Tis not for us to shirk or shrink,
  Though out in fearful weather:

We know some comrade's doom'd to sink,
And we, too, hang on Danger's brink;
But fear ye not!—don't stop to think!
Pull bravely all together!
Row, brothers, row! row, brothers, row!
One long strong pull together!

III.

Bend to your oars, good brothers, row!
Give way with hearty courage!
Death's just as nigh on land, as now,
When seas are wolves at forage:
And Heaven's as near on sea as shore,
However wild the weather;
We've but to ply the manly oar,
And shut our ears to ocean's roar,
Nor heed the Fate, behind, before,
And bravely pull together!
Row, brothers, row! row, brothers, row!
One long strong pull together!

IV.

Bend to your oars, dear brothers, bend!
We may not 'scape this danger—
But times of peril prove the friend,
And we've escaped even stranger;
'Tis something of God's law, I think,
When out in angry weather,
And men are dashed on Danger's brink,
And all seem doom'd, and many sink,
That one and all their hands should link,
And bravely pull together.
Row, brothers, row! row, brothers, row!
We sink or swim together!

YE SONS OF CAROLINA.

Ye sons of Carolina,
  Our Eutaw flag that bear,
And glory in a glorious name,
  That knows not shame or fear;
The sacred trophy that ye keep,
  The matchless names ye own,
Ever need that your deed
  Shall not shame the triumphs known:
Shall not shrink from battle's raging fires,
  Shall not shame the triumphs known.

The memories of battle
  Should be living in your souls,
While the crimson plains of Eutaw rise,
  And the stream of Ashley rolls;
On shores where gallant Moultrie fought,
  Your hearts shall gather flame,
Which shall light, through the fight,
  To as proud and pure a fame;
Though the storm of battle rages wild,
  Which shall light ye still to fame!

Your souls shall need no succor,
  Though the tempest rages fast,
While ye prize the mighty memories,
  That have famous made the past:
While ye think of Marion's rifles,
  And of Sumter's gleaming blade,
And the name, and the fame,
  In your Eutaw flag displayed:
Of the proud and matchless name ye bear,
  And our banner yet displayed.

That banner still shall triumph,
  In the troublous storm at hand,
And ye shall joy, beneath its folds,
  To light each meteor-brand;
Wild then shall rise, ye warriors,
  Your shouts above the blast,
As ye claim, for each name,
  A brave triumph like the past:
As ye wave your Eutaw banner high,
  In a triumph like the past.

OH! WHAT IF THE PROSPECT BE CLOUDED?

Oh! what if the prospect be clouded,
  And what if the sunlight be fled?
The bright Sun himself may be shrouded,
  And the bright crown be torn from his head
But he yields never long to the rigor
  Of the tempest that beats on his form;
And he comes forth, anon, full of vigor,
  More glorious because of the storm.

From the Sun let the Soul take its moral,
  Nor shrink 'neath the battle of life;
Near the cypress grows ever the laurel,
  And we pluck, as we please, from the strife.
Though the foe presses fierce with his legions,
  And ye stoop for the hour to his will,
Keep your calm in the turbulent regions,
  And the triumph inures to you still!

SERENADE.—THE STARS ARE HIGH.

I.

The stars are high up in heaven,
  Look out, belovéd, and see
What a countless train hath been given
  To light my steps to thee.
Come forth with those stars of thine,
And mock these hosts as they shine,
Not brighter, nor half so divine,
  As those which shine for me!

II.

I bring a song for thy waking,
  And now, while the vestal Night
Her maiden walk is taking,
  Put on thy slipper of flight.
The tell-tale moon no longer roves
With searching eye through our shady groves,
And there's not a star, that longs and loves,
  But will wink as she holds her light.

III.

There's one, you see how she blazes,
  As if glad to show us the way;
And well may the lover who gazes
  Rejoice in her rosy ray.
Ah! thousands for ages have seen her rise,
How suddenly bright, with a sweet surprise
Holding her light, but shading her eyes,
  And with never a word to say.

WE 'VE SUNG AND WE 'VE DANCED.

I.

We 've sung, and we 've danced, while the hostile power
  Stole subtly upon our noon-day rest,
Nor knew that he waited the dreaming hour,
  To leap in his rage on his victim's breast!
    We wake; and have found
    Our free limbs bound,
  And the foe of his feeble prey possess'd!
  Oh! the shame of that waking—the sorrow!
  The grief, and the guilt, and the horror!
  But yesterday free—what, To-morrow
    Shall tell our children the rest?

II.

What hope for the race, when such is the story,
  Told of the nation a thousand years?
The peasant strides on, in a progress to glory,
  And his valor, the State in the forest uprears.
    But his sons grow base,
    And the coward race
  Yield their necks as the braver foe appears!
  And we can but weep o'er the pages
  That tell of the ruins of ages;
  Deeds of Men, songs of Bards, thoughts of Sages,
    All vain, 'gainst the shame and disgrace!

GIVE ME, WHEN DAYLIGHT SETS.

I.

Give me, when daylight sets,
And stars are on the sea,
The thought that never all forgets,
And I'll give mine to thee!
Think, at that sacred hour,
That I am watching too;
And if the stars and the night have power,
Both shall be true!—be true!

II.

I bear, wherever I fly,
The tokens my truth that keep:
I see thee in shore and sky,
In day, night, land, and deep!
The breeze that stirs my hair,
The stars that light the sea,
The whisper of twilight, earth, and air,
All tell of thee!—but thee!

SLUMBER.—FROM THE ITALIAN.

Sweet is slumber—it is Life
Without its sorrow, sin, or sighing:
Death, without the fearful strife,
The mortal agony, of dying.

BETTER LUCK ANOTHER YEAR.

I.

Oh! never sink 'neath Fortune's frown,
But brave her with a shout of cheer,
And 'front her fairly, face her down—
She's only stern to those who fear!
Here's—"better luck another year!"
Another year!

Aye—"better luck another year!"
We'll have her smile, instead of wile—
A thousand smiles for every tear,
With home made glad and goodly cheer,
And "better luck another year"—
Another year! another year!

II.

The damsel Fortune still denies,
The plea that yet delights her ear;
'Tis but our manhood that she tries;
She's coy to those who doubt and fear
She'll grant the suit another year!
Another year!

Here's—"better luck another year!"
She now denies the golden prize,
But, spite of frown, and scorn, and sneer,
Be firm, and we shall win and wear,
With home made glad, and goodly cheer,
In "better luck another year!"
Another year! another year!

BATTLE ODE.—A TYRTÆAN.—FOR MUSIC.

[SCENE.—A rocky promontory, beetling over a plain. Troops defiling below— horse, and foot, and artillery. Martial music; the Bard stands upon the edge of the promontory, his beard streaming in the wind—his arms extended. His chaunt, as the columns are passing, and as the events follow, mingles with the martial instruments that severally sound below, in correspondence with the movements of the masses, and the action which succeeds.]

TIRA-LA! tira-la! tira-la!
  Tira-la! la! la! la!
Hark! the glorious trumpet how it rings!
  Tira-la! tira-la! tira-la!
As our eagle when she flings
The deep slumbers from her wings,
And, sonorous screaming, sings
  As she goes—"tira-la!"
As she darts upon her prey,
  Like the lightning from the height,
And tears her spoil away,
  With the matchless speed of might!
    Tira-la! tira-la! tira-la! la! la! la!

Sleep ye still when roars the flame?
  When ye hear the battle-cry,
Which should fire the weak, the tame,
  Death around, and Doom on high?
    Answer trumpets!—tira-la!
Hark! the only summons for the brave!
    Tira-la! tira-la! tira-la!
And it calls alike from mountain and from wave:
A call to wake your fathers from the grave!
    Tira-la! tira-la! tira-la! la! la! la!

III.

Know that to the soul of honest Fame,
In the arts of peace is nought but shame,
  Follow'd, when the foe
    Stands o'er Home and Altar,
    With his Brand and Halter—
Stands in scorn, and braves ye to the blow!
    Tira-la! tira-la! tira-la!
Blow free, blow wild, ye bugles, once again!
Blow till ye blast these rocks, and rive this plain!
Blow till ye rouse the living, like the slain—
  The mighty brave who perished long ago!
      Blow! blow!
Blow with your eagle voices, bugles, blow!
  Tira-la! tira-la! tira-la!
      Tira-la! la! la! la!

IV.

Sing welcome, bugles!—welcome to the strife!
War to the very knife—
In Freedom's hour of need, war is her only life!
  Tira-la! tira-la! tira-la!
Blow for the coming land-sturm—bugles, blow!
Blow death into the nostrils of the foe,
And stir with shame the sleepers now so slow!
      Blow! blow!
  Tira-la! tira-la! tira-la!

V.

Peace is but the reign of rest,
Out of season never bless'd;
  War is vigilance!—

Soul, and strength, and virtue!—all,
When the Despot would enthrall,
To bestow, at Freedom's call,
  Meet deliverance!
Sound your trumpets—tira-la!
  Hark! the echoing sound,
  From the grave—the ground!
Hark! our dead are stirring in their graves!
  Sound, ye sonorous summoners, once more
    Tira-la! tira-la!
From their cerements see them start—
See the vaults that quake and part!
They are free—they stand
With a flaming brand
In each bony hand!
    Tira-la! tira-la!
Each a hero mighty as of yore—
  In each bosom thrice a heart,
  In each eye a fiery dart!
    Tira-la!
  Shall they rise to see
  The children flee—
See them recreant—see them slaves—
  Whom they left so free?
  And in horror feel the dread
  Which flings dust on every head,
Lest the mothers of the recreants lie dishonored in
      their graves?
  Tira-la! tira-la! tira-la!

VI.

Blow, ye rebuking bugles, shrilly blow!
      Tira-la!
  With such allies from the dead,

We shall feel the brand of shame,
We shall feel the spur of fame,
And be ready, soon be ready for the foe!
Find our heroes at our head,
Raging with the torrents as they pour
Down the heights, to gather on the shore,
Where the cannon of the foe begins to roar!
Tira-la!
Blow for the battle grandly—bugles, blow
We are ready now—all ready for the foe!
Blow! blow!
Tira-la! tira-la! tira-la! la! la! la!

VII.

Lo! the horsemen, and the chariots, where they come,
To the shrieking of the bugle, to the rolling of the drum!
Tira-la! tira-la! tira-la!
Lo! the billows of the battle, how they rise,
As the hurricane goes surging through the deep!
Ha! the wonder in the skies! *
Behold the shadowy hosts,
A thousand trooping ghosts—
Your spectral sires, are marching in the air,
And their cloudy banners flare,
As if tempests in their wrath were gather'd there!
Starting from uneasy sleep,
To the ancient fields they sweep,
Battling with the ancient foe,
Whom they baffled long ago:

* To the natives of this country, whose ancestors were in the Revolutionary war, the omen here illustrated is a familiar and general tradition. The seven years' conflict was preceded by a grand phenomenon in the skies, of marching and contending armies. It seems to have been witnessed in most of the States. I have heard of it in several. My grandmother has often told me that she was taken out of bed by her father to behold it.

Shadowing forth the fiery strife that threatens all below,
Where the emulous bugles blow – grandly blow!—
While the vultures scent the carnage from afar,
And scream with lust, impatient for the war—
Tira-la! tira-la! tira-la!
Which shall spread on mighty board the bloody prey,
And dress with crimson horrors all the victims of the fray.

VII.

How it howls, the howling rage,
As the mighty hosts engage—
As the masses roll together in the strife,
With the rush of death and life!
Tira-la! tira-la!
The elements of destiny set free,
Like the storms upon the sea,
When the shattered navies flee,
Tira-la! tira-la!
Lo! the torrents of the legions, as they bound,
A thousand mailéd horsemen from the steep,
Charging down upon the deep,
As the ocean, with a roar,
That rolls in terror all the white billows on the shore!
Tira-la! tira-la!
Ha! the crimson fires of battle, how they sweep
With a hiss and horrid rush along the ground,
As the angry bugle blows
In the nostril of our foes,
Tira-la! tira-la!
Now the grapple—the death-grapple—and the more than
mortal throes!
All the agony of action, all the bitterness of blows!
Tira-la! tira-la! tira-la!

Do not shrink! do not cower! do not fail!
Hurl again the hail—the iron hail:
Tira-la! tira-la!
And the fiery arrows fling!
Tira-la!
The bolts of death and terror how they sing,
As with loving hate they dart,
Each fiery-eyed, and seeking out the passage to a heart!
Tira-la! tira-la!
Swept with thunders, see the columns, as they sway aside and part,
Like the shivered forest branches, when the wild tornado goes!
Again! again! again!
To the grapple—the death-grapple—with our foes!
We have thrice a thousand slain,
But ten thousand more remain:
We must stretch them with their comrades on the consecrated plain!
Blow, ye bugles, blow!
Grandly, fiercely blow!
Tira-la! tira-la!
The triumph to our people, and the terror to the foe!
Blow—the charging to the grapple—the last grapple—with the foe
Blow! blow! ye bugles, blow!
Tira-la! tira la! tira-la! la! la! la!

IX.

Seas of blood rush redly on the sight!
Eyes flame out like stars of hellish ire!
Ha! the glorious, horrid, rush fight,
And the very fields and skies are fire!
Tira-la-la-la! tira-la!

Ha! the war-steed, as with nostril wide he plunges
Through the thunder-cloud and thick of fight!—Hurrah!
How he shouts and cries:
"Ha! ha!"
And the bugle with a volumed blast replies,
"Tira-la! tira-la! tira-la!"
And it goads him, through his frenzy, to delight!
Hurrah! hurrah! hurrah! Tira-la! tira-la!
And he maddens with the fight,
And with death-dilating sight,
Tramps headlong through the masses—tira-la!
See! see!—levelled bright, where the bayonets' serried
lunges
Try the muscle and the soul—tira-la! tira-la!—
Roars afresh the mighty cannon—rives anew the iron hail!
Tira-la! tira-la!
On again! On again! Freedom's battle shall prevail!
Tira-la! tira-la!
None be living left to tell the tale!
Tira-la! tira-la!

X.

Hurrah! hurrah! hurrah!
Tira-la! tira-la!
The foe is stricken down!-
Tira-la!
Or in terror hurries on!
Tira-la!
Panic stricken, flying,
Howling, groaning, dying,
And the field of freedom's won—forever won!
Tira-la!

While the lordly trumpet rallies
  For the final charge, that brings
Peace to all our valleys;
  And our ensign eagle sings,
  As she spreads aloft her wings,
Tira-la! tira-la! tira-la! la! la! la!

SONNET.—WHY THE TYRANT?

We make our monsters as we make our gods!
  The ideal shapes the creature. In our *aim*
  Lies all the difference betwixt pride and shame;
Thus are we whipt at last by our own rods!
Thus are we slaves and victims! We create
  The tyrant that subdues us; who but comes
  The creature of our call; and, if he dooms,
Why groan? We've made him master of our fate:
The scourge that whips for virtue in decay!
  And, if a tyrant, not for us to curse;
  We needed ere we call'd him—needed worse;
And proper is submission to the sway
That chastens to reform us. He may be
A monster—but what baser things are we!

II.

Take to thyself one living truth, and know
  That never yet, while virtue in a race
Presided dominant, did tyrant grow;
  He is God's absolute angel—in his place;
  The best for sway when men grow weak and base.

We nurtured him in hot-beds of our lust,
  Low aims, and foul desires, and mean pursuits;
  And it is proper, when men sink to brutes,
They should be leash'd and scourged! We may not trust
  Free will to those whose will still foully shows;
  Must mock them with denial: nay, give blows,
And bondage, if it needs! And this is just!
  And though we slay the tyrant when we can,
  He's one of the necessities of man!

THE LIFE MARCH.

I.

In doing is blessing,
  And he is most blest,
Who learns the grand lesson
  Of doing his best.
And the best gifts of Heaven,
  Most fruitful of spoil,
Are the fields it has given
  For the freedom of toil.
No lack of the region
  For culture and art,
If the proper religion
  Be warm in the heart.
And in doing is living,
  In feeling the soul,
The gain is the giving,
  The march is the goal.

II.

Now, give me the vigor
  To join in the strife,
And try me with rigor,
  That the training be Life:
And let the warm feeling
  Gush swift through the heart,
That its fountains unsealing,
  Its strength may impart.
The bravest will falter
  When the danger is worst,
And the fancies will palter
  With the passions athirst;
But if thou wilt arm me,
  O God! for the strife,
They'll not chide me, nor charm me,
  From the toil which is Life!

III.

But a single step onward,
  And how the fields spread;
Whether seaward or sunward,
  Under foot, overhead!
The forests, the mountains,
  The valleys, the sea,
The life-giving fountains,
  All open to me!
With my axe, I am sovereign
  O'er empires of wood:
With my vans, I am hovering
  O'er oceans of flood:
With my shaft, I am baring
  The rock to its core:

With my ship, I am steering,
  New worlds to explore:
With my share, I am plowing
  The waste for the close:
With my art, I'm endowing
  The wild with the rose:
And sending, each dawning,
  My blessings abroad,
My labor is crowning
  My people for God!

IV.

And my pride's in the power
  With which I embrace,
In the toils of the hour,
  The good of the race:
That in plowing, or clearing,
  Lifting up, hurling down,
My people are nearing
  The sceptre and crown.
New mysteries shown them,
  Which art shall lay bare:
New provinces won them,
  For culture and care:
And with plowshare, or sabre,
  New toils to be wrought—
New fields for the labor,
  New labors for thought.

V.

On the wayside, one's sinking,
  To whom I must bear
A life-draught, for drinking,
  To keep from despair!

In the cell is a student
  The world never knows,
In the world's ways imprudent,
  He dreams while it goes!
He is working the problem
  Of Beauty for Thought,
But the crowd never trouble 'em,
  Though the problem be wrought.
He will make them a model
  Shall last them for aye,
But they care not a boddle,
  Seeing only to-day!
And while the crowd fly him,
  He droops and he dies,
Unless I draw nigh him,
  And see with his eyes;
See where the true story
  Grows under his hand:
Where the grandeur—the glory
  Are at his command:
Where it needs but the master
  To rise to the toil,
And—*sic itur ad astra*—
  To conquer the spoil!

VI.

And that spoil?—not the bubble
  Of flatulent praise:
The fever, the trouble,
  The crackle, the blaze,
The cry of vain fashion,
  Which speaks for a hall—
But a world's heart, in passion
  That cries out for all!—

The catholic emotion
  Unschool'd, with a gush,
Like the great heart of ocean,
  That swells with a rush;
Stifling envy, denial,
  The doubts, which still shame,
Every great heart's first trial
  In the struggle for fame!

VII.

Yes, if true to the mission
  Which calls me, I bear
A far nobler commission
  Than plowshare or spear!
Not the conquering only,
  But the soothing is mine:
And I seek out the lonely,
  Who hope, yet repine!
Alas! for the duty,
  When men shall contemn
Invention, thought, beauty,
  As unworthy of them:
When all question of being
  Shall be question of bread—
Of clothes, shows, and seeing
  How draped, ranked, and fed:
When the blockhead in splendor
  Shall be foremost in place,
And the brave, true, and tender,
  Wanting wealth, shall be base:
When the noble in thinking,
  Shall be worthless in state,
And good eating and drinking
  Alone shall be great!

VIII.

These forests, these mountains,
  Hide fruits of delight;
There are life-giving fountains
  For draught and for sight;
But no pathways open
  For those who would gain,
And the blind man, still groping,
  Would pierce them in vain!

IX.

I must tear down and cut out
  A path for the weak,
That no more they be shut out
  From good which they seek!
And yonder's a tower,
  Where brave captives groan:
I must arm me with power
  To break through the stone;
Help the myriads now striving
  With their burden in vain,
Other myriads scarce living,
  That know life by pain!

X.

Oh! great is the harvest
  That burdens the soil,
And he alone starvest
  Who shrinks from the toil.
Of God's gifts, most gracious
  Are those which bestow
Fields so various, so spacious,
  For the brave heart below.

Where the humblest ambitions
  May rise in the race,
And the meanest conditions
  Find a sun-lighted place;
Where we lift up the lowly
  From depths of despair,
And make sacrifice holy,
  On heights of Good Cheer:
Purge the vision through beauty,
  Through feeling, the heart;
Teach the love that's in duty,
  The religion in art!

XI.

Oh! the fields how they widen,
  The more that we gaze;
Fields for souls to take pride in,
  And triumph to praise:
Fields for culture all hours,
  Laid bare to be wrought,
Tasking all the best powers
  Of soul and of thought.
By this working, we're gaining
  Best use of the soul;
The grand life-march maintaining
  Which is progress and goal!

EPIGRAM.—FROM THE SAXON.

QUILP says, on such as I he still looks down;
  Nor doubt I this, provided he can show,
That, in the moral pillory of the town,
  The scoundrel can see any thing below!

THE HERO WORKER.

Alas! how low he lies,
Whose spirit, through his eyes,
Was ever aiming upward to the skies!

How silent that deep voice,
That ever cried: "Rejoice!
We soon shall reach the mountains of our choice!"

How cold the heart whose glow
Made sunshine in the snow,
And warmed his people's faith when fires burnt low

We see no more that aim,
That, like a shaft, all flame,
Ever shot upward to the heights of Fame!

Will he no more aspire,
With his great soul's desire,
To sway, to soar, highest, and ever higher?

Will he not pluck his wreath
Even from the realm of death,
For realms which know no forfeiture of breath?

Shall all that brave desert,
That will, that regal heart,
Magnanimous in passion, all depart?

His purposes of might,
His grasp, beyond the light,
Of things, and thoughts, left shrouded now in night?

The grand ideals of good
And beauty, watch'd and woo'd
While other men lay sleeping, stuff'd with food?

The faith—the courage—will
To work and conquer still,
Assured 'gainst every prophecy of ill?

Shall these great aims, this power,
Be quell'd in one brief hour?
These goodly growths of virtue have no flow'r?

Was the fond toil in vain,
Pursued through mock and pain;
Grief in the heart, while grandeur ruled the brain?

Cut short each noble toil,
Ere yet was won the spoil,
That would have crowned with fruit the natal soil?

There, at the quarry, lies
The half-hewn block—your eyes
See that in vain each meaner workman tries.

And shall the great soul keep,
Henceforth, unbroken sleep,
Nor ply the subtle thought, nor work the problem deep?

Is he, who now lies mute,
Denied each fond pursuit,
Nor let to work until his toils bring proper fruit?

Doth the transition break
The progress? Shall it take
The master from the fields where he had learn'd to make?

Shall he not still pursue
The favorite plan—though new,
Field and material be—imperishable too?

Not to dull earth he clings,
And now he puts on wings,
Shall he not rise to yet sublimer things?

Perfect each sovereign thought,
Which he so fondly sought?
Achieve the ideal good on which he long hath wrought?

To consummation fine,
Work out the grand design,
Elaborate beauty born and blooming in each line?

Life, here, was but a term
Of ordeal, whence the germ,
Training, to lift the angel from the worm;

And, with his growth of soul,
Prepared for loftier goal,
He but flings off the bonds that would control.

His task was but to leave
Grand models, which should grieve,
And make the emulous race with nobler births conceive.

This done—himself endowed
For toils beyond the crowd,
He makes his way to spheres more pure and proud:

Where nobler, better spoils,
Await superior toils,
And Art at will creates, and Nature never moils.

New spheres, new stars await
His presence—and a state,
That lives in beauty, and that mocks at fate!

A grander model grows
Before his soul—he glows
With ideals far beyond the all he knows.

His wisdom, in great aim,
Makes mortal knowledge tame,
And finds a motive far beyond all mortal fame.

For fame, the human lure,
Though, in degree, most pure,
Is yet of mortal birth, not purposed to endure.

When higher flights we take,
Then loftier motives wake,
The horizon spreads—new suns upon the vision break.

The ambition then dilates,
Nor soon with conquest sates
That soul which learns to move 'mongst spirits, stars, and fates.

Itself a Fate—a God—
It flings itself abroad—
All thought, and will—nor asks if men and stars applaud.

The "Still Beyond," alone
Appeals with heavenly tone
To souls that, ne'er content, o'er each achievement moan.

Not their's, with drowsy thought,
To brood above the wrought,
Nor deem aught won, with something yet unsought.

This woos, while baffling will;
The ideal mocks them still,
The wing must soar, the eye see yet a loftier hill.

And every summit won,
Unveils a "*farther on!*"
Alps rise o'er alps, and more must yet be done.

This is the eternal round
Of nature; and the found,
Makes nothing for the soul that knows no bound.

From star to star it speeds,
Each flight a flight of deeds,
And every night in holier pasture feeds.

Ah! vainly we pursue,
The eternal progress through,
God, the Ideal that woos, yet ever keeps from view.

CICADA—THE KATY-DID.

Sing me summer,
Sweet Cicada!
Chirruping gay in the bristly pine;
Though thy song hath made me sadder,
Yet my heart must thank thee for it!
Were each comer
But as welcome,
With no better song than thine,
What a bit of Eden were it,
In this forest nook of mine!

AH, ME! THE SAD MISDOING.

I.

Ah, me! the sad misdoing,
The watching, weeping, wooing,
The sueing and pursuing,
So fruitless as with pain;
Ever doubting, ever dreaming,
Yet beguiled at every gleaming,
With some newer scheme still scheming,
And with every scheme in vain.

II.

'Neath ancient oak tree lying,
Still languishing and sighing,
Drooping ever as with dying,
Yet with keenest sense of life;
Oh! for the storm, the clangor,
The battle—war's wild anger,
Aught but this wretched languor,
Where Slumber's self is strife.

III.

Sing me the storm—the battle—
The tempest's shriek—the rattle
Of cannon, when, like cattle,
Men headlong march to Fate!
Rouse me, these griefs assuaging,
To Passion's wildest raging,
Till, as with foe engaging,
I rush from Love to Hate!

THE CHRISTIAN WARRIOR.

The wing is down, that, when the day was dark,
  Soar'd upward ere the lark;
The eye is dim, that, when a people slept,
  True watch above them kept;
The soul is fled, that, with a holy blaze,
  Warm'd all within its gaze;
The fearless form is blighted, which had stood,
  Strong, battling like a god;
Firm against ancient error, and as true
  In conflict with the new;
And hopes, that from his presence sprang elate,
  Lie blasted, in his fate!

Tears, that to all we give, however low,
  Speak ill our sorrows now;
Fame, that belongs to rabble tongues, were vain,
  And might his worth profane;
The monument is frail, the pageant dim—
  What could they speak for him?
Prayers were more vain—the soul we honor thus
  Might better plead for us:
Ascending high would be his holy pray'r,
  While ours were lost in air!
Who shall requite the love he bore to man?
  His God!—none other can!

I'LL BUILD FOR THEE AN ALTAR.

I'll build for thee an altar,
  And truly, day by day,
My heart shall never falter,
  Its solemn vow to pay;
A sacred fire shall crown its height,
  And sweeter shall its incense be,
That I will burn at morning's light,
  Than ever came from Araby—
From 'neath its dark green wave, from off its spicy tree!

I'll build for thee a palace;
  And many a slave shall bring,
From thousand happy valleys,
  The sunny gifts of spring;
No treasure brought from Lebanon,
  Uraba's pearls, and Ophir's gold,
Though art hath wrought and valor won,
  Shall match with thine when thine is told—
Oh! thine shall be a state most wondrous to behold!

They mock! but Love hath stories
  Of greater wonders done:
Of realms of richer glories
  Than hath the setting sun:
Of power no earthly monarch owns,
  From lowly woodland hut to raise
A temple richer than his thrones,
  And heroes better form'd for praise,
With gifts of soul, and spells, that still the world amaze!

SING ME THAT SONG.

Sing me that song, that ancient song,
  That won mine ear in boyhood's hours,
And made me come, and linger long,
  A happy listener in thy bowers;
Dear were the simple notes that rose
  In artless triumph through the grove,
Soft-stealing as the brooklet flows,
  Yet every murmur steep'd in love!

Thou had'st no cunning, wanton strains,
  To strike and startle, as if Toil
Had brought to music Labor's pains—
  Hard labor in unfruitful soil—
But from thy lips, as from the heart,
  The unconscious strain in music flow'd,
As brooklets from the greenwood dart,
  And ripple o'er the pebbly road.

Sing me that strain, that ancient strain,
  That told of love on Scotia's hills:
Of love that did not once complain,
  Though still the hapless love that kills!
Once more that tale of simple wo:
  The maiden sinking to the grave,
And he, for whom she perish'd so,
  Unconscious that he still might save!

SONNET.—TO ONE DEPARTING FOR ENGLAND.

The bark is ready for your carriage hence,
Dear friend, and o'er the waters soon your eye
The shores of glorious Albion shall descry,
Whose merry cheer shall more than recompense
The pangs of every parting. It may be
You shall forget, in dear ones at your home,
The friends that here you leave beyond the sea—
For such is still the wont of those who roam.
But if it chance that you should think of me,
Think of me only as of one denied,
Who fain would go upon a pilgrimage,
Seeking his absent friends; and would assuage
His sorrow, by beholding them in pride,
Stately, in ancient halls, where reverence grows with age.

LADY, I KNOW THY HEART.

Lady, I know thy heart, like mine,
Endures the crowd, but loves it not;
We do not see its gay lights shine,
Its music does not soothe our lot;
Yet not an ear hath heard the wo
That works unceasing in my breast:
And ah! too well thy pride, I know,
Hath never yet thy pain confess'd.

Ah! if in heaven our souls may find
  That refuge calm—that union there—
Such as no mortal may unbind,
  Our separate souls but dream of here!—
Happy, if future spheres may bless
  The love that here we dare not own:
Nor thwart the hope, earth makes not less,
  Though still denied—though still unshown.

GUARANTIES.

OH! the rose is a sweet one thou givest me to-night,
        But it dies in a day;
And that star which would hallow our loves with its light,
        With the dawn wastes away;
    Ah! dearest, the token must be
    Much surer, which tells of thy passion for me.

Methinks the sweet bird which is carolling now,
        Will too soon spread his wings;
And I always have found that a musical vo
        Is the fleetest of things!
    Ah! dearest, the token to bind,
    Is surely a something of different kind.

Vows sworn by fond lips on fond lips, are, methinks,
        Much more rational ties;
And whether one fudge or fidelity drinks,
        Matters not to the wise;
    But 'tis certain, my dear, when the guaranty's such,
    One never can have an assurance too much.

IF NOT READY.

If not ready,
Stern and steady,
When the insolent foeman braves,
Then I see ye, doom'd already,
Cowards fitted to be slaves!
If ye falter
At the altar,
Ye would take the field in vain;
Rather stoop ye to the halter,
And as bondsmen wear the chain!

What a story,
Writ in glory,
By the hero-hosts of old;
To become, ere trees grow hoary,
Shame for fame, by cowards sold!
Where's the ranger,
Braving danger,
That beneath these old trees stood?
Every feeling sternly steeling
For the land that drank his blood!

Oh! the sorrow,
That can borrow
From the past no braver thought:
That leaves basely to the morrow,
Deeds we should to-day have wrought!
In the Hour
Still lies the Power,
But if not ready to seize it then,
We lose the power, losing the hour,
And never for ages shall find it again.

THOU'ST WAKED ME FROM THE HAPPIEST DREAM.

THOU'ST waked me from the happiest dream,
And, with a single word, hast chill'd,
Of sweetest thoughts, the fairest stream
That e'er through boyish fancy thrill'd;
I dream—alas! I sleep—no more,
But with a phrenzied memory,
Still destined idly to deplore,
I turn in hopeless pain to thee!

I turn to thee, but turn in vain;
Thou hear'st me not—thou wilt not hear,
Nor heed, that daring hope again,
As fatal quite, to me, as dear!
Ah! could'st thou but one hour restore,
That hour would make me more than free;
And yet, though destined to deplore
And curse the past, I curse not thee!

Yet, was it well to use the game,
Thy web of witcheries—tear and smile—
To fan boy-fancies into flame,
Thou mocking faith and love the while?
Where was the merit in thy art,
On one so simple—all untaught
In that base school that sells the heart,
And lives a lie to love and thought?

I HAVE WANDERED MUCH.

I.

I have wander'd much, and wander'd far,
But ever I had a particular star,
  That carried me back with an eager bound;
The syrens, they wooed me to stay with a boon,
But, lipping them swift, I fled them soon,
  And followed my star, till my home I found;
Where the pleasures lived on through the fleeting years,
Bringing me sunshine and bringing me tears,
  But leaving me stronger with every wound:
While my star still brighten'd as time flew by,
Till at last it lightened the whole of my sky.

II.

Yet still do I wander, day by day,
And the syrens woo, and awhile they stay,
  For I cherish a feeling for every bliss;
And my heart grows glad with a fond embrace,
And my fancies pursue each winning grace,
  And my lips yet burn with a beauty's kiss!
Oh! never, I wot, do I aught deny,
Of the charms that hallow the earth and sky,
  And to love them deem never a thing amiss;
But they keep me not long from my proper star,
And I hurry me home where my treasures are!

YOU MAY MUSE O'ER GLORIES GONE.

I.

You may muse o'er glories gone,
  Gazing on these glowing skies,
But when droops the setting sun,
  Then my dreary memories rise:
Then the thick'ning glooms I see,
  No sun-glance may penetrate:
Then the waste opes wide for me,
  Sterile, pathless, desolate!

II.

Vain your boyish heart's lament,
  By no lasting sorrow made;
Mine's a mournful monument,
  With a thousand glooms arrayed;
There the death's-head on each shrine,
  Column, court, and spire behold;
And some spirit, mocking mine,
  Starts from every ruin old.

III.

On my path the spectres dart,
  Not from tomb and cave alone—
The choice places of my heart
  To their searching sway are known;
And they bitter all of life,
  And they banish all of joy,
Till I murmur, through the strife,
  Wherefore do they not destroy?

SONNET.—RESIGNATION.

His eye was tearless, but his cheeks were wan;
 There sorrow long had set her heavy hand;
 Yet was his spirit noble, and a bland
And sweet expression o'er his features ran!
Care had not tutored him to sullenness—
 The world's scorn not subdued the natural man:
The sweet milk of his nurture was not less,
 Because the world had met him with its ban;
He is above revenges, though he drinks
 The bitter draught of malice and of hate;
And still, though in the weary strife he sinks,
 They can not make him murmur at his fate;
He suffers, and he feels the pang, but proves
The conqueror, though he falls, for still he loves.

FLIGHT, NOT FREEDOM.

I.

Is it freedom—speeding lonely—
 Reft of all that being brought—
O'er life's ocean—brooding only
 Over past resource of thought?
Freedom!—all abandoned, steering,
 Loose from every tie and stay,
With the currents idly veering,
 Heedless where they stop or stray—
Still unfeeling, still uncaring,
 If the billows serve or sway?

II.

Ask the cloud, when sadly drifting,
  With the rising wind it goes—
Ask the billow, storm-uplifting,
  Into terror from repose—
Ask the meteor, sudden gushing,
  Into darkness, shorn of light;
Or the river, helpless rushing,
  Down to ocean from its height:
Ask of these, which Fate is hushing,
  If 'tis freedom follows flight?

SONNETS.—WITH MY PORTRAIT.

I.

My portrait! will it serve when I am dead,
  To bring me to thy memory, as beside
  Thy cheerful fire thou sitt'st at eventide—
Thoughtfully resting on thy hand thy head:
And, from thy mantle, with unconscious glance—
  How full of speech to friendship!—I look down,
  And catch thy sudden glances upward thrown,
Or note thine eyes fixed on me in a trance,
  Speaking dear memories of sweet seasons gone,
Precious to both, and full of that fresh faith
  That won the heart by fond soliciting
  Of the true nature, and the generous spring,
Ere Hope had found denial, or Love scaith,
And to believe in all we feel and see,
Is youth's delight and best necessity?

II.

Yet why the portrait? If to thee as me,
  That Past be still a memory of delight,
And Love and Faith, with hands for ever free,
  Brought goodly fruits; and these were, in thy sight,
A precious boon of blessing, such as still
Recalls their perish'd blossoms with a thrill,
Even while the winter, with an aspect chill,
Takes absolute place upon thy lonely hearth:
  Then do I sit with thee beside the fire;
Share all thy solitude; help thee to thy mirth;
  And smile with thee to see the glooms retire:
If such my presence in thy heart's desire,
Such the keen quickening of thy soul with mine,
What need my portrait? I need none of thine!

III.

The indelible hues of memory on my heart,
  Have limn'd thee in perfection rare as true;
  I see thee rise before my present view,
Each lineament all living as thou art—
As Art can never reach! Thy pale white brow,
  Lofty and massive; the keen falcon eye,
  Eager, yet with that arch vivacity
Which argued well the merry heart below;
The brown curls scattered o'er thy forehead fair;
  The Roman beak; the sweet mouth free of guile;
  The very girlish dimple in thy smile,
That still betray'd the quip before its birth,
When the sly thought, half satire and half mirth,
Made thee the happiest Yorick at our cheer.

I SEEK TO SING OF GLORY.

I SEEK to sing of Glory,
  And, for my deathless name,
To win from future story
  A high and holy fame!
I strike the faithful lyre
  The high design to prove,
But, ah! the sounds expire,
  And Glory yields to Love!
Ah, Love! wherefore Love,
When the soul would soar above!

In vain I turn the pages
  Of sad and sacred lore;
And still, through buried ages,
  Dread, solemn truth explore:
Alas! through all the ashes
  Of ancient years, arise
The soft, but piercing flashes
  From Love's triumphant eyes!
Ah, Love! look not thus,
Or no glory shines for us!

I turn'd me to the sages
  For wisdom, to arrest
The wild, consuming rages
  Of passion, in my breast:
But they, with eyes of sorrow,
  Did each lay bare his own,
And lo! still ruling thorough,
  Love sate as on a throne!
Ah! ruling every where the same,
He leaves to Glory but a name!

THIS LONELY HOME AT LEAST IS FREE.

This lonely home at least is free,
  And here my harp may wake,
Unheard, the song that tells of thee,
  Remember'd for thy sake;
That lyre, so loved in other days,
May well recall the words of praise,
  That soothed its infant fears—
When thou and Hope, alike, were young,
And Feeling, as each lay was sung,
  Repaid the toil with tears.

Those chords in mournful silence long
  Deplored thy hapless fate,
Till Memory came to wake the song,
  Which yet sounds desolate;
When thou grew'st silent all was dumb,
No fancy could the spell o'ercome,
  Thy loss o'er life had cast;
But as the sorrow grew subdued,
Thy image fill'd the solitude,
  Though still it mock'd the past.

Oh! Memory still her chaunt renews,
  Though not with former tone;
She can not, and she would not choose,
  Forget that she is lone:
That, if thou hear'st her tribute strain,
Thou dost not answer it again,
  As still thou didst of yore;
She dreams that thou art nigh, but sees
No more, as Love and Fancy please,
  And weeps and sighs the more!

THE LIBERTY TREE.

[IN Colonial times, when the spirit of Seventy-Six was fast maturing for the issue which tried men's souls, the people of the Southern Colonies were wont, in each community, to select a favorite old oak as the Liberty Tree, where they met in consultation and to inspirit each other. The Liberty Pole is an unsightly substitute for the noble oak, vigorous in its green, great in column and spreading branches, and venerable with its streaming beard of moss. Most of these trees have disappeared—cut down by the sacrilegious axe. It will be well if the spirit which was fostered beneath their branches shall not disappear also, with that veneration which should have held them sacred to the last.]

HURRAH for the tree!—the old oak tree!
The Liberty Tree of the Colony;
How grandly it stood,
The King of the Wood,
With its bearded moss of a century!

How grand was its growth of a thousand years,
As the nation grows by its hopes and fears,
By the storms that wring,
By the birds that sing,
And feeds on the very strifes it bears:

Till it grandly spreads with the arms that wave,
For a thousand years o'er a people's grave;
And the race that lives
In the shade it gives,
Grows strong, like itself, the storm to brave.

Hurrah for the tree!—the proud old tree!
Where the brave old men of the colony,
When the land was aflame,
Together came,
To brood o'er the toils which should make it free.

And for pious rite, and for godly grace,
And valiant counsel, what holier place
    Than the shade of the tree,
    Of a century,
The sire so long of so great a race?

Would it speak but now, that brave old oak,
As in Colony days it surely spoke,
    Oh, what would it say
    To the sons to-day,
Of the shame they bear and the galling yoke?

Be sacred the valor that guards the tree,
That saw the bright dawn of our liberty;
    And under its boughs
    Let us make our vows,
To die if it needs for our Liberty Tree!

HOW STILL THE HOUR.

How still the hour—how still!
  As if night had all her own,
And her sway, without a will,
  Were a Queen's upon her throne!
No voice to break the calm,
  And but the west wind's breath,
Soft, over beds of balm,
  That make sleep akin to death!

Ah, hark! as from afar,
  Love's murmur of delight;
'Tis some fair girl's guitar,
  That sounds from yonder height.
It breaks the liquid air,
  Yet soothes the wound it makes;
And though it breathes of care,
  'Tis love alone that wakes.

Hush! o'er the wave it swells,
  And the waters seem to sleep;
A murmur only tells
  Of the depth within the deep:
And the west wind, late in play,
  Now droops upon the beach,
As if it felt the sway
  Of a strain it could not reach!

Alas! for the young heart,
  Whose song so sweetly takes
Winds, waves, and with an art,
  So sovereign, nature wakes:
It mourns the song in vain,
  That fails one only ear;
All others it may chain
  But the one it fain would hear.

QUEEN HECATE'S TRIUMPH.

I.

Midnight clad in brightness,
  Beautiful in calm,
Walked her realm of starriness,
  Through a breath of balm;
Softly-rising zephyrs
  Swept along the way,
Where the Lord of Mazzaroth
  Held his regal sway:

And the sad-eyed sisters
  Of the Pleiades,
Weeping still the lost one,
  Watch'd o'er smiling seas;
Fleck'd with stars, the mantle,
  Floating free, of Night,
Stream'd o'er northern summits,
  Trailing robes of light.

Never the blue gardens
  Of the firmament,
With such starry blossoms
  Were so brighty-sprent;
As the twiring beauties
  Sped, each glorious form
Was at once the proof and pledge
  'Gainst the growing storm.

II.

'Twas a realm all faerie,
And o'er Eastern waves,
Sweetly sad, Queen Hecate
Rose from Ocean's caves;
Thousand pure white zephyrs
Sped along her way,
Signalling a thousand tribes
To come forth and play.

How the little billows
Lifted their green heads;
Each a foam-wreath wearing,
Torn from ocean beds;
And with these commercing,
You might fancy swarms
O'er the gray beach gambolling,
Light, fantastic forms.

Gayly, little islets
Floated o'er the deep,
Breasting sky and ocean,
Each a shining sleep;
And great birds were spreading
Vans for either shore,
While in green groves, little birds
Sang back to ocean's roar.

You might deem, with reason,
That, from every land,
Longing hearts were linking
In a loving band:

Souls for flight had pinions,
  Won from music's wing,
And with never a care, the heart
  Could everywhere go sing.

III.

Yet the very brightness
  Hath its birth in gloom;
And the dreary blight stands evermore
  Waiting on the bloom;
And the skyey gardens,
  Hanging soft in air,
Feel the Presence rising
  Of a grim Despair.

Twin-born with the Zephyr,
  From one ocean bed,
In the West ascending,
  Lo, the Shadowy Dread!
Speeding on with pinions
  Breaking through all bars,
Spreading vans that threaten
  To submerge the stars!

IV.

Insolent! all vainly
  Would thy hate assail
The silver-footed Huntress,
  Guarded with bright mail:
Arrow after arrow
  Rends thy sable wings,
While the shaft that wounds thee,
  Beauty o'er thee flings.

Oh! how vainly flying
  Her pursuing gleams;
O'er thy murky mantle
  Pour the radiant streams;
Far, the floating edges
  Of thy pall of night,
She hath ermined lovelily
  With delicious bright.

On thy brow sepulchral
  There's a gleam—a glare—
And thy great black shoulders
  Suddenly grow fair;
Through thy folds of murkiness
  Speed the silver darts,
As the arrowy lightning
  Gilds the gloom it parts.

Thus, in horrid Hades,
  Midst the realm of gloom,
Beauty strives with Terror,
  Gladdening blight with bloom!
So fair Proserpina
  Soothes the storm to rest,
With silver tresses streaming,
  Flung fond on Pluto's breast.

THE ECLIPSE OF HECATE.

I.

Long I watched the doubtful struggle
  'Twixt the rising storm and night—
One with vans of fearful blackness,
  One with smiles and shafts of light;
Till at last, o'ercome by Beauty,
  Back the vampire form had sped,
Arrows sharp, of wondrous brightness,
  Swift pursuing as he fled:
And, with sympathetic triumph
  Cried I, to the baffled storm,
As pursued, and still retreating,
  Sullen growled the lurid form:
"Where is now the hateful triumph,
  Speaking late in wing and eye?
Where are now those savage squadrons
  Swooping lately through the sky?
And, along the fields of heaven,
  Where is now thy haughty sway—
Crouching now and baffled, driven,
  Wrecked and shattered, far away?"

II.

And I laid me down exulting
  In the conquest still in sight—
Love o'er Hate, and Peace o'er quarrel,
  And, above the Black, the Bright!
Sailed the Queenly Hecate o'er me,
  Squadrons white, in grand array,
Heralding her perfect conquest
  To the embraces with the day;

And, as fanned by zephyr-angels,
  Slept I in the moonlight pale,
Never dreaming once that legions,
  In such glory clad, should quail.
And I dreamt of mortal beauty,
  That me-seemed immortal too:
Such as youthful fancy summons
  Out from blessing realms of blue.
And I felt the loving ardor
  Of her bosom near mine own;
And my heart upsprung exulting,
  Like a hero on his throne!

III.

Bright as soft, like streams of sunset
  O'er a fond and placid sky,
Fell her tresses round my bosom,
  Shone her blue and blessing eye.

IV.

Oh! the wondrous charm of Beauty,
  Soothing with a dear delight!
Oh! the loving calm of Beauty,
  Making Rapture out of Night!
Oh! the true and deep religion
  Nursed within a loving breast,
Like a gleam of holy sunshine,
  Hiding in a happy nest!

V.

Dreaming thus on Earth, of Heaven,
  How deliciously the bliss
Of that summer night enwrapt me,
  With embrace and balm and kiss!

Steeped in all the spells of Beauty,
  Drank I in the immortal breath;
Straight forgot that skies had tempests,
  And that life was full of death!

VI.

But I woke with chill upon me,
  And the sky was bright no more;
And the ocean, hoarsely howling,
  Hurled its billows on the shore.
All the sky was in commotion,
  All the hosts of storm were there:
Troops and squadrons, fresh from ocean,
  Swept the starry fields of air.
Great, in central state of terror,
  Hung the vampire form on high,
Roaring wild, with angry clamor,
  For possession of the sky.
And the whirlwind shrieks, and rouses
  All his storms, and sets them free;
And the spout of ocean throws his
  Great black banner o'er the sea!

VII.

Where the queenly Hecate's crescent?
  Where the shafts of light she sped,
When, before her gay white legions,
  Late, the sullen vampire fled?
Where the islet forms of beauty,
  Soft reposing o'er the deep,
When I laid me down, of rapture
  Dreaming, in delicious sleep!

VIII.

They are gone, the forms of brightness,
  With the dreaming joys they brought,
The forgetfulness, in pleasure,
  Of the sterner things of Thought!
And the soul deplores in sadness
  The wild triumphs of the Form,
Black with billow, red with lightning,
  Sire of wild misrule and storm!

IX.

But, even while the Terror triumphs—
  As a bird within its nest,
Though the tree with storm is rocking,
  Sings the blessing in my breast;
And the Beautiful, still hopeful,
  Though with hooded brow she lies,
Patient waits the hour of freedom,
  When the storm shall leave her skies!
And I knew that all the blackness
  Should, in passing from her face,
Leave her far more bright than ever,
  And with lovelier spell and grace.

X.

And my thought was like an arrow—
  Like the shaft by Hecate sent,
Piercing all the sullen storm clouds,
  Opening up the firmament!
And, beyond, I felt the beauty
  Calm reposing in the sky;
Saw the pure bright eye triumphant,
  Like a star for storm too high!

Thought and Love, and Faith and Fancy,
  Made the Beautiful still mine;
Priestesses, white-handed, tending
  On the soul's superior shrine—
Making lovely still the Terror,
  Till the very brows of Gloom,
And her trailing pall of blackness,
  Glow in beauty, grow to bloom.

SWEETHEARTS AND WIVES.

SATURDAY NIGHT—IN AN INDIAN CABIN.

I.

Sweethearts and wives, boys,
  Sweethearts and wives;
Fill high, heart high, boys,
  Drink for your lives!
Who drinks with meet heart, boys,
To his wife or his sweetheart, boys,
  Lovingly thrives.
Drink—Ada or Zoe,
Drink—Clara or Chloe—
  Sweethearts or wives!

II.

Virgin or wife, boys,
  Woman is still
The spell to give life, boys,
  Making hearts thrill!

To husbands—drink sweethearts, boys;
To bachelors—meet hearts, boys;
  Drink with a will!
Drink—Janet or Carrie,
Drink—Nellie or Mary,
  Sweetheart or wife!

III.

We may be wild, boys,
  Roving and free;
Quickly beguiled, boys,
  With all we see;
But sweethearts are yet, boys,
What we never forget, boys,
  Even on a *spree*.
Drink—Kate or Christina,
Sue, Sally, or Lena—
  Sweethearts or wives.

IV.

We are from home, boys,
  Risking our lives,
Still forced to roam, boys,
  From dear native hives;
But like men, and with meet hearts, boys,
Drink wives and sweethearts, boys,
  Sweethearts and wives!
Drink the dear one, though nameless,
And the pledge shall be blameless,
  Sweethearts and wives!

NO MORE!

I.

My heart is in the yellow leaf,
  I feel that spring of life no more,
That once, when all my hours were brief,
  Could every blessed hour restore:
Could bring to life each perished joy,
  And still recall, with morning hours,
The evening rapture—sweet but coy—
  That waved my fancy on with flowers!—
That waves me on no more—no more!

II.

Oh! very sad to memory's heart,
  The mournful truth that all is o'er:
That all the precious things depart,
  Still murmuring—though we plead—"No more!"
Our bird, whose gay beguiling song
  Still won our way through Love's domain;
And all that countless, wooing throng,
  That we shall never woo again—
That woo and wave us on no more!

III.

Oh! words that strike with icy thrill,
  That chide us with defrauded hours;
That rob us of our moonlight still,
  The charm of song, the sweet of flowers;
Our faith in fancy; all that glows,
  For boyhood's day, and nightly dreams;
His shadows crowning for repose;
  His love, that most immortal seems;
Dreams, love, that woo and charm—no more!

NOW ROUSE THEE UP, OLD ENGLAND!

A BALLAD FOR OUR BRITISH BRETHREN, FROM THE BACKWOODS.*

Now rouse thee up, old England,
  And sharp anew thy spear,
And clothe thee in that valor
  That hath made the nations fear;
A thousand years thy banner
  Hath o'ershadowed sea and shore,
And thy soul hath never faltered,
  Since the day of Azincourt!

For a lion spirit in thee,
  With a stern and simple might,
Born of purpose frank, and wisdom,
  Made thee stronger from each fight;
Thou had'st native virtues growing
  In thy soil, that led thy race
To performance, through a Genius
  That had ever foremost place.

But thy blood-red cross is paling,
  And the sinews of thy strength,
Thy calm wisdom, Genius, failing,
  Bring the threat'ning fate, at length;
Thou hast shown, by fatal error,
  That thy legs are made of clay;
And thy brass of front and forehead
  Will not keep thee from decay!

* Written during the Crimean war.

And but vain the simple valor
  Of thy people in the fight,
Though they fling themselves on danger
  With the wrestler's fierce delight—
If the Genius that once led them,
  In the brave old days, be gone:
The Eye that went before them,
  And the Wing that bore them on!

Where the stern old Norman virtues
  Of thy Sidneys, Hampdens, now?
Where the Cromwells, Blakes, and Nelsons,
  That wreathed laurels round thy brow?
Great master-souls, that ever
  Shone out bright, with solar burst—
With a might to meet the trial,
  When the danger threatened worst!

'Tis in these thou lack'st, old England!
  Not the sinews but the soul—
The grand genius still for guidance,
  The grand wisdom for control!
But the jackal plays the lion,
  Where thy ancient statesmen stood,
And thy blood-ennobled virtues
  Have been changed to things of wood!

Lo! thy monkeys in high station
  Chatter welcome to thy fate;
Mock with impotence each effort
  That would still maintain thy state;
Thy brave souls receive no summons
  Such as saved thee still of yore:
Not thy nobles now—thy commons,
  Can alone thy sway restore!

Face the truth in season, England!
  Let thy wisdom seek, at length,
In the *genius* of thy *people*,
  The true secret of thy strength;
Purge thine altars of the jackals
  That sit gibbering thy disgrace;
And to competence plebeian
  Let thy puppet peers give place!

What to thee the Gaul's alliance,
  After years of Waterloo?
What the Russian's—world's—defiance,
  To thyself, had'st thou been true?
Had'st thou kept the simple England,
  Stern of virtue, with an aim
To ennoble manhood only,
  To the grand results of Fame?

How had the noble Norman
  Of the days of brave Queen Bess,
Loathed alliance with that foeman
  Whom thou load'st with thy caress!
Thou hast pass'd, in briefest season,
  With a wondrous brass of face,
From the speech of scorn and loathing,
  To the kiss and the embrace!

'Tis a Judas kiss between ye,
  Like the viper's, to be feared,
For ye loathe, even while ye drivel,
  Slavering o'er each other's beard!
False and hollow each profession,
  Each with purpose that betrays,
And the kiss is but the prelude
  To the treachery that slays!

Think'st thou, as France beholds thee,
Struck down in single fight;
All thy feebleness made patent;
India's treasure full in sight—
That her keen and fierce ambition,
Rival she for sway and fame—
Yearning, with revenge impatient,
For a long account of shame—

Think'st thou, thy kiss will blind her
To the bait thy weakness shows?
Hollow truce and treaty bind her,
When her blows were fatal blows?
That thy glozing, honied phrases,
Will prove soothing, salving things,
For the race and man so lately
Grided by thy sneers and stings?

Believe it not!—The hour,
Sating hates of thousand years,
Nigh approaching, brings the power
That may well alarm thy fears:
Golden spoils, as well as passions,
Urge the speedy foe's advance,
And thy Indian empire opens
To the Russias and to France!

Not for thee the false alliance,
Frail as false, with Turk or Gaul!
One alone, of all the nations,
Still had succor'd thee from fall!
To thy genius kindred—springing
From thy loins—the sister race,
Here, in Apalachian forests,
Still had kept thee from disgrace!

In the Old World thine—and ours,
 Stretching, conquering all the New,
'Gainst the world, in arms united,
 We had proved each mission true:
Earnest pressing, still securing,
 With each sunset, what the day
Yielded up of golden empire
 To our mutual arms and sway!

For we loved thy glories, England,
 Felt thy genius—felt it ours;
Shared thy fame—thy Norman spirit—
 All its purposes and powers;
Loved the mother-land that bore us;
 And, with instincts truer far
Than the teachings of the schoolman,
 Followed still our natal star.

But thou did'st not suffer, England,
 That our love should share thy fate;
And, as resolute on ruin,
 For our fondness gave us hate;
Still pursued, with vexing quarrel,
 Still assailed, with cruel blows,
Goading still a kindred people,
 'Gainst their nature, to be foes!

Could'st thou rob, or wrong, or trample,
 Could'st thou mock, or flout, or shame,
Thrust thy spear against our weakness,
 Spoil our lands or taint our name—
Rampant, with imperious passion,
 We beheld thee, all elate,
Fiercely hostile, foully working,
 Glad to do the work of hate!

Yet, remembrance of thy glory,
  What is noble in thee still,
Makes us weep to see thee failing,
  Overborne in strength and will:
Though we know that, in alliance
  With our foes, thy hostile aim
Means us malice; still would cripple;
  Seeks to conquer, flout, and shame!

Yet thy blood is in our bosoms,
  Kindred genius, aims, and powers,
And no policy can stifle
  Pleas of nature such as ours:
Though we know that in thy triumph
  Grows thy insolence and might,
Sworn to bring us future danger,
  And one last and fearful fight!

Yet we would not see thee quailing
  From thy ancient pride of place;
Would not see the red cross trailing,
  Lily-dusted, in disgrace!
Rouse thee to thy Norman birth-right,
  Braving Europe's odds and powers;
And if foreign arm must save thee,
  Be it kindred—be it ours!

WELL, IF THAT DREAM OF BLISS.

Well, if that dream of bliss be over,
  That moved so deeply heart and brain,
I am not that insensate lover,
  To lose, and then to love again;

The hour that tells me hope has vanish'd,
  An hour of freedom can not be;
As well assure the wretch that's banish'd
  From home and country, he is free!

'Tis true that gallant barques may bear him
  To other climes as fair as this,
And eyes may warm, and lips may cheer him,
  With memories of a former bliss;
Yet, were he blind to every aspect
  Of storm and sorrow in his gaze,
He could not lose that ancient prospect
  That stamp'd his soul in earlier days.

The exiled heart bears still an anguish
  That never leaves his fancy free;
And doom'd on foreign rocks to languish,
  Still dreams of homes he can not see.
Far back o'er waves of memory roving,
  Decreed to feel, yet still deplore;
His passions, like their tempests proving—
  His hopes, the wrecks that strew the shore.

If thine's the heart which yet can cherish
  Each fancy of thy childhood still,
'Tis well, perchance, that mine should perish
  'Neath broken faith and fickle will!
The heart which thou discard'st so cheaply,
  Thine ear shall never hear repine;
It loves thee still, too dearly, deeply,
  And fondly bears the doom of thine.

OH, HAD I BUT THE POWER!

Oh, had I but the power,
I would twine for thee a bower,
Such as love might ever fancy of the gadding vine and flower;
Such a sky should arch above it,
As should win thee still to love it;
Such birds should sing within it, as should soothe thy saddest hour.

They should gather from thy beauty,
A meet sense of love and duty;
They should image forth the sweetness from thy angel nature breathing,
And the song and sunshine meeting,
Should be evermore completing
The bright circle of delight, which for thine my love is wreathing.

They would take from me the feeling,
They are fittest for revealing,
That still joys to yield the joys which thy dreaming heart but fancies;
And the love of mine they sing thee,
With the homage that they bring thee,
Should possess thee with a magic such as glows in old romances.

THE CHIMNEY CRICKET.

I.

WHEN the dusky shadows glide
Through the porch at even-tide,
And the wintry faggot's blaze
O'er the wall fantastic plays;
And the household forms appear,
Each in the accustom'd chair—
Grandsire old in seat of pride;
Son and wife on either side;
Urchins on the knee astride;
Slender maid, in volume lost,
Reading rapt of true love cross'd—
Ere the evening board is set,
While the urn is hissing yet,
Then—as if the whole were met,
Unto whom his song is bound,
In his circle gather'd round—
Then, with lay of measured mirth,
Sudden, from the silent hearth,
Our chimney cricket chirps refrain,
Fitting the domestic strain—
Singing of the pleasant peace,
And the household's fair increase,
And the quiet gliding on
Of the years, from sire to son;—
Of old house and ancient state,
Not too high to anger Fate;
Modest worth, and working brave,
Which, of yore, the homestead gave,
And maintain it, with a fold,
Growing well, though growing old:

Planted like a rock, and strong
In God's favor, just so long
As the cricket sings his song.

II.

For, 'tis not a fable all,
That predicts the household's fall,
When the cricket leaves the wall.
Household insect—bird that clings
To the roof-tree, while he sings,
Which, for full a hundred springs,
He hath held, and rear'd his young,
Speaking each the self-same tongue,
Of safe homestead, happy still
In the blessing of good will,
And God's bounty;—
Dog that waits,
Watching nightly near the gates,
Like a sentry—faithful guard
Of the dwelling and the yard;
Puss, that purring, coil'd up snug,
Keeps the centre of the rug;—
All have instincts fine, that teach
Presciences, we can not reach—
All domestic, all designed
Waiters, watchers on mankind,
With the family allied,
Sharing in its pain and pride,
Shrinking never from its side,
And, by chirp, or howl, or song,
Signalling the threatened wrong.
Hurt, or hindrance; beast of prey;
Sudden tempest; sad decay,
As the household wastes away;

Or, in hours of peace like this,
Chirrupping domestic bliss.

III.

Grateful to my thoughts and ear
Is, at dusk, the song I hear
Of our cricket in the wall,
Timéd well to sober fall;
With a strain monotonous,
Suiting the well-order'd house;
Suiting well the set of sun,
Conflict over, toil well done,
And the pleasant calm which brings
Sweet repose for striving things.
Song of grave solemnity
For his spouse and children three,
As for mine, though more there be—
Three or thirty, which you will—
But a well-train'd household still;
Making, it would seem, a grace
Fitted to the homely place;
Giving thanks for daily food
To the Giver of All Good,
Even as we, who smile, declare
Bounty that receives no prayer—
Needs none, if the thought be there.

IV.

By the lonely hearth I sit,
Watching, while the figures flit
O'er the walls; or, in the fire,
See the phantom shapes expire—
Cities, and their domes, in flashes,
Till they fade in the gray ashes—

Start, to hear the sudden shock,
The knell'd hours upon the clock;
But never lose the cricket strain,
Changing seldom his refrain,
Which would seem in purpose vain,
Murmuring:
——"Wherefore all this stir?
Half life's struggle is to err!"
He, the best philosopher;
Satisfied with lodging small,
But a dry one, in close wall,
And a single burden ditty,
Dull enough to move the pity
Or the scorn of captious city,
Ever bent on insect ranges,
Constant only seeking changes,
With a lizard lust for sunshine;
And, 'twixt mammon, gammon, moonshine,
Showing butterfly propensity,
With scarce butterfly intensity.

V.

"Better," quoth he, "watch the fire,
See sparks kindle and expire,
Than indulge in vain desire—
Half your strifes of men are flashes
That go out in smoke and ashes!
Half your struggles, but a run
Of brown lizard after sun!
Half your pleasures, or your pains,
But a worm's, for silken gains,
The best part of life made bitter,
With its cares, for idle glitter;

And the soul's most noble powers
Flung away, through fruitless hours,
In a fond pursuit of flowers!
Flowers, or phantoms—vainer far
Than the hope to pluck the star—
Prison rays of fancy, gleaming
Through the fairy realms of dreaming!
Every power of virtue wasted—
Flowers tainted soon as tasted—
All because of that vain struggle,
Still pursued through strife and juggle,
To assert, on painted pinion,
O'er still meaner things, dominion;
Moving motes of meaner station
Into vulgar admiration!

VI.

"Better far, my evening prattle—
Purr of cat, or low of cattle,
Bark of dog, or chirp of sparrow—
To avert of Fate the arrow;
Take the sting away from being;
Teach your young ones truthful seeing,
And conduct them to the beauty
That lies sure in homely duty!
Here, beside the evening fire,
You shall guide the young desire;
Train the heart, with modest lesson,
And the noble soul, to press on
In the walks, or high or lowly,
Which the endowment renders holy!"

VII.

They are sleeping, all my young,
And their mother. Not a tongue,
Save that whose moral hath been sung,
Makes a murmur through the house.
O'er the carpet runs the mouse;
Heedless of the cricket, he,
Though still rather shy of me,
And the cricket's song, but late
Full of meaning, sinks to prate,
The mere click-clack, dull debate,
Such as to the common sense
Offers little recompense.
Yet, methinks, he might have said,
What's been running in my head?
And, with such a notion, he
Shall never be dislodged by me.

VIII.

Ah! dear drowsy chirper, why
Should I lodging place deny,
Though thy prattlings never cease,
When they promise household peace?
Till the house itself shall fall,
Take the freedom of the wall,
While it pleaseth thee to hold
Tenure in the mantle old!
Rear thy tribes to teach mine own,
When both thou and I are gone!
It would please me much to know
That when hence, perforce, I go,
Thou, or thine, shall sing for mine,
Teaching them the instincts fine,
Which may lead to the divine;

All the sweet morality
Of that constancy in thee,
Which thou still hast taught to me!
They shall keep the household fires,
And home evenings, like their sires,
With a love that never tires!
And a gentle, calm content,
Which, at close of day well spent,
Keeps the evening innocent;
And, with placid mood, surveys
The slow sinking of the blaze,
Till each golden gleam decays!

MY HOPE IS IN THE YELLOW LEAF.

My hope is in the yellow leaf,
  My dream is of the Past;
My early joy hath brought me grief,
  My early profit waste;
And still, the greatest grief of all,
  Is that too late I know,
How easy 'twas to scape the fall,
  That laid my fortunes low.

We shed the tear from vain remorse,
  To think, could Time restore,
How easy 'twere to sweep the course,
  That opes for us no more.
Forgetfulness! Forgetfulness!
  O Lethe! where art thou,
The thought to hush, that can not bless,
  And brings no wisdom now?

BATTLE HYMN.—NOW RAISE THE MIGHTY SONG!

Now raise the mighty song—the brave old Doric song—
  The trumpet strain that tells of Liberty!
For, oh, too long! too long! we've borne the cruel wrong!
Let us now be strong, for the work of vengeance, strong!
  Let us now be free, as the winds of winter, free!
  Shout high the stormy chorus, shout, for Death or Liberty!

Hark! the sovereign anthem, how it floats
  From our mountain summits, swells and goes,
Bearing, terrible, and swift, like our native eagle's notes,
Mighty as the storm, from thrice ten thousand throats,
  Terror to our foes, and fate!—fate and terror to our foes!
  Shout, to their insolent souls, of the terror in our blows!

Ay, shout as one, ye thousands, all! The chorus
  Shall rouse anew the souls that long have slept!
Teach the insolent foe that gathers now before us
  How the vigil of our sorrow hath been kept;
  How we crouched in our shame; how we wept!
But we wake to sleep no more with the tyrant's banner
      o'er us!

To the field! to the field! where the long account of shame
  Shall be satisfied forever to the freedom in our souls!
Where we wash away the blot, the dark stigma on our
      name!
Where our anguish, as we dare once again to think of fame,
  Grows to gladness, even in danger, and with every peal
      that rolls,
  We fling off the foul fetters that were crushing in our souls!

Shout to battle! shout to battle! Raise anew the noble song—
 The eagle note of hate and of vengeance on the foe!
Our fathers' spirits waken, and no more we suffer wrong;
We are strong in souls and thousands—for the field of carnage
 strong—
 And with joy of battle raging, with a death at every blow!
Shout the chorus, brave and free! the Doric song of Liberty!
Death or Liberty be ours—and in death we may be free!

NOW WEAVE YOUR SPELLS, YOUNG MAIDEN.

Now weave your spells, young maiden—
 Love's sweet and mystic charms;
For the old moon now comes laden
 With the young moon in her arms.
And 'tis the auspicious season,
 When maiden spells have power;
When the rhyme becomes the reason,
 And the fruit is in the flower.
So, weave your spells, young maiden,
 Lo! the sign, and this the hour!

Bring Faith, the all-confiding,
 And Hope, that sings by night;
Love, through all seasons 'biding,
 And Duty, grown Delight;
Truth, that from feeling borrows,
 And Care, that, watching fondly,
Knows but to soothe all sorrows,
 And cheer the heart most lonely—
These be thy charms, dear maiden,
 The best for love—the only!

SONNETS.—DEFEAT—DISAPPOINTMENT.

I.

A LITTLE farther on, the shadows deep
Of this great forest give security,
And here, the pageant o'er, the crowd gone by,
Pride may assert the privilege to weep—
Acknowledging the earth, Humility,
That better knows the sense of pain than life,
May, for a season, yield the outward strife,
And suffer the o'erburden'd soul to sigh!
Alas! in lowliness of soul like mine,
That loathes it in a world of so much state,
How precious is this still obscurity!
Where even Fear may mock the hurt of Hate,
And the poor heart, long baffled, cease to pine,
As if new freedom rescued it from Fate!

II.

If the good star that quicken'd at my birth,
In spiritual tie and consciousness,
With that frail life, decreed a toil on earth
Which earth hath never yet allow'd to bless,
Be at this moment gazing from its place,
In search of mine, a sympathy with shame,
And the dread cloud that settles on my fame,
Will blotch for aye the beauty in her face!
Yet have I struggled till all stars grew pale,
Nor shamed them by that struggle—was it mine
To make, like theirs, the face of fortune shine,
To shield her ever from the night-cloud's veil?
Was not the struggle much, that brought distress
And pain? and is't my shame that cannot make success?

QUIET IS ON THE EARTH.

I.

Quiet is on the earth, and in the sky
The moon rides pale and high;
Silence is o'er the city, and the gush
Of the sweet South is all that breaks the hush;
Oh! wonder not, while Earth thus lies at rest,
If thy dear memory stirs within my breast,
And from my bosom's depths my soul should rove,
Still seeking thine, dear love!

II.

How should I sleep, though daily toil be o'er
Doom'd vainly to adore?
Like some heart-humbled devotee, I bow,
Yet the stern idol still rejects my vow;
Hopeless, like him, my erring prayer is sent
Into the bright, cold, loveless firmament,
Which, by its scorn, would seem to mock the prayer,
Whose worship is despair!

III.

In the deep blue, how graciously the stars
Smile from their twiring cars;
And Earth, beneath the dewy-dropping gleam,
Sleeps, as if favor'd with some happy dream!
Oh! while all nature laps it in delight,
Why should'st thou rise thus coldly on my sight?
Thou marr'st the music in the scene I prove,
Yet oh, be there my love!

AWAKE! AWAKE! DEAR LADY!

Awake! awake! dear lady!
  Nor lose these Eden hours,
For the moon grows bright in the balmy East,
  With the breath of the incense flowers!
The breeze, like a spirit-bird, comes on,
  O'er the crisp waves of the sea;
And a voice goes forth through the air that soon
  Will swell into melody!

It is for thee, dear lady! 'tis for thee,
  These murmurs rise and fall!
With me they plead; with me,
  On love, and thee, they call!
Wake from the sleep that brings
No rapture on its wings!
Wake to delight that bears
Its tribute in its tears!

Awake! awake! dear lady!
  And hark the passionate song
That taught by Love in his fondest mood,
  'Neath thy lattice I now prolong!
Oh, let me not mourn a planet lost!
  Nor longer, thus cold, delay to shine!
But, like a sweet star to the tempest tost,
  Look down on this heart of mine!

It is for thee, dear lady! 'tis for thee,
  These tribute flowers unfold!
Stars shine, skies smile, winds murmur, all with me!
  They murmur—"Thou art cold!"

Thine is the crowning part
That beauty seeks from heart!
Thine the sweet boon to bless,
And soothe the soul's distress!

BATTLE HYMN.—COLUMNS, STEADY!

Columns, steady! make ye ready—with the steel and rifle ready!
Wait the signal! wait the moment—soul and steel and weapon steady!
Hark! the bugle! Music! march! we are on the foe already!
Quick step, column! swift, though solemn!
Let them feel ye! bravely steel ye—
And the field shall soon be won!
Hurrah! hurrah! hurrah!
Bravely steel ye! make them feel ye!
Every man and mother's son!
Hurrah!

They are looking from the house tops, they are listening from the wood,
Mothers, wives, and sweethearts, and the children of your blood!
And they ask of all the wounded, as we bear them to the rear,
"What of him whom my soul loveth? doth he turn away in fear?
Is he coward? is he recreant? Let me take his place and spear!"
Hurrah! hurrah! hurrah!

Charge! ye gallant legions, bravely, as one soul and body, charge!
Ye have souls of strength among ye, though your number be not large!
Bravely steel ye!
Let them feel ye!
On 'em! over 'em!—Hurrah!
On!—every mother's son—
And the field is won!
Hurrah!

'Tis not blood, thirsting madly, that we crave!
No wild passion for the strife;
But our honor, and our glory, more than life,
We would pluck from bloody grave—bloody grave!
'Tis for this we have thrown aside the plow!
In earth's sterile furrows let it rust—
'Tis our manhood, we must lift up from the dust;
And to fields of strife and slaughter hurry now—
Our only fields of freedom and of fame!
To work in others now,
With the brand upon our brow,
Would be shame—the worst of sorrows—would be shame!

Columns, rally! make you ready for the final charge and sally!
Skirmishers, in front! and cover, with your rifles, height and valley!
Let each pass be sighted deadly—range with eye of fate each alley!
Wings, be swift! and centre, steady!
Firm and steady, make ye ready
For the grapple now at hand!
Hurrah! hurrah! hurrah!
Make them feel ye! bravely steel ye!
Bullets down, and bared the brand!
Hurrah!

Waiting, watching, trembling, weeping, they are crouching in
the wood,
Wives and sweethearts, mothers, sisters, and the children of
your blood!
As they bind the wounds of comrades, cowering, sheltered in
the rear,
How they toil in silent terror! how they weep in silent prayer!
"Husbands, brothers, do not fail us! doom'd to bondage and
despair!"
Hurrah! hurrah! hurrah!
Charge, ye legions! bravely, sternly; as one soul and body,
charge!
Ye are sons and brothers—men—though your number be not
large!
Let them feel ye!
Bravely steel ye!
On 'em! over 'em!—Hurrah!
Be the work well done,
And the field is won!
Hurrah!

And if joy should be ours, when the storm of battle rolls,
'Tis because that we have burst
From the sleep of shame and sorrow that accurst,
And feel the fresh air of freedom on our souls!—
See the dawning, in its glory, of the light
Which shall bring us to the day—
Though it be through all the horrors of the fray,
Though our sun shall forever set in night!—
Yet, welcome be the trial storm and strife!
Ay, welcome, Fate and Fight,
Though our day shall set in night,
Since, in perishing for freedom, we prove worthy of its life!

THE AMULET.

I.

Here's a spell of power I've wove—
  Woven at night, in the moonlight pale:
It was wrought to rouse to a happy love,
  And to cure a heart of its hapless ail!
Take it, and make it thine, I pray;
  Bind its leaves to thy wounded heart—
Every pang it will steal away,
  Every sorrow 'twill make depart!

II.

More than this, when thy soul is sad,
  A mystic pleasure 'twill quickly bring—
Wingéd fancies, to make thee glad,
  Fresh from the wizard's haunted spring!
'Twill make thy drooping eye to glow,
  Bright with fresh hopes and youthful fire!
'Twill make thy bosom once more to know
  The purple gush of its young desire!

III.

Mine's the alchemist's charm, to give
  To the withering heart all its native powers;
To bid, with a voice of song, revive
  Every grace of thy youthful hours!
Buried treasures, and banish'd joys,
  What the Fate preys on evermore,
And Hate pursues, and Time destroys—
  Mine are the powers that still restore!

IV.

Then, if thine eyes would again behold
  The long-lost dear one, too early blest;
The loved, that in living were never cold,
  Won back again from their sainted rest—
Lo! as you lift your tearful eyes,
  Softly stooping, each starry wing,
Won, at a word, from the opening skies,
  By the sacred force of the spell I bring!

V.

Sovereign for hurt of heart the spell,
  Woven by midnight, in moonlight pale;
Strove the auspicious spirits well,
  That its virtues of healing should never fail.
They taught me to rear the flower whose fruit
  Hath given me power the sad to free,
Whenever Love shall make mournful suit,
  For healing and hope, to Memory!

WHILE THE SILENT NIGHT.

While the silent night goes by,
And the winds have scarce a sigh,
And the hours seem not to move,
Do I think of thee, my love!

And the moonlight's on the hill,
And the voice of man is still—
Lonely, in our walks, I rove,
And but think of thee, my love!

Star and shade recall thee now;
Gleams thy pale white maiden brow;
Flash thy dark eyes through the grove,
With a gentle fear, my love!

Walks thy spirit now with mine,
In the calm and sweet moonshine?
Dost thou seek, in dreams, the grove
Where I dream of thee, my love?

GOOD-NIGHT!

Good-night, my love! while blessings
  Like vigil spirits, keep,
Around thy dreaming pillow,
  Sweet watch above thy sleep!
May no rude vision rouse thee
  From fancies taught by mine!
But be the dream that woos thee
  Pure as that heart of thine!
Good-night! good-night! dear lady–
  Love's angels guard thy sleep!
      Good-night!

Heart that, forever gentle,
  Ne'er knew the taint of sin!
Eyes that, like evening flowers,
  Shut sunset hues within!
Lips, like the rose just budded
  That shrines heaven's sweetest dew—
Sleep with no beauty clouded!
  Sleep with each feeling true!
Good-night! good-night! dear lady—
  Love's angels guard thy sleep!
      Good-night!

WOODLAND VESPERS.

Hark! as rises now the moon,
  And the star of day declines,
Soaring with night's growing noon;
  Hark! along yon mount of pines,
Slowly sweet, the memories rise,
  As of spirits born to sing
Of the loves of earth and skies,
  In the coming of the spring—
    Jubilate!

Pleasures, born of faith and prayer;
  Dreams, from angel whispers caught;
Memories pure, and visions rare,
  Grow from memory to thought.
And in diapason sweet,
  How, together, do they rise
Into music; joyous, meet,
  For the peace, in peaceful skies—
    Jubilate!

Voices of the secret heart,
  Mingling with the voice of groves;
Birds that, with a natural art,
  Sing together of their loves—
And so pure the happy strain,
  Gushing from so sweet a spring,
That our hope grows young again,
  With renewal of its wing—
    Jubilate!

Oh! the peace that crowns the shade,
  When the passion fires, subdued,
Leave the soul, where once they sway'd,
  To the careless solitude!
Not the wild delirium now,
  That once fever'd heart and mind,
But a milder, gentler glow,
  Leaving love and peace behind—
      Jubilate!

BE IT FOLLY OR FRENZY.

Be it folly or frenzy—so sweet the delusion—
  I would not, for worlds, it should cease to be so!
And great were the guilt of that busy intrusion,
  Which would argue the folly or frenzy to show!
The world's but a painted deceit, and the pleasure,
  The only true pleasure 'tis left us to share,
Is found when we shut our eyes to the measure,
  So brimful and acrid, we drink of its care!

What better than frenzy—the evil disguising—
  If, mentally blinded, we see not our chain;
And the dream which beguiles us, predominant prizing,
  Refuse to look down on our fetters of pain?
We see not the straw in the cell that receives us,
  We feel not the scourge as it tortures us still;
We know not the guile in the heart which relieves us,
  And fancy no evil, and suffer no ill.

Why waken the dreamer, when bright to his vision
  Seems the life that on waking his spirit deplores?
Why torture the soul all whose dreams are elysian,
  With the gloom of that reason which blackens all yours?

Call it folly, or frenzy, but, oh! let my madness
  Escape without question! My heart is at stake!
I dream, it may be, but the dream is all gladness,
  All grateful, all glorious—and why should I wake?

FRIENDS ARE NIGH.

Friends are nigh; despair not,
  Though fast in the despot's chain!
True, they may fly, but fear not,
  They'll surely return again!
Never more true the season,
  Bringing its fruits and flowers,
Than, through fortunes freezing,
  Come these friends of ours!

Virtue can patiently languish,
  Though under the scourge of pain,
When round its bed of anguish
  Glides a ministering train!
True, they are all hid from us,
  Though waiting around they stand;
But they bring us an angel promise
  Of happiest help at hand!

Though in chain and prison
  Valor and virtue sigh,
Yet a generous host arisen
  Are working in secret nigh!
Here's Courage and Faith, who lead 'em,
  And they'll gnaw through the wall and chain,
Ay, die! but they'll bring to freedom,
  The comrade they love, again!

NOW FARE THEE WELL, SWEET RIVER!

Now fare thee well, sweet river—
  A long and last farewell!
I am borne from thee forever,
  By another stream to dwell!
But I feel, thus sadly roving,
  That, beneath the blessèd sky,
There is none so worthy loving
  As the noble stream I fly!

Thou hast filled me with a beauty
  Like a smile from the Most High;
Thou hast cheer'd me with a murmur,
  Still of music, melting by;
I have seen thee in thy glory,
  When the loved ones saw thee too;
But I see them now no longer,
  And to them and thee, adieu!

Farewell, O billowy water
  That still tells me of my youth—
When every sight was gladness,
  When every song was truth!
Dark clouds have come about me;
  Thou, too, hast felt the change,
And thy billows only flout me
  With a murmur sad and strange!

Yet well my heart hath loved thee,
  And it dearly loves thee still!
I can not choose but love thee,
  Let me roam where'er I will!

Thou art still unto my spirit,
  Like a smile from the Most High!
Thou art still most worthy loving
  Of all streams beneath the sky!

WHAT! AFTER LONG SEASONS!

WHAT! after long seasons of strife,
  Where the sorrows so thickly were strewn,
That, through the wild storm which has troubled my life,
  Thy love was the starlight alone!
To come with expectancy's glow,
  In the dream of a meeting with bliss!
To hail such a shadow as darkens thy brow,
  And a glance—oh! ye Heavens—like this!

Oh! how had the exile from home
  Been cheer'd by the dream of this hour!
It succor'd his heart in the season of gloom—
  The rich rainbow spanning the shower.
And I said to the tempest: "Rage on! while the light
  Of that promise attends me in sorrow and strife,
All vainly your storms gather black on my sight—
  My love is the star of my life!"

Had I dream'd of such meeting while far,
  'Mid trial, temptation, unloved and alone,
One pang had been spared in that terrible war,
  The worst that my bosom has known!
Thus, the warrior who combats all day with the foe,
  And singly the hope of his country defends,
In the moment of triumph, receives the death-blow
  From the arm of the traitor, 'mid ranks of his friends.

OH! LINGER WE NOT?

Oh! linger we not, dear love, thus lonely,
Of the wide world the unwise ones only,
When the buds and the blossoms persuade to fly;
When spring is beside us, with all her dower
Of bloom and of beauty, and breeze and flower,
And, merrily pour'd through the perfumed sky,
Is the song of a thousand birds of pleasure
That woo to a thousand fields of treasure—
Love's fields, and the worlds of delight that lie
Every where spread in the eye of the breeze,
Deep in the forests, and out on the seas,
By the blue lake, and the billowy shore—
Wherever the soul may fly, and be free,
With none to mock, yet with *one* to see—
One kindred soul to requite, restore,
Bring back the lost rapture, the new to cherish,
While fresh-risen hopes, which shall never perish,
Persuade the glad spirit to seek no more!

Linger we not, while the storms pursue us;
Hasten we far, where the seasons woo us,
And let us unfold our mutual wings,
Till we rest where the waters of Pacolet
Murmur welcome in song that for sweetness yet
Surpasses the minstrel that sweetest sings!
I know the deep glens, and the fertile valleys,
The green brow'd hills, and the verdant alleys,
And the mountain runnels and secret springs!
Oh! dearest of all the young hearts glowing
Where Etiwan's lordly waves are flowing!

Be this song of mine in thine ears a spell,
To win thee hence, ere the summer hours
Shall wither the leaf in thy maiden bowers,
Make thy cheek pale, and thy bosom swell
With a feverish thirst; which the mountain breeze,
By the foaming torrent, 'neath shadowing trees,
And with love to sing thee, alone shall quell!

BALLAD.—THE SIGH THAT SAYS.

THE sigh that says our love is vain
Would teach us not to sigh again,
But that it would not pain the less
To part with such a sweet distress!

If this be true, 'tis not in vain
We feed the fire, and nurse the pain,
With hope of no success, but this,
To keep the faith, not win the bliss!

We know that never more shall ours
Be the sweet couch we spread of flowers!
No more the fire, so dear below,
Shall warm the hearts that bade it glow!

Yet that the flowers are fresh and fair,
Fed by fond smiles and heavenly air,
That bright ascends the holy flame
That we may neither hope to claim:

This is a rapture mid the wo,
That soothes with sweetest overflow!
And, though our hopes bring no success,
Nor you, nor I, would have them less!

Nor you, nor I, though taught to know
That we may meet no more below,
Would have that mournful passion gone,
That leaves us two, yet made us one!

Within thy bosom, still my shrine,
I feel thy altar-place in mine!
Our faith still bless'd by tendance sweet—
Of love—though we no more may meet!

GLORIANA.

Thou hast won me, fondly following, very far,
Gloriana!
Thou hast led me, as the shepherd by his star,
Gloriana!
Thou hast been, of all the blessèd host, the only star for me!
And I've follow'd, with fond worship, through the desert and the sea;
Through the danger and the strife,
As if seeking for the life—the breath of life—
The beauty, and the blessing, and the rapture—all in thee,
Gloriana!

And thy smiles, for many seasons, cheer'd my way,
Gloriana!
Till I fancied I had reach'd the perfect day,
Gloriana!
That with eye forever gazing on the grandeur of the sun,
The sovereign heights of power that had wooed me all were won,
And thou—the glorious prize,
The blessèd star-ideal of mine eyes—
With hands that bore the laurel, to thy bosom waved me on,
Gloriana!

Oh! with promise to my heart of such a spoil,
Gloriana!
How little did I think of the peril and the toil,
Gloriana!
How my young heart bounded onward to each trial with a cheer!
How I braved the storm of battle, till it back recoil'd in fear!
How, forgetting all beside,
I wooed the lovely danger as a bride—
For she smiled with all thy smiling, and I felt that thou wast near,
Gloriana!

And I scorn'd the common joys of the humbler things of earth,
Gloriana!
All the human hopes and homes seem'd to me of little worth,
Gloriana!
What were common mortal beauties to the eye that look'd on thee?
What the treasures of the cottage—what the fruitage of the tree—
What the charms of mortal face—
What the pleasure and the pride of mortal race,
To him who sought thy beauty, shining far o'er mount and sea,
Gloriana?

And in this proudest worship my fond spirit went alone,
Gloriana!
'Twas enough that thou wast wooing—that thine eye upon me shone,
Gloriana!
That I rose from height to height, that I rush'd from star to star,
But with eye set ever 'yond them, to the sovereign height afar,
Where thou wast throned in state—
The beauty of my passion, and my fate!
Not a cloud upon thy loveliness, the perfect charm to mar,
Gloriana

Alas! even while I watch, while I gaze upon thy face,
Gloriana!
I faint—I sink—I sicken—I am dying in the race,
Gloriana!
Ah! sudden I remember the long seasons that have flown—
Toiling, striving, watching fondly the one star that for me shone!
Never once I held the fear
That another should keep pace with me so near!
Alas! the bearded Saturn that now mocks above my moan,
Gloriana!

He recks not of thy beauty—he but mocks my fond pursuit,
Gloriana!
His eye he loads with terrors, but his ashen lips are mute,
Gloriana!
Step by step, beside me, hath he ever gone before,
But I knew not of his presence—he will follow me no more!
He breathes with icy breath,
And his very look goes through me like a death!
He would strike at life and hope alike, and blast them in the fruit,
Gloriana!

Thou dim'st before my vision, and the mist grows o'er thy face,
Gloriana!
Ah! me—have I then worshipp'd but a thing of mortal race,
Gloriana?
Have I won no human friend, not a loving woman nigh,
My burning lips to moisten—my soul sweeten with a sigh?
The simplest cottage maid,
The home obscure, but safe, in the humblest forest shade,
Were now above thy beauties, far more precious to mine eye,
Gloriana!

But I have not idly striven, in pursuit as fond as vain,
Gloriana!
My faith hath never failed me, nor in danger nor in pain,
Gloriana!
Thou hast fail'd me—not my faith; nor the purpose fix'd, which knew
But the one bright star for homage; and my heart was ever true!
I was erring in mine aim,
But the faithful, fond pursuit of the glory still is Fame—
And thou wilt shine above his grave thou didst to ruin woo,
Gloriana!

NO, NEVER! THOUGH LOUD BE THE VOICE!

No, never—though loud be the voice that upbraids me,
And sad be the stigma that blackens my fame!
Though malice assails, and though slander o'ershades me,
And the lips that once worshipp'd, breathe nothing but blame!
While thou, all unmoved, art relying as ever,
And still keep'st thy faith as in earlier days—
My soul shall succumb to the destiny, never!
I live in thy love! I am proud in thy praise!

Yet, were it not so, and wert thou not before me,
Confiding and fond, as when blessing and blest;
Did thy smile shine not still, all the past to restore me,
Bringing sunshine and calm to this desolate breast—
I know not what else, in this life, could sustain me,
Thus blacken'd by slander, thus sinking in fame;
I live, for thy bosom will never disdain me!
I love, for thy spirit has shared in my shame!

OH! SPRING HATH THE GAYEST GARMENTS!

I.

Oh! Spring hath the gayest garments,
 And she putteth bright jewels on:
Pearls of the dewy morning,
 And gems of the ruby sun;
And weaving a garland of flowers,
She dances away the hours.

II.

And the sweetest of zephyrs attend her,
 That float from the Mexique sea,
With tribute of tenderness laden,
 And a musical liberty;
As they seek, 'mid the forest roses,
Where her beautiful form reposes.

III.

Nor sad, though the sun be sinking
 In his sorrow of dusk from the sky,
She warbles a song of the twilight,
 For the Evening's lullaby;
And, fond, with the nursing Hours,
She hushes to sleep the flowers

IV.

O beautiful Spring! I love thee!
 Thy blessing of odors and airs,
The April caprice in thy smiling,
 And the April blooms in thy tears;
For the rich red blossoms thou bringest,
And the bird at thy shoulder that singest.

WHAT SHOULD WE CARE FOR STATE?

I.

WHAT should we care for state?
Love's never desolate!
I love thee, spite of Fate,
And, loved by thee,
A gorgeous realm is ours!
Love plants the waste with flow
Wings bright the summer hours,
And sets hearts free!

II.

What if the proud should scorn?
That makes no heart forlorn!
Are we not free this morn,
To woods and skies?
May we not sing, not soar—
Dart wide, ascend, explore—
And what would Love ask more,
That Love denies?

III.

Love's the sufficient state
With such a charm 'gainst hate,
That it disarms each fate,
Asking no more!
Love found, as soon as sought,
Leaves us no need for aught:
Who lives in love that's bought,
Though rich, is poor!

IV.

We live, as birds that fly,
Having free woods—free sky
Free wings, and satisfied eye—
Thou me!—I thee!
No state—no hate—no strife—
All love—and love is life!—
And these are ours, dear wife—
Hearts fond, yet free!

AH! DREAMS, YOU SAY!

I.

Oh! not for sleep in such a night!
'Tis now, while earth and heaven are bright,
That blessing spirits speed in flight,
And, as they tell,
Glad, on green slope and starry height,
Weave magic spell.

Glide to the well-known walks and homes,
Steal softly through the midnight rooms,
Breathe, o'er the sleeper, gracious blooms
From happier spheres,
While sweetest dream the eye relumes,
Late fill'd with tears.

Could we but see—were but our eyes
Purged by befitting sacrifice
Of lowly thought, and for the skies
Made pure by prayer,
Methinks dear forms should quickly rise,
Our hearts to cheer.

So bright, so calm, so soft the close
Of day—so holy the repose
Which now the blessèd scene o'erflows,
        That, in the soul,
Faith at each airy whisper glows
        Beyond control.

She asks to see!—once more retrace
The once bright eye and vanish'd grace,
The happy smile, the glowing face
        Of youthful hours,
That left their light on many a place,
        Yet left no flowers.

II.

Ah! dreams, you say! Well, call them dreams.
And what are all your precious schemes,
Your daily arts, your midnight themes,
        Well conn'd, that show
How substances are wrought from gleams
        As fires from snow:

How half the world—the veriest child,
With all its reason, dreaming wild—
May, by the cunning, be beguil'd,
        And you, more wise,
Work subtle plans, which, unreviled,
        Bear off the prize!

Win from the simple, plan the snare,
Take in the flies—the spiders spare,
Achieve success, and—rest you there—
        What the success?
An erring, simple brother's share—
        An Esau's mess!

Your's, too, a dream!—a sorry toil
Of goodly wits, for lowly spoil;
How long you strive, how basely moil,
In what low arts;
And what your care, which in its coil
Mocks heads and hearts!

III.

Dreams all!—But what is all the bliss
That Heaven to life accords in this?
A flower upon the precipice,
That, as we take,
Our senses swim, our footsteps miss,
And we—awake!

What's Passion's triumph, but the wild
Delirium of the feverish child,
With fancies fed, by dreams beguiled—
The sudden light,
When skies have for a moment smiled,
To burst and blight?

What's Love? Hast loved?—Then such the flower,
New blown, and fresh with morning's shower,
Sweet, pure, as if some heavenly dower,
By seraph given:
Place it within thy breast an hour,
And where thy heaven?

Fame!—Ask the echoes of the past,
The exulting shout, the trumpet blast:
Would'st deem that Fate its shroud shall cast
Such fortunes o'er—
Such echoes die away at last,
Heard never more!

Yet where the hero? where the acclaim,
The myriad shouts that promised fame,
The imperial column to his name?
Another ear
Wins shout and trump and tower, the same,
And he is—where?

IV.

Dreams all! The fame, the love, the gush
Of passion, from its virgin blush,
To the wild fever of its flush,
That, soon or late,
Will lose their bloom, their voices hush,
And yield to fate!

Not less delicious that they die
While yet the fire is in the eye,
The sweetness in the shout or sigh,
That love, or fame,
Brings, with delusive ministry,
Our souls to claim.

Dear spectres, that, from dream or heart,
Thus cherish'd, never quite depart;
Still on our sight their phantoms dart,
And still they woo,
As from the shroud, at night, they start,
To smile and sue!

V.

We may not lose them all: the bloom
Still breathes from where the flowers found doom;
Their memories lighten up the gloom
Their parting brought—
Still hang sad chaplets o'er the tomb
To solace thought!

Still come by night, when all is still,
Persuade us to the grove, the hill,
Speak through the leaflet, through the rill,
And all the breast
With happiest, sweetest instincts fill
That make it blest!

Survive the wreck of common things,
Bring Hope its eye, and Faith its wings,
Conduct where flow the eternal springs,
While, o'er the sight,
A sacred moonlight memory flings,
Eternal bright!

DESTINED TO SEVER.

I.

Destined to sever,
Thrice hapless, for years;
Perchance again never
To meet, or in tears!
What, in the dreary hours,
Then, shall repay,
For the blooms, for the flowers
Fate tears away?

II.

What shall restore thee
That sweet sunny clime,
When life rose before thee,
Unshadow'd by Time?

When Hope, in glad bowers,
  Sang like the young bird,
Born of beams, 'mid the flowers,
  Childhood first heard?

III.

To me, what can Being
  Then bring, to restore
Those young joys that fleeing,
  We win never more?
Those nights when no sorrow
  Brooded over Love's sky,
And no gloomy To-Morrow
  Stood frowningly by!

IV.

With nought to endear us
  To what is left now;
And nothing to cheer us
  In the Future's dark brow:
Where look we, sweetest,
  For the pleasures that last—
The brightest, the fleetest?—
  Ah, me! to the Past!

RENDER THY TRIBUTE TO BEAUTY.

I.

Render thy tribute to Beauty,
  Nor question with doubt the decree,
That makes the sweet service a duty,
  Though without seeming profit it be;

'Tis something to bend at the altar
  Where Beauty is priestess, though still
The heart of the worshipper falter,
  As the smile of the goddess grows chill!

II.

'Twere sadder, the fortune which found thee,
  From the bondage of Beauty set free;
For the fetters with which she had bound thee,
  Did'st thou love them, were blessings to thee!
She might scorn the poor captive's devotion,
  While holding him fast in her snare;
But the freedom of earth and of ocean,
  Were but exile, were Beauty not there!

THE FAMILY VAULT.

I.

Come from the halls of mirth, and drink
  The cup of memory now I bear;
Turn from the festive board, and think
  'Tis still a guardian wins thee here.

Here, where the silent grave-stones rise,
  Beneath the stars, in dusky white,
And, from the grass, great mournful eyes
  Look upward through the ghastly light.

Here, where they sleep, the noble dead,
  To whom thou ow'st thy name and blood;
Thy mother's heart, thy father's head,
  The brave, the generous, great, and good!

Their bones, for quite an hundred years,
  Are shrined where loving hearts may seek,
Fit altar-place for anguish'd prayers
  Of him whom vice hath rendered weak!

II.

Here should thy heart recall the hours
  When life had nobler aims than now:
When, if thy fingers toy'd with flowers,
  Great thoughts were struggling in thy brow!—

And thou could'st shape in will the deed,
  And well conceive, and high aspire,
Thy spirit bounding to be freed,
  And all thy youthful soul on fire!

When she, thy inspiration then,
  Blest to behold thy eager aim,
Look'd proudly for the hour when men
  Should hail thee with the shouts of fame!

And thou, responsive to her prayer,
  Had but the single thought, to stand,
A Hero-worker, bold to dare,
  And strong to save thy native land.

With noble passions moved, and cheer'd
  By voice that never idly taught;
Anguish'd by very hopes, that dared
  Beyond the flight of youthful thought:

And sending up the famishing shriek,
  Such as the eagle pours, who lies,
Struck down beneath some mountain peak,
  And struggling for her native skies!—

Mixed pride and pain in every scream:
  Now Doubt that shudders with despair;
Now Hope, exulting in the dream,
  To stretch again her wings in air;

Conscious of one great want alone,
  And burning with the will that brings
But wo to him that can but moan
  The brave desire without the wings.

III.

Thou had'st th' ambitious aim to rise;
  Chafed with the eager will that strove
To break from earth, to break through skies,
  Range o'er all realms, and rise above!

Nor did the sinews lack—thy youth
  Gave earnest of a strength to soar—
Well found in wisdom, bright in truth—
  Where youth had never risen before.

And, with the yearning—in the sight
  Of her who watch'd thee then, there grew,
Even from her watch, the wing for flight,
  And all the pride and purpose too!

And Love grew happy to behold,
  As proudly darting up from earth,
Thy vans, when first they did unfold,
  Declared the mountain eaglet's birth!—

No feeble flight—no doubtful aim—
  But straight, with joyous pride, they took
Their upward course, through fields of flame,
  While every plume with rapture shook!

IV.

How glorious in that mother's sight—
  An eagle she, without a mate—
The fearless aim, the brilliant flight
  Of the sole offspring of her state!

And all the secret fear was gone,
  That long had vext her heart—the thought
That ere thy flight was fully flown,
  Her eye and heart should both be nought!

For dim already grew that eye,
  And death was in her heart; her prayer
But asked to see thee, mounting high,
  Endow'd to do—resolved to dare!

And all the bitterness of death
  Was soothed and sweeten'd, as it grew,
That hope, within her soul, to faith
  In what thou could'st, and yet would'st do!

V.

Fond dream!—How well do I recall
  Her parting words: "For him, my son,
I have no fear! He can not fall,
  With such a flight so well begun!"

VI.

He can not fall!—Alas! we stand,
  Even as our rise is swift and high,
Upon a beetling, shelving strand,
  A trembling, steep acclivity!—

A precipice!—a gulf beneath!
  We hang between two worlds; and Fear
Shrinks trembling though upheld by Faith,
  While Hope is mute beside Despair!

A breath will shake the mountain down—
  A silent Terror work beneath;
And we who deem the world our own,
  Will sudden sink in jaws of death!

Of death?—perchance a darker fate!—
  Of hate, and shame, and sore disgrace;
And curse the pride—alas, too late!—
  That sought such treach'rous resting-place.

And thus thou stood'st that very hour
  When she, within her hopeful heart,
Beheld thy strength, thy promised power,
  And calmly heard the word: "Depart!"

No doubt of Heaven—no doubt of thee;
  How beautiful her life in death,
The spirit wing'd for liberty,
  Through worlds of doubt, to skies of faith!

VII.

If from itself thy heart may pass,
  And o'er the griefs of virtue brood,
Here shalt thou see, as in a glass,
  How precious was the heart that woo'd:

How fond the love that pray'd in vain,
  To crown thy soul with strength and will,
And free thy spirit from the chain
  That pleasure winds round weakness still!

That woman was thy genius! She,
  From Love the sweet persuasion caught,
That thou a chief of men might be,
  The sov'reign in the popular thought.

She knew thy native strength—the powers,
  That, in her training, had been true;
Nor in yon false and sensual bowers
  Forgot her love and lessons too.

She knew thy powers, but did not know
  The lurking weakness in thy soul,
That secret lay, to work thee wo,
  When she no longer might control:

To watch the hour—the fearful hour,
  When guardian love and guide were gone,
To blossom with pernicious flower,
  When first in life thou stood'st alone!

VIII.

Ah! had'st thou heard her secret prayers,
  With Love pursuing still thy quest—
Thy triumphs nurtured by her tears,
  And all thy virtues in her breast!

Here, by her grave!—How still she lies,
  Whose voice was such a charmer!—still
As those wan lights that haunt the skies,
  Looking out with neither love nor will:

Stars, as we call them—and admire,
  Unwitting how brighter far were they,
That sought us with affection's fire,
  Warm in all seasons, night and day!

She was the star of all thy host—
  Thy guardian star, whose loving art,
Unseen by thee, was ever most
  The impulse to thy mind and heart:

So wast thou loving—loved, and brave—
  And daring in thy aim to rise,
Till that dark hour, when in her grave
  The light went out that spell'd thine eyes!

'Twas she who fram'd for thine the thought,
  And, by a word, a look, a tone,
Th' unshaped ambition within thee wrought,
  Till, through her love, it grew thine own.

IX.

And she is gone!—and thou!—look back
  Upon the past; if there be heart
Within thee, bold enough to track
  That past, while conscious what thou art!

'Twill task thy best of strength—the all
  Of soul that's left thee now, to gaze
On what thou wast before thy fall,
  In those best, bright, ambitious days!

How bold thy heart! how strong thy flight!
  What noble purpose made thy aim,
While she, with eyes, tears dropping light,
  Sang in thine ears a song of Fame!

X.

Think'st thou those eyes no longer see,
  Those ears no longer hear—while thou,
In halls of wretched'st revelry,
  Shout'st high in chorus with the low?—

Each noble purpose dead!—Design
  That struck out pathways to the skies,
And strove with consummation fine,
  In labors worthy of the wise!—

And now, o'er rudest wassail bowl,
  With fever'd veins and flushing face—
No longer conscious of a soul,
  Or purpose—herding with the base!—

Well pleased, with wanton jest and jibe,
  The lecherous tale, the ribald song—
Dregs of thy better powers—to bribe
  The applausive shout from rascal tongue!

XI.

Think'st thou she hears not—does not see?
  That, lock'd within these walls of stone,
That noble spirit walks not free,
  Beside thee ever, making moan?

I tell thee that before us now,
  With folded hands that stretch to Heaven,
And weeping eyes, and pale white brow,
  She prays that thou be saved and shriven.

That, for her love, surpassing show,
  A sudden light from heaven may break,
A seraph gleam, a meteor glow,
  A voice, thy better self to wake:

To tear thee from the thrall which binds
  Thy heart and will in basest bond;
Unseal the eyes which glamour blinds,
  And show the nobler heights beyond!

Oh! could'st thou see—nay, could'st thou feel,
  Thou 'd'st win from love the needful power,
And woo the angel of thy weal
  Beside thee, as in boyhood's hour.

XII.

Hast thou a thought, the revel o'er,
  Of all its gross and wanton shame?
Doth conscience never once restore
  The moments, peaceful, free of blame?

Dost never feel the bitter wo,
  In calmer hours—if such there be—
At sight of these, thy comrades low?—
  To hark their foul and foolish glee?

She prompts thy conscience—wakes the pain;
  Her secret soul to thine reveals;
Sends subtlest whispers to thy brain,
  And through thy dream of midnight steals:

Would rouse thee yet to noblest aim;
  Thy heart make pure, and strengthen will,
And teach thee that the paths to fame,
  Spite of the past, lie open still!

But hast thou manhood? Can'st thou brave
  The scorn of fools—the wretched sneer
That's only potent o'er the slave,
  Who dare not walk alone with Fear:

To whom th' applause of vulgar tongue
  Suffices for those baffled powers,
Which, when thy soul was pure and young,
  Scaled heights of hope on mountain towers?

Oh, grief! Oh, shame! Oh, bitter wo!
  To think how such a flight was check'd!
By lure so foul, by spell so low,
  Such wing of fame forever wreck'd!

THE APPROACH OF THE PESTILENCE.*

I.

Let those who will, with anxious dread,
  The coming danger still deplore,
And, with dark boding fancies fed,
  View all with fear that fills our shore;
Though not less fond of life than they,
  And warmed by many a glowing hope,
Let me in calm the plague survey,
  And with each threat'ning terror cope.

II.

Let me not watch, with idle fears,
  Long in advance, the approaching doom,
And, before Death himself appears,
  Prepare the shroud and build the tomb;
But, with a heart securely calm,
  Still on that Providence rely,
Which, if it blights, yet brings its balm,
  And strengthens, though it bids us die.

III.

Still let me hold to that high truth,
  The best that God to man hath given,
To cheer in age, to teach in youth—
  There is no certain hope but Heaven.

* Written in 1832, on the first appearance of cholera in this country.

And if I fall, and if the fate
  That strikes the thousand, strikes at me,
And makes my fireside desolate,
  And blights the bud and blasts the tree:

IV.

And from my fond affection rends
  The child that still my heart hath blest,
And robs my eyes of many friends,
  At least 'twill give them peace and rest.
And though the fate thus comes, 'twill be
  But the same fate we still should meet,
When time hath brought infirmity—
  Without repair, without retreat.

V.

A few years lopt the human lot
  Will only lose us years of care,
Affection's blight, and Memory's blot,
  And Love's defeat, and Hope's despair—
A fate no human skill can foil,
  No place avert, no care evade—
A fate that brings release from toil,
  And yields us mansions heavenly made.

VI.

Father! thus lesson'd, let my soul,
  In calm the coming stroke await;
Yet do thou still the plague control,
  And lengthen life and limit fate;
And bid the stricken sufferer live,
  And bid the city smile, and take
The curse away, the crime forgive,
  For weeping nature's, mercy's sake.

EVA.—IF, 'NEATH THE SUNSET TREE.

PARAPHRASED FROM THE SWEDISH.

If, 'neath the sunset tree,
Musing, I dream of thee,
And the delights that we,
  Loving, might share—
Thou, with a thought like mine,
Gently should thus incline,
And in that heart of thine,
  Hold mine as dear:

Ah! then, methinks, that joy,
Ever to fond hearts coy,
Led by that wandering boy,
  Love, might be ours;
Then should delight restore,
Fresh from its home once more,
What made the heaven, of yore,
  In Eden's bowers.

Yet if, in fancy vain,
Thou from this proof refrain,
Think not that I complain,
  If hopeless, *free;*
Never you doubt but love
Holds still, in sweetest grove,
One dear heart, glad to prove,
  Eva, to me!

'TWAS A VISION OF FAIR LADYE.

'Twas a vision of fair ladye,
Kept, and still must keep me here,
Sadly sighing, when I should be
Happier in another sphere:
Such the fetter thrown around me
By her witchery, it hath bound me!—
That fair ladye, that fair ladye,
Holds me fast in subtle snare!

Many a hope would sweetly woo me,
And, in other regions blest,
Love and Glory both pursue me,
Seeking place within my breast;
Yet I linger, never fleeing,
Losing fame and bliss and being—
That fair ladye, that fair ladye,
Makes a captive of her guest!

Like the bird around whose pinion
Serpent spells have wrought a chain,
I am held in close dominion,
Seeking to be free in vain!
Vainly words of wo I utter—
In her bonds I fret and flutter—
That fair ladye, that fair ladye,
Oh! she laughs to see my pain!

Yet with spirit uncomplaining
Would I in her bonds repose,
Were she not the while disdaining
The poor captive in her close;

Would she now and then smile on him,
Though her bonds have still undone him,
That fair ladye, that fair ladye,
Still might keep him bound, Heaven knows!

FORGET NOT THE TROPHY.

Forget not the trophy we made her,
The country so glorious and dear,
When, to grapple the ruthless invader,
We took up the rifle and spear.
He came with his engines of power,
And he spoke with the despot's decree,
But we rose in our wrath, and the hour
That saw us enslaved, saw us free!

We struck down the fool for his error,
When arm'd for our freedom, we rose;
And he shrank from the combat in terror,
Never dreaming the weight of our blows!
Did he deem that so feeble a spirit,
Though arm'd by such sov'reign desires,
Could seize on the rights we inherit
From a race of such true-hearted sires?

Oh! forget not the trophy then made her—
That freedom so fondly we boast,
When we struck down the ruthless invader,
And scattered his insolent host;
When our banner of palm, proudly waving,
Shone out o'er the perilous plain,
And our eagle, all destiny braving,
Grew drunk in the blood of the slain

LOVE ON TO THE LAST!

Oh, fly!—but remember,
  We can not forget!
They may rob us of rapture,
  But not of regret;
They may tear us asunder,
  Our hopes may deny,
But love's thought is freest
  Of all 'neath the sky!

They call thee a traitor,
  And say, when we part,
Thou wilt banish my image
  In scorn from thy heart;
But the love in thy bosom
  I judge of by mine;
And enough, that my faith is
  A sure faith in thine!

And were I to doubt thee,
  And thou to deny,
To live on without thee
  Were vain—I should die!
But I wrong thee to whisper
  A doubt which would blast;
Hear my heart's only pleading—
  Love on to the last!

I make thee no promise,
  I ask not for thine;
Keep thy faith but as fondly
  As I shall keep mine!

If like me thou dost cherish
  One living regret,
We may part—we may perish,
  But never forget!

GO, THOU FAITHLESS ONE!

Go, thou faithless one, go wander,
  Fickle heart with sunny brow;
It were base in me to squander
  One poor thought upon thee now!
Far, in other regions roving,
  It may be that thou shalt find
Nobler hearts—but none so loving;
  Brighter eyes—but none so blind!

Both are free, though one with ruin
  Sits beside a lonely hearth;
While the other, still misdoing,
  Revels in his wanton mirth!
Though I droop, with broken pinion,
  By the spoil'd, abandon'd nest,
And thou soar'st with wide dominion,
  Robbing other homes of rest:

Though my foolish heart be breaking,
  Yet no plaint its grief shall show;
Not a nerve within me shaking,
  While, with scorn, I bid thee go!
Every maiden hope hath perish'd,
  Yet no mortal eye shall see,
That my heart hath ever cherish'd
  One fond, foolish thought of thee!

TO THEE, WHEN RUDDY CUPS.

I.

To thee, when ruddy cups are glowing,
And boards are gay, and hearts are light,
When song takes wing, and wit is flowing,
And eyes and thoughts alike are bright:
To thee still ever wedded only,
My thought returns, my fancies flee;
And 'midst the merry crowd still lonely,
I long, oh how I long for thee!

II.

The wit that shines—the song beguiling—
Have not a charm to take thy place;
The smiles, the tones, whate'er their wiling,
But tell of thy superior grace:
They lack the art to teach forgetting,
And fail, of all their spells, to me;
The present chills—the past regretting—
I long, oh how I long for thee!

III.

Their songs but tell of music sweeter,
In shady groves, with thee but near;
Their slowly-lapsing hours were fleeter,
If tones of thine were in mine ear;
These shouts of mirth, they do but sadden,
When memory, whispering soft to me,
Tells of thy sighs, that did but gladden,
And makes me long to sigh with thee.

IV.

Ah! 'midst the crowd, the gay confusion,
  Mix'd song and shout, and jest and cheer,
A spell o'er all, with sweet illusion,
  These all expel, and bring thee near:
I see no wild and eager faces,
  I hear no clamorous burst of glee;
Thou tak'st my gay companions' places,
  And I am all alone with thee!

THIS FLOWER, IT BLOOMS 'MID A RUIN.

This flower, it blooms 'mid a ruin,
  But its sweet is more precious to me
Than the wreaths which thy fortune is strewing
  Round the shaft of thy family tree;
For it speaks to my soul of the blessing
  Which in deepest of wo was my gain,
That love, which mine own is possessing,
  And for which thine hath striven in vain!

Thou may'st joy in the splendor around thee,
  The state which makes gallant thy halls;
In the crowd that with homage surround thee,
  And exult when thy enemy falls!—
I turn from the sting of their malice,
  And envy no pomp which is thine;
I look from the lights in thy palace,
  To the one in this low cot of mine.

AH! LOOK NOT THUS UNKINDLY.

I.

Ah! look not thus unkindly now,
  Fling not my hand in pride away;
The cloud is on thy heart, thy brow,
  But there it must not, shall not stay!
    Ah, no!—No! no!
  If love hath power it shall not stay!

II.

There's not a bliss thy heart hath known,
  But it hath suffer'd mine to share;
Wrong me not now, when joy hath flown,
  Denying me to feel thy care!
    Ah, no!—No! no!
  Deny me not to feel thy care!

III.

Fling off the shadow of thy grief,
  And all thy secret wo reveal;
My heart would seek from thine relief,
  Still taught by thee to love and feel!
    Ah, yes!—Yes! yes!
  Still teach me how to love and feel!

IV.

Then look not thou unkindly now,
  Fling not my loving hand from thine,
But let me share, with love, the care
  That glooms the soul so dear to mine,
    Ah, yes!—Yes! yes!
  Thy grief as well as joy be mine!

WERE I A BIRD!

"WERE I a bird!" thus runs her song,
When days are dark, and nights are long,
"How soon I'd fly to thee!
Though far thou fliest, though wild the way,
Nor cloud should stop, nor storm should stay
The happy wing set free!"

Alas, poor bird of love! how frail
Thy loving wing to face the gale!
Woman or bird—thy fate
Is still to pine o'er hopes that fly,
A storm forever in thy sky,
And, matchless, find no mate.

SERENADER IMPLORES HIS MISTRESS TO COME FORTH.

WHILE the evening star is tender,
Softly flashing o'er the deep,
Open eyes of equal splendor,
Dearest maiden, cease to sleep!
Here are worlds of fairy treasure,
Such as woo the virgin heart;
Here are songs of youth and pleasure,
True to nature, dear to art!

Here thy cavalier delaying,
Lingers with a loving joy;
Duteous, with a true song, praying
That his heart may have employ.

Look thou forth in all thy beauty,
Bright for conquest, thou, and He,
Glad to hail, with happy duty,
The first faintest smile from thee.

Come thou forth, with step of fleetness,
As the birds through air advance;
Beam out bright, with eye of sweetness,
Swaying hearts with starry glance.
Come, while hearts and hours are sighing,
Still ungladden'd by thy sight;
Come, with soul and smile complying,
Bringing blessings on the night.

SONNET.

Moonlight is down 'mong shadow-keeping hills,
And bright o'er placid waters—let us go:
I would not seek my couch while such a show,
Of beauty, all the blue empyrean fills.
Give open brow to joy—throw wide the vest
To the fair angel that would make us blest;
Welcome the vision, fresh and beautiful,
And shame to snatch it with a spirit dull!
Look, where the shadows of the houses cast,
Grow sick with the gay loveliness of night;
And as her living beams flock hurrying past,
How shrink they, as if shuddering at the bright—
Let us away, dear heart, 'tis beauty's hour,
And we must share her smiles, and smiling seize her flower.

COME OUT TO PLAY!

I.

Give thyself freedom to-night!
  Hence with the cares of the day;
And dreaming alone of thy boyhood's delight,
  Bid the young heart come and play!
Oh! for that precious child ditty,
  The sweetest that bard ever sung,
That summon'd to sports of the highway and city,
  The hearts that knew how to be young!
    And still, methinks, they say,
    As in that happy day:
"Come, boys and girls, come out—come out and play!"
And oh! the sweet assurance in the lay—
"The moon—the moon is shining bright as day!"

II.

Even with the memory I see
  The lakelet, the hillock, the vale,
The green-sward, the old oak tree,
  And the round moon, bright and pale.
And ho! for the shouting and leaping,
  Headlong, o'er hillock and plain;
As if boyhood knew nothing of weeping,
  And play-day must ever remain!
    Oh, girls and boys, away!
    Renew the ancient lay!
Come out, as then, come out—come out to play!
Fling not the innocent joys of youth away,
The moon still shines for youth, as bright as day.

SONNET.—CONCEALED CHARACTER.

RUFFLE him not by wrong, and he will keep
As tranquil as the sunbeam in a brook,
Where the winds seldom whisper, and scarce look—
A season still of calm, akin to sleep!
Yet hath he in him fiery qualities,
That need but provocation for the blaze,
And, of a sudden, will his spirit rise,
The wanton or the heedless to amaze.
Sport loves he, and he will not heed your jeer,
If still he deems no malice taints your mirth;
But, with his first suspicion, leaps to birth
The unwonted anger, unallied to fear—
As sudden, under wrong, reveals his ire,
As smit by hostile steel the flint gives fire.

CHAUNT OF LONELINESS.

AH! Hours, how sad and lonely
Ye move, when from the breast
The first fresh glow of feeling
Is gone, that brought its wing to Thought,
While Rapture did the rest!

Ah! Hopes, why mock ye ever,
The gleams that once ye cast;
And on the dark horizon,
Still linger lone—though all be gone—
Sad spectres of the past?

Why conjure memory ever,
  When well ye know how vain
Would she recall the rapture,
That known too late, 'tis not in Fate,
  Or Love, to warm again?

Sweet swallow—wanton soaring!
  Oh, for a wing like yours,
Not seeking hopes departed,
Nor one delight, but only flight,
  From memory-haunted shores!

Oh! for some powerful pinion,
  That, with the speed of light,
My form may speed to regions
Which still, in dreams, of joyous gleams,
  Bring blessings to my sight!

Ah! thither, at the shutting,
  At eve, of flowery eyes,
How blest to wander idly,
And lose the care, the pang, the tear,
  When all but sorrow dies!

No bird that skirrs the mountain,
  No fish that darts the lake,
Would speed more gayly onward,
Just taught to sweep, through air or deep,
  Its joy or prey to take!

Ah, me! how dread the morning
  That ushers in the night!
How silent all of sweetness,
To spell with art, the thought or heart,
  Or wing the soul in flight!

HANNIBAL; PASSAGE OF THE ALPS.

I.

O Faith and Will! maternal birds that lift
The wing of Genius, and make sure its gift;
How do ye strengthen for the audacious flight,
The soul whose eyes still open for the light;
How train the feeble fledgling whence to rise,
O'er rocky heights, commercing with the skies;
To brave the bolt, and with careering form,
Break through the cloud, and wrestle with the storm!
Ye are the wings of Purpose, the Desire
That flies to Fame, and wins its way through Fire;
Ye keep the eye still resolute in aim,
The heart still faithful to the imperial fame:
Chasten each passion which would thwart the toil,
And teach the fitting enterprise and spoil;
Prepare the soul for struggle, train the Power,
Till both mature, the Mortal and the Hour;
Then fling aside the veil that hid the goal,
And cry the spell word for the conquering soul!
O mightiest birds of Genius, that in cloud,
And earth, and midnight, still your secrets shroud,
I see ye busy, in mysterious rite,
Training one bold young eaglet for its flight;
The altar smokes in sacrifice—the rock
Shakes with the lightning-bolt, and thunder-shock—
Lurid, the fires from gloomy temples rise,
And the black Doubt hangs threatening in the skies!
But your twin voices reassure, and Fate,
Submissive, seconds the great hope of Hate:
The mighty Vengeance ye would rouse to strife,
Starts up before you, armed with death and life:

Waiting the last commission, forth he stands,
The red bolt quivering in his fateful hands:
Your pliant wings beneath his arms ye bend,
And the rocks open, and the wings ascend;
From the great peaks your spectral eyes explore,
While all the Hounds of Horror hunt before!

II.

The chosen spirit, on its forward march,
Armed with just courage that makes great it's cause,
Stands mightier than the force of common laws,
And grows, beneath the heaven's broad favoring arch,
Into an eminent stature, like a God,
Whose distant-piercing vision, all abroad
Sends fiery brightness, which informs the nations
With a life-giving virtue, like the sun's!
Thenceforth, rise other spirits to their stations,
And a new blood through all the people runs.
Thus animate for conquest, o'er the earth
They spread; and conquest by a generous race,
Endowed with high commission at its birth,
Is blessing, and brings messages of grace
And great encouragement to the struggling low!
They look up as they see the brightness glow,
As Shepherds at the Day-Star, and arise
With welcome; and their progress thence, though slow,
Is certain, and most worthy of the skies!

III.

Methinks, when sworn to an eternal hate,
Against a reckless tyranny, the soul
Of Hannibal was robed in regal state,
And held upon his race divine control.
The Boy before the altar, with his Sire,

Sworn to his country's glory and her fate,
Grew thenceforth into manhood, from desire
Of work in a great office; as the Priest,
Or Prophet, dedicate to Heavenly ire,
Grows lifted, while his lips, with tongue of fire,
Bid the doomed city to her fatal feast!
Thence evermore a dread Necessity
Walks by his side. Thence evermore his ears
Drink in the voices of the Awful Three,
And yet a single sound is all he hears.
Thus is it with the Dedicate! They march,
Following one blazing star, that shows the way
Over the gloomy crags, till the black arch
Grows azure, and the night melts into day!

IV.

Alps fling themselves before him—giant alps,
With their dread gorges—with their savage shade,
Mocking the sun, and sending their white scalps
Into the very heavens, that shrink afraid,
And crouch into their bluest caves afar;
Pursued by other pinnacles, that dart,
As with the ambition of a human heart,
Sending their snowy shafts higher and higher,
Till the bridged void, accessible to the sight,
Persuades to travel where the sovereign star,
The central eye of the Universe, with fire
Due to her wants, rests on his noonday height,
And looks encouragement to the eager aim,
That soars, on wings of Will and Faith, to Fame!

V.

Yet there had grown a weariness in the breast
Of the young chief; the mortal man, o'ercome

By an immortal labor, longed for rest;
And with a craving appetite for home,
Lay prostrate for a season—saw no sun
Making a passage o'er the mighty piles—
No wingéd eye of wooing that beguiles
To conquest, through new promise. Toil had done
Her work in deep exhaustion; and his thought
Challenged the truth in that same faith it taught:
The merits of that mission which, unsought,
Had sworn his young soul to the work of Hate!
The weakness tutored him the work to shun;
Counselled the ingenious fear, the shrewd device,
The false Philosophy, that knows to prate,
By calculation close, and caution nice,
In fashion fatal to the great design;
Making depend on square and measure fine,
The grand achievement, and the purpose great,
By which the mighty Genius conquers Fate.

VI.

"If Rome must perish, as the Gods decree,
Let the Gods work her overthrow!" quoth he;
If Carthage be the care of Heaven, let Heaven
See to her safety! Wherefore is it given
That I, to sacrifice of my young delights,
Home, love, and safety, should ascend these heights,
That grow before me ever as I rise,
Until the mountain crags shut out the skies,
Or show the sun at rest upon their peaks?
'Tis not for such as this my spirit seeks,
And wherefore am I chosen for the toil?
My soul delights not in the strife and spoil:
Would cherish peaceful sports—would lie at ease,
Where idle sails disport on summer seas,

And flowers of pleasant odor court the breeze;
And Love and Beauty, to the mock of care,
Join evermore in pleasures, sweet as rare,
And Hope itself folds up the satisfied wing,
While Fancy, witless, with no farther guest,
Lapsing in dream, beside the wizard-spring,
Needs never farther seeking to be bless'd!
Ah! the dear glimpses now that memory bears
Of the well-satisfied heart in boyhood's years—
Its smiles, and songs, and sports—its very tears—
That woo me back to wildering stream and grove,
Where Rapture, panting, sits with flowing locks,
While, eager, with delight, the impetuous Love
Bounds in pursuit adown the headlong rocks,
Sings bounding, and with purple, flowery twines,
Makes fast the glowing captive 'mongst the vines.
Ah! wherefore to the loss of these delights,
Pursue this toil, along these perilous heights,
While Bliss entreats me to the shade, and Life,
Assured of every rapture, free from strife,
Makes pictures from possessions, and so moves
Hope with enjoyment, that no more he roves,
But in the lap of Rapture feels content,
In very slumber finding ravishment?

VII.

"Oh! by the banks of Mœtis, ere I came
To this dread service, which hath nought to woo,
Stood one that, weeping, waved me to return:
A palm branch in her hand; her eye of blue,
With smile to make the gazer's bosom flame,
And beauty, of such mingling smiles and tears,
That but one single lesson might he learn,
How Love hath promise that much more endears,

Than any in the glozing speech of Fame!
  Yet did I fly the seeker—oh, the shame!—
Making Love the price of Glory! Yet what claim?
Hath it a higher altar? Doth it burn
With lights more precious? Wherefore, for its powers,
Crush the dear life-blood from one innocent heart,
Tread with the hoof of war on holiest flowers,
And with the despot's malice, say 'we part,'
When in the very utterance lies a death!—
And she to whom our love hath been the breath
Of being, and the odor of its bloom,
Beside the very altar droops to doom!

VIII.

"Thus have I done beneath this destiny,
Pitiless in power! and must I still deny
The sweet seduction, and go forth for Hate,
Renouncing Love, and raptures that so late
Were mine—with promise to be ever mine?
Where is my hope of youth—the life—the Bride?
Methinks the voice still murmurs at my side,
A murmur born of music!—and I see
The grove beside the brooklet; and the flowers
Breathe blushingly, nor tell of fleeting hours,
How joyful!—and the sweet repose of bowers,
Where sits and smiles the innocent Deity,
That sways without a consciousness, and deems
Herself the subject!
"These are not the dreams
Of truant fancies. Love is yet a thing
Of truth and bliss, that never spreads a wing,
Till we forswear his worship in desires
That cloud with smoke, and taint his altar fires!
Have I thus wander'd?

If to Hate decreed,
Am I not also sworn to Love, as well?—
My sovereign still, that never yet has freed,
And now invokes me with imperious spell!
The fascination of his eye still warms;
Still doth he woo me with a world of charms;
How glorious is the vision of delight
He paints for Fancy, on the memory's sight;
How sweet the forest shade, how cool the air,
What songs delicious rise and murmur there;
How peaceful all the pleasures, and what balm,
The breathing zephyr in that world of calm—
No strife, no doubt—the valley's wealth of shade,
Cool brooklet, and calm sunset!—unafraid,
Peace sits within her bowers, and all the grove
Murmurs experience of devoted Love!"

IX.

He rises slowly, and with weary gaze
Looks forth, and upward, on the perilous ways
That challenge manhood, yet defying, grow
To bulwarks that but mock th' audacious foe!
Alps gather still before him; alps arise,
Above him piled, stupendous, to the skies;
Eternal summits, each with snowy crest,
Bar the steep passage, and the march arrest!
They wear no more the mantle of the sun,
But each, with aspect fierce and garment dun,
Stands forth, a terrible champion in the path,
With giant bosom, mocking mortal wrath,
As mortal purpose? Whither shall he shape
His progress, and the perilous strife escape?
Even while he muses, the great mountain flings
Its toppling masses thundering down the steep;

From the great gorges rise a cloud of wings,
That darken daylight as they upward sweep:
Thunders the rolling avalanche, that tears
New pathways, down to gulphs that mock the gaze:
And the new pinnacle its tower uprears,
And wingéd shafts of ice the vision daze;
While shrieks from unknown birds of fearful might,
Tell of abysses where they lurk in night,
Waiting their victims!
Still, beyond his eye,
On every side, where'er he bends his sight,
All is a dread and terror—all a doubt—
And the dark fear arrests activity,
Lest he shall pass where bird may never fly,
Or, flying, never gather his way out!

X.

He saddens—we have seen him—o'er the joy,
So well remembered, which had blest the boy;
Feels all the terrors which still rise before,
And mock the curious thought which would explore.
But doth he shrink or tremble? Doth he stay,
With more than moment pause, his venturous way,
Though the dark piles inclose him from the day—
Yield to the weakness of his dreaming mood—
Shrink from the peril that still warms his blood—
The hope forego, forgetful of his aim,
And all the fervid courage caught from Fame?
When did Ambition pause upon his march—
Generous Ambition, whose wide-seeing eye,
Following the sun's proud passage through the arch—
Forget the resolute will, the purpose high,
That teaches still the single course to run?
So the brave eagle in his native skies,

Steering with giant pinion to the sun,
Bathes in the blaze that blinds all humbler eyes!

XI.

The gloom and doubt are gone! The drooping hour
Departs, and leaves him to a nobler power;
The very terrors which would fright his soul,
But teach him of the greatness of the goal.
No more the enslaving passion now persuades,
To dreaming raptures in remembered glades,
Of blossoms opening in the smiles of even,
And songs that woo'd, like music caught from Heaven;
Till all his soul, in the delicious dream,
Lapsed in diffusing weakness, straight forgot
The flight, the conquest, glory, and the gleam,
Which make ambition loathe the inferior lot.
The soft, beguiling reverie, which had made
Each form of Beauty start from out the shade,
Triumphant over Terror as o'er Fame,
Dissolved, departs as swiftly as it came!
And the delirious rapture of great deeds,
Kindling up images of triumphant strife,
Wings him anew for the great path of life,
While all the spirit of his father leads;
Sudden, he sees a mighty phantom rise,
Towering in evening sunlight, from the brow
Of an imperial alp, and stretching now
His shadowy arm beyond him, to the skies!

XII.

"Thou droop'st, my son!" the royal spectre cries;
"These seem dread barriers to thy feeble eyes;

But know that Faith o'erleaps the Impassable,
And the Impossible succumbs to Will!
And Love is but a faint and perishing flame,
Scarce worthy the girl's worship, and *her* shame,
While that burns ever which belongs to Fame!
Rocks rise, and dread abysses cross thy path;
But did'st thou dream that roses strew'd the way
To glory? Would'st thou feed eternal wrath,
And great revenges, by a shepherd's lay,
Piped dreamingly at eventide, when gleams
The softening light of sunset on the streams,
That dance to flitting star-light? Weaving flowers,
One scales no heights, o'erthrows no enemy's towers,
Plucks never the rose from Danger's rocky heights,
And wins no conquest save o'er base delights.
Who yields himself to the enslaving moods
Of the boy-passion, and with Fancy broods
O'er the supposed perfections of a life
Pass'd in delicious luxuries of repose,
Barters his birth-right for a world of woes!
The best security for Peace is strife;
At least, the prompt and resolute will to brave—
Nay, seek the danger, ere we fall, its slave!
He only merits love who joys in war;
Love follows on the conquest—is its close,
Not its condition—must be kept afar
From any estimate of the absolute need;
To be enjoy'd in peace, securely nigh,
The enemy conquer'd and the duty freed!
Thy heart is in thy home; thy love is there;
She, whose bright visage, ever in thine eye,
Gleams with persuasion, making all thy care
Lie in the very comforter! What is here,

Of wisdom, home denied security?
But home thou hast not: Carthage has no home—
Love no security or life—while Rome
Endures upon her hills, and sends abroad
Her ravening legions—conquers like a God,
To torture like a fiend! If *she* survives,
Thy country falls! A hundred thousand lives
Share in the deep perdition of her fall,
And all her cup of blessing turns to gall!
Thou art her life! In thee her hope revives;
And if *thou* fail her!—But look back and see
What sort of home and life hath Italy
Decreed to Carthage!"

XIII.

Ceased the awful shade,
In the prophetic speech. The chief obey'd,
Look'd back, and trembled in his great surprise.
No alps behind him rose!—yet had he striven,
Toiling upward, till the heights grew into heaven,
And the great marches backward had become
Themselves a terror, making manhood dumb,
As did the heights beyond.
His eager eyes
Beheld the happy and sweet vale, that late
He left in bless'd security. What Fate
Had now usurp'd its beauties? Dread the shape,
Coated with serpents, that made fiery rape
Of all its dear possessions! Cottage and grove,
Fair hamlets, orchards ruddy in the sun,
And Youth and Rapture dreaming in the shade,
Forgetting danger in the joys of love—
All by this terrible enemy overrun;
Suddenly crushed and perishing; suddenly made

A blended ruin: while a deathly roar,
The crash of falling cities, mixed with shrieks
Of women, heard a moment and no more,
Drove the warm blood in whiteness from his cheeks!

XIV.

"Thou see'st!" resumed the phantom of the sire,
"That terrible shape is War! And such the doom
Of Italy or Carthage! Do thou choose
Whether such fortune fall upon *thy* home,
Where all that is most dear to thy desire
Harbors, or on the country of thy foes!
Such is the fate of Carthage or of Rome!
They are two rival destinies, that strive
In conflict, and one only may survive!
Look not again behind thee, but before!
There speed that terror! Let the ravaging form
Spread forth on every side, in fire and storm!
Be pitiless, that ye may better prove
Tender and merciful where most you love.
There rend the city; bid the temple flame;
Man yield to hate, and woman sink in shame;
While Rome succumbs to Carthage and to thee,
Even as thy will and courage shall decree!
But look not back—and dream no more! The hour
That finds thee thus unfaithful to thy fame,
Finds thee and Carthage lost to pride and power
Fate on her roof, disgrace upon thy name.
On, though alps tower on alps; though perils crowd
Thy legions, through the tempest and the cloud;
Though thousands perish in the pitiless strife!—
Even in their fate shall Carthage gain new life!
Heed not the rocks that ever round thee rise,
These bring thee hourly nearer to thy prize;

They are thy steps to triumph—steeps that bring
The conqueror to new uses of his wing;
Thence, down upon the valleys shalt thou spring,
With tenfold power to crush; thence shalt thou grow
Resistless, in the struggle with thy foe;
And when thy soul is saddest, and thy form
Grows weariest, let one thought thy courage warm—
Rome is beyond! That empire of thy Hate,
Thy foe and victim She, and Thou, her Fate!"

CANZONE.—IF THOU COULD'ST SEE THE TEARS!

I.

If thou could'st see the tears,
  That I so long have shed for thee;
If thou could'st know the fears
  My thoughts have hourly bred for thee;
If thou could'st dream of all I've done
  To make thy lot in life more bright,
Thou would'st not, could'st not dare to shun
    My gaze to-night!

II.

I watch thee through the festive hall,
  The fairest in the spacious round,
Where all is sweet to sight—where all
  Is more than exquisite in sound;
My glance is never from thy brow,
  And, in the whirling dance, alone
Of all the crowd I see thee now—
    The only one!

III.

Without a thought on him who stands
  From all that festive throng apart—
Whose thought, afar—in foreign lands—
  Those foreign lands, thy heart, thy heart!—
Thou glid'st among the insensate crew,
  And speak'st the idle language there,
And smil'st, and wear'st the features, too,
    Thou should'st not wear!

IV.

I come not now to tell thee aught
  Of all my sad and lonely hours;
Be free of censure—free of thought;
  Sport, if thou canst, with silliest flowers;
Be bless'd—be happy—if, perchance,
  Thou hast sufficient heart for bliss;
I will not blight thee with a glance,
    So fell as this!

V.

Away! away! yet whither fly?
  No aim or purpose guides me now—
My bark must take what sea or sky
  Shall wing or warp her wandering prow!
On to the ocean's dreadest deep,
  Where Cunning holds her crowded mart,
And pain, that dies not, still must keep
    Close in the heart!

SONNET.—DREAM-LAND.

One might sleep ever in such dear delight,
Thus dreaming of Elysium—of bright eyes,
Still glimpsing, with an ever-sweet surprise,
Beneath the lids that open for the light,
Yet close again with rapture that it brings!
Oh! the most precious of a thousand things,
Thus to accumulate the various bliss
That comes with such dear 'tendance; and, with this,
To know the treasure, o'er all earthly price,
Is still beyond all purchase, save of faith—
That quits the giver with his own device,
And finds self's better profit in its death.
Each generous gift of love to kindred worth,
Calls thousand worshipping spirits into birth.

STANZAS.

When life deserts this lowly sphere,
And earth receives the form it gave,
Can wildest hope expect a tear,
From Love or Friendship, on my grave?

The pangs of life, the dread of death,
It might repel, and sure would soothe,
To feel that, with the parting breath,
All is not lost to love and truth.

And with conviction sure to know,
  That she who sits in silence nigh,
With tears too deep for overflow,
  Will cherish long the grateful sigh.;

Will long, with yearning soul, go back,
  In fruitless quest, through vanish'd hours,
Wherever love has left its track,
  Or duty wove its way in flowers:

Still fond to trace the memories dear,
  Of joys so precious to the soul,
That love forgets each living care,
  In that which can no more control.

And with what soothing, through the range
  Of future hours, their grief and glee,
To feel that he, whom nought could change,
  Still lives in changeless memory:

Still lives for friendship—for the heart,
  That, with his own, in emulous strife,
By glory lured, in love with art,
  Began the ambitious race of life.

To dream that one, with joyless eye,
  Will seek him still through realms of gloom:
To baffled hopes accord the sigh,
  And crown with precious tears the tomb;

And from the herd's pursuing hate
  Will still, with generous warmth, defend,
Declare the ambition mock'd of fate,
  How bold its aim, how pure its end!

Ah! these are hopes that well may still
The vulture in the hour of pain;
The dying heart with solace fill,
And soothe the fears they may not chain.

Were these but mine!—but ah, the doubt
Even now is struggling at my breast;
I feel the deep desire, without
The assurance which should make it blest!

Alas! if, at the parting hour,
The eye that sees my sad decline
Shall watch unmov'd life's fleeting power,
And coldly meet the glance of mine;

Shall turn with heedless haste away,
When o'er me sinks the heavy pall,
Nor shudder when the oppressive clay
Is heard upon my lid to fall;

Shall seek the crowd, the festal board,
The revel and the rout, to hush
Those memories love should fondly hoard,
With hopes that to the future rush,

To ask of stars, and winds, and skies,
Of thoughts by day, of dreams by night,
If faith may yet secure the prize
Still precious in affection's sight;

If ties, so dear to earth, may be
Acknowledged in that happier clime;
And there, if eyes of love may see
Once more the things so dear to time!

Ah! take from me the fear, that all
The friends so dear, so cherish'd long,
Shall from their deep allegiance fall,
A precious, but a faithless throng.

Let me not doubt that in the hearts
To mine most dear, I still may see,
Ere yet the pulse from life departs,
Love's better life—fidelity!

BATTLE OF FORT MOULTRIE.

Soft is the veil of moonlight o'er the waters,
Soft is the swell, upon the shore, of billows,
Soft, in the distance, the great city's spires,
And soft the breeze.

Peace is upon the land and on the ocean,
Peaceful the slumbers of this ocean hamlet,
And the blue concave, by a cloud unshadowed,
Looks loving peace.

Before us sleeps a mound, whose solemn shadow
Beseems the red man's tumulus of ages,
As keeping in its deep and vaulted chambers
A realm of dead.

With gentle light the moon stoops down to hallow
The deep repose that wakes not to sweet voices;
She leaves her smiles, where sad, in seasons vanish'd,
Man left but tears.

No sleepless bird is heard, with cry or music,
Unsuited to the quiet, deep and sacred,
Where Silence, in her own primeval temple,
Still reigns supreme.

Who that beholds that ocean wrapt in brightness;
Who that enjoys embrace with these sweet zephyrs;
That feels the beauty and the calm about him,
Would dream of strife?

Would dream of tempests raging o'er this ocean;
Clouds in that azure vault, its charm effacing;
And for this breeze, so meek, yet full of fondness
Would look for storm?

Yet will the tempest, with a wild transition,
Stifle these gentle breathings of the zephyr,
While great tornadoes sweep the face of heaven,
With all its charms!

Yet will the seas, in beauty now reposing,
Boil up in madness and o'erthrow their barriers
Defacing lawny shore and verdant meadow,
Now blest with peace.

Thus, in a moment—let the foe but threaten—
That silent mound becomes a fiery fortress,
Whose flashing death-bolts, hurtling o'er the waters,
Ring out his doom!

Such awful change of old this shore hath witnessed,
When first our young republic, bold but feeble,
Claimed, though at peril of all wreck of fortune,
Her place of pride.

Thus calm the seas, when o'er the waters raging,
Rush'd, swollen with wrath, the giant form of Britain,
Her thunders hurling on our peaceful hamlets,
With hate of hell!

Thus silent lay our bulwarks of palmetto,
Behind them little groups of youthful heroes,
Waiting the signal when, with answering thunders,
To meet her wrath.

How patient was their watch beneath that banner,
The slight blue streamer, lighted by one crescent,
That show'd the modest hope that warm'd their courage
In that dark hour!

How doubtful, yet how fearless of the struggle,
When, in the strength assured of thousand battles,
Britain, in armor, 'gainst the youthful shepherd
Came fiercely on!

Doubtful our young men stood, but undespairing,
Not blind to all the fearful odds against them,
But sworn in faith, that finds it better falling
In fight, than fear!

How beautiful, as serpents fang'd with venom,
Glided the swans of battle to the conflict,
Their streamers flaunting with Britannia's lion,
Rampant in red!

How silently they moored beneath our fortress,
Unmuzzled their grim ministers of vengeance,
And waited but the signal, to send terror
Among our sons.

One awful pause preceded the wild tempest,
Then roared the storm, and fell the hail of battle;
A thousand fires were lighted, in a moment,
At Moloch's shrine!

One look of yearning to the distant city,
Where hung, in tears and fondness, wives and mothers,
Forms of most fond delight and dear devotion,
Weeping in prayer:

And then, the brave hearts of our youthful warriors,
Nerved with new couragê by those sweet spectators,
Conscious what hopes and eyes were set upon them,
Rushed to the strife!

Thunder for thunder, and defiant voices,
Bore witness to the love that faced that conflict—
How the brave spirits, battling for their homesteads,
Defied the Fates!

Through the long day of summer, still unshaken,
They stood beside their cannon, while each broadside
Shook their frail simple bastions of palmetto,
But shook no hearts.

There Moultrie coolly stands, the scene surveying,
Ranging his muzzles on each mighty frigate,
Speeding each fearful missile on its mission
Of blood and wreck.

There Marion ministers, his young lieutenant,
Wheels the swift piece, and sights the flaming cannon,
Or, when the bullet rends the reeling vessel,
Shouts loud with cheer!

There, stout McDonald, slain upon the rampart,
The first brave martyr in the fearful battle,
Shrieks, as he falls: "I die, my gallant comrades,
But not our cause!"

Down sinks the crescent streamer of the fortress,
While o'er the city sudden darkness lowers,
As if a star, the only one in heaven,
Had sunk in night.

But lo! it rises from the cloud, and waving,
Reveals the lithe and active form of Jasper—
He plucks it from the beach, and rears it proudly
Through all the storm!

If then one heart had trembled in its terror,
It gathers hope and pride from that glad omen,
And hears the whisper'd cry from each fond mother,
"Be strong, my son!"

And they were strong, as for the rock, the eagle,
Who hears the cry of young ones in his eyrie,
Assailed by subtlest foes, and bends his pinion
To guard his nest.

Day wanes, and Night hangs out her starry banner,
Blue spread the curtains of the sky for slumber,
Peace soars aloft, as if in prayer imploring
For peace below:

But still the cannon thundered with its mission;
Still spoke fierce music to the hearts of valor;
Still shouted high the brave and shrieked the dying,
Till midnight fell!

The lion-banner sank, at length, in darkness,
The crescent soared, in every eye triumphant
While in the distant city rose the shouting
From hearts made glad.

With dawn, the shattered hulks to sea were drifting;
Upon the shores the gentle waves were breaking;
And, with the triumph of our virgin valor,
Came peace once more!

THE WINGED STEED.

I.

What! laugh they to behold my steed?
They little know his blood and breed,
His fiery heart, his lightning speed—
How soon he cleaves the height!
What glorious impulse gives him way,
When, breaking bonds of time and clay,
He sees the clouds around him play,
And beats them down in flight!

II.

They saw him first on lowly plains,
The harness crushing on his reins,
Grief in his soul, and in his veins
A feverish sense of wrong;
The lowly herd, with brutal force,
That baulked him ever on the course,
Baffling his native free resource,
And trampling on it long!

III.

They saw him with his fires subdued,
In weary hour, in abject mood,
Worn in the conflict, driven to brood
  In pastures not his own;
They saw him droop beneath the yoke,
Shrink, smarting from the thong and stroke,
His limbs o'erborne, his spirit broke,
  Scourged, scorn'd, and still alone.

IV

They saw him ever by the herd
Wronged or abandoned—crushed or stirr'd
By usage base—still unpreferred—
  To service vile decreed;
They knew not that, by instinct taught,
Unerring, every heart was fraught
With rage, and into hatred wrought,
  As conscious of his meed.

V.

He was not of their race—he bore
A power to them unknown before,
And still a haughty carriage wore,
  That goaded pride to hate;
He loved not with the rest to rove,
Still went apart—still went above—
And lovely, seemed to seek no love,
  And matchless, found no mate.

VI.

For this they hated!—strange, how well,
With what foul art and blasting spell,
How worthy all the fires of hell,
  They wrought for his annoy!
How they pursued—how banded still,
To vex the soul, the spirit kill,
And goad, with ceaseless work of ill,
  As seeking to destroy.

VII.

For long they triumph'd—oh! how long
He sunk and suffered 'neath the wrong,
Gnawed vainly at the cruel thong,
  That bound him to despair:
But still in soul and strength he grew,
When none beheld, or but the few;
The secret power his spirit knew,
  Still taught him how to bear!

VIII.

How should they deem—the vain, the blind,
That tramp the noblest of their kind—
That he should rise at last, nor find
  Obstruction in their hate;
That he, the meanest of the herd—
So held—should be at last preferr'd—
Should win the world's applauding word,
  And speed without a mate?

IX.

They mock, they hiss—with scorn they cry,
Still seeing with their ancient eye:
"Behold, what crude deformity—
He hath nor grace nor might!"
Armed with their former fires of wrath,
They fain would blast the powers he hath,
And set their snares upon his path,
And seek to mar his flight.

X.

With jeer of malice, howl of hate,
Blind fury, and bad hopes, elate,
They crowd his course, and strive with fate,
To crush and conquer still:
They laugh to scorn the few who cheer,
O'erwhelm the applause with fiendish sneer,
Would bar his passage, could they dare
Encounter whom they kill!

XI.

He comes—he treads the course—they see,
And wonder, with what motion free,
What ease of limb, what majesty,
He passeth o'er the plain;
Whence got he that imperial grace,
That makes him native to the place,
And lifts him o'er the lowlier race,
That watch his steps with pain?

XII.

They never saw before the fires
Blaze in that eye, which now aspires,
As with a wing of fierce desires
That need no mortal rest;
Such vigor in those limbs; and still
They dream not of the seraph will
Which nerves—the impulsive, holy thrill
That lightens through his breast!

XIII.

How should they see—the wilful blind—
Or wish, in him they hate, to find
The soul that makes him, of his kind,
The conqueror, born to sway?
'Tis ruled that, as we toil, we gain;
Who seeks not, finds not; and in vain
The pleasure, born of others' pain,
That feeds not those who prey!

XIV.

Still laugh they to behold my steed!
They pamper thus the ancient need,
Though yet they doubt his strength and speed
To win the imperial goal:
They know not of the power that grows
From patient watch and mighty woes,
Well borne, for long, through fiercest throes
Of the ambitious soul:

XV.

What muscle springs from patient toil,
What soul from commerce with the soil,
What impulse, when the world, with foil,
  And force, hath baffled long;
What—in the hour of wild delight,
That opens fair the field for flight—
The hope that then dilates the sight,
  The will that makes it strong!

XVI.

He speeds, he bounds, he darts away—
At once unfold the gates of day;
The skies come down; with joyous ray
  Suns round his pathway grow!
Ha! Now they start—they see the wings
Spread from each side, as off he springs,
With flight that leaves all meaner things
  Afar, behind, below!

XVII.

Where, now, the favorites of the crowd,
Hailed late with plaudits long and loud,
The pride of hosts, themselves too proud
  To toil with patient brow?
Shouts, plaudits, nursing friends, and aid—
Sleek service, and the hirelings paid
To lie for pertness in brocade—
  Are all but mockery now!

XVIII.

The strife is o'er, ere yet begun!
The courser, kindred to the sun,
Sweeps o'er the field—the goal is won!
  The hooting hosts of Hate
Depart in fury; shut their eyes;
Deny—for Envy still denies—
The right to him who takes the prize,
  The master, he, of Fate!

XIX.

See, where he speeds—how proud the flight—
What giant wings to win the height,
Where, on the mountain tops, alight,
  He sways the plains beneath!
How changed the shout, the cry, the song—
The servile mass that mock'd his wrong,
Most clamorous now, with echoes long,
  That speak their perfect faith.

XX.

Believe them, and they always knew
The wonders that his wing could do,
His matchless grace, his empire true,
  And all the gifts he bore!—
Alas! how blasting first to sight,
The sudden glory of his flight,
That wing of majesty and might—
  That sway they curse no more!

XXI.

Blind mouths! that ponder as they breed,
That never knew their better need,
Still, for a life, on garbage feed,
  Nor dream how base their fare;
While daily, nightly, from the skies,
The quail and manna fall, their eyes
See not the heavenly food that lies
  Around, and bids them share!

XXII.

They wander wide in sterile ways,
Self-led, self-blinded, all their days;
The shepherd comes—instead of praise
  And thanks, the wolfish crew
Set on him with keen fangs and rend!—
Ah, God! be merciful—still send
The shepherd, these to save, befriend—
  They know not what they do!

EPIGRAM.

Within her breast, more white than snows,
Fair Amaryllis plants the rose;
Not that the flower should bless your eyes,
But the rich garden where it lies.

THE SLAIN EAGLE. (SALUDA.)

I.

THE noble bird! What mighty stretch of wing—
Seven feet from tip to tip! And what an eye,
That glares in death, as with the will to spring,
Spurn earth, and rush into the blazing sky!
What talons!—that shall lift the lamb on high,
And bear it to its heights, nor feel the weight!
Emblem of power, and might, and majesty,
Yet victim of the feeblest stroke of fate,
Transfixed by Indian shaft, when soaring in thy state!

II.

The eye that stopt thy flight, with deadly aim,
Had less of fire and beauty than thine own;
The arm that cast thee down could never claim
Such matchless vigor as thy wing hath shown,
Yet art thou, in thy pride of flight, o'erthrown:
And the great rocks that echoed back thy scream,
As from the rolling clouds thou sent'st it down,
No more shall see thy red-eyed glances stream,
From their wild summits round, with fierce and terrible gleam!

III.

Lone and majestic monarch of the cloud!
No more shalt thou o'ersweep the mountain's brow,
Mocking the storm, when from its vampire shroud
It pours wild torrents on the plains below!
Thou, with thy fearless wing, yet free to go,
All undebarr'd, undaunted in thy flight,
As scorning, while defying, every foe;
Shrieking, with clarion burst, thy conscious might,
That, for a hundred years, hath kept the unchallenged height!

IV.

Thou had'st no dread of danger! Thy great pride
  Kept thee from fear! Breasting the wintry storms,
Thy mighty pinions have stretched far and wide—
  Have triumphed, struggling with a thousand forms
  Of terror! Thou hast felt such strife but warms
The sovereign courage; and with joyful shriek,
  Sang of the rapturous battle—its wild charms
For the born warrior of the mountain peak,
He, of the giant brood, sharp talons, bloody beak!

V.

How hast thou, in thy very mirth, stretched far
  Thy wings in flight; with freedom that became
Miraculous in license; still at war
  With winds and clouds and storms, that could not tame
  Thy spirit, nor arrest thy sinewy frame!—
Such power and courage, such a billowy flight,
  Man wonders to behold, and calls it Fame!
His soul, when noblest soaring into light,
But follows in thy track, at once of aim and might!

VI.

Morning, above the hills, and from the ocean,
  Ne'er sprang aloft into the fetterless blue
With such a glorious grace and godlike motion,
  Nor from her amber pinions cast the dew
  That hung about her path, and dimm'd her view,
With greater ease than thou—resolv'd to steer
  Onward, through storm—hast sped with courses true,
Though winds pipe high, and arrowy lightnings glare,
Thy Day-Star wrapt in shroud, through fathomless fields
    of air.

VII.

Thus eminent in vision as in wing,
  With ever paramount purpose to achieve
The highest; scorning to keep low, and cling
  To earthy thraldoms; but, by might, to grieve
  The emulous crowds who vainly would conceive
Thy secret, and o'ercome the height and space;
  I find a faith that sways me to believe
Thou wast designed, the model of a race,
For conquest born, like thee, and wing'd for loftiest place!

VIII.

Let men but once behold thee in thy sweep
  O'er mountain heights to heaven, and straight they grow
To stature; and the big thought, fond and deep,
  Works in them with a restlessness like wo,
  Till they have put on wings, and felt the glow
Of flight and might, like thine; and with their eyes
  Have sought the secrets of the cloud to know;
And bathing their grand plumage in the skies,
Feel ever, with the will, the wing and power to rise!

IX.

Alas, for thee! Even from the chosen race,
  The antagonist nature, loathing thy estate,
With subtle arts, the virtue of the base,
  Barbs the sharp arrow that becomes thy fate.
  The very bright of glory 'genders hate;
The grandeur of the sun himself will bring
  The clouds about the shining of his state;
And he who hath no moral, but a sting,
Will hound with hate the steps of each superior thing.

X.

And thus it is that such as thou go'st down,
  Even at the highest; thy imperial flight
Stay'd, sudden, in career; when, all thine own,
  The sun had made thee brother of his light,
  And earth and skies maintained no eminent height
Baffling thy pinion; rival wings no more
  Waged conflict; and thy might had grown to right!—
Supreme, o'er sky, and rock, and wood, and shore,
Thine was the sovereign wing, as thine the will to soar!

XI.

Of all the race, from out the ranks of men—
  The million moilers, with down-looking eyes—
Perchance but one, beholding thee, as when
  Thy wing was bathed in beauty of the skies,
  Grew lifted by thy flight, and thence grew wise:
To struggle through the cloud, with emulous aim;
  Achieve the grand condition; and arise,
Through hate and envy, rivalry and blame,
To sway, on loftiest terms, in highest homes of fame.

XII.

How hath he watch'd thy wing, to see how vain,
  From his great central eminence, the sun
Shot forth his brazen arrows to restrain
  Thy triumph!—how the storm, with aspect dun,
  His ice-bolts vainly might they beat upon
Thy buckler!—To their presence didst thou fly,
  And Eblis-like, undaunted and alone,
Thou didst confront the Unknown; his power defy,
And to thy sun-god's face uplift thy rebel eye!

XIII.

And he who watch'd thee then had hope to soar
  Even with a wing like thine. His daring glance
Sought, with as bold a vision, to explore
  The secret of his own deliverance,
  As of his thraldom; eager to advance
To sovereign sway like thine—above his race;
  To rise and rule, the better to enhance
The virtues in their gift, with gifts of grace;
Lifting them proudly up to his superior place.

XIV.

He triumphs in his flight; but not in aim!
  He strives for those who, with a resolute will,
Reject the blessing; loathe the very fame;
  Prone to the dust and eating of it still,
  As did the serpent, never having fill!
To the base spirit, obligation grows
  A torture, and all gratitude is shame!
Hate finds increase with sense of what it owes,
And while one hand receives, the other 'quites with blows.

XV.

He triumphs, but he perishes, like thee,
  O sun-brow'd eagle!—scales the sovran heights;
Cleaves clouds; mounts tempests; feels his pinions free;
  Wantons in worlds of empire; and, in flights
  That fill his soul with paramount delights,
Endows his race with provinces of pride;
  New thoughts and attributes; new fields and rights;
Then sudden, when on topmost height astride,
Falls—smitten by hand so base that even the base deride!

XVI.

O glorious bird! whose wing hath pierced the cloud;
Nor sun nor storm had barrier proof to thee!
Thine was the soul, magnanimous as proud,
That stoop'd not; but, majestically free,
Won heights whose secrets man shall never see.
Ah! where thy spirit now? the wing that bore?
Thou hast lost wing, and all—save liberty!
Death only could subdue—and that is o'er—
Alas! the very hind who slew thee might deplore.

XVII.

The missile sped, the victim at his feet,
How looks he now, with sense of sudden shame,
At the great vans, the pinions that so fleet,
Held pace with winds, and on their wings became
A pioneer to realms that have no name!
Wings broken now: and dim the dying eye,
Dilating with the effort still to claim
Its summits; straining upward for that sky
Which vainly woos its vans to light and liberty.

XVIII.

A proud exemplar hath been lost the proud!—
Oh! he that smote thee in thy fearless flight,
Had wiselier follow'd thee, and fled the crowd,
That babbling now take measure of thy might,
Stretch wide thy pinions, and with wondering sight
Compute thy talons! Had he not been base,
With wretched comrades, he had found delight
To take the lessons of thy nobler race,
And make his way, through thought, to some superior place.

XIX.

'Tis he should weep for thee: for he hath lost
  The model of dominion! Not for him
The mighty eminence; the gathering host
  That worships; the great glittering pomps that dim;
  The tribute homage and the hailing hymn!
He might have had a life, that, to a star,
  Rises from dust, and sheds the holiest gleam,
To light the struggling nations from afar,
And show to kindred souls where fruits of glory are.

XX.

Behold him now, where, clamoring o'er his prey,
  He tells you how his secret shaft was sped:
He lurk'd within the rocky cleft all day,
  Till the proud bird rose surging o'er his head,
  At sunset, when he slew him! O'er the dead
Exults he now; yet, had those eyes their fire,
  Were but those talons unclasped, those vans outspread,
The dastard had shrunk trembling from the ire
Whose very glance had quench'd each foe's most fierce desire.

XXI.

How basely do we seek to overthrow
  The thing we are not! The ignoble mind
Thus ever aims to strike, with secret blow,
  The nobler, finer beings of their kind;
  In this their petty villany is blind:
They smite their benefactors; men who keep
  Their homes from degradation; men designed
Their guides and guardians; well, if they may creep,
At last, to honoring shrines, and o'er their victims weep.

XXII.

Farewell, proud bird!—this human homily,
How vain for those who fall, and those who hate!
Who now shall teach thy young ones how to fly?
Who fill the presence of thy longing mate?
Ah! type of Genius, bitter is thy fate!
The shaft of meanest boor may leave them lone—
Thy eaglets and the partner of thy state:
Shaft from the very fen whence thou hast flown,
And feather from the wing thy own wing hath struck down!

HORACE TO POLLY.

ODE (XXIII) "AD PYRRHAM."

You fly from me, Polly, my dear, like a fawn,
That, trembling still at each breeze that blows,
Seeks for its dam on the mountain bawn,
With a terror that suffers her no repose;
With feeble limbs, and faltering heart,
That shrinks from the rustle of leafy spring,
And deems the green lizard, as bushes part,
Some very fearful and terrible thing!

Believe me, Polly, no tiger wild,
No panther of Buncombe to tear you, child;
And now that you're quite of a marrying age,
And I'm not the worst-looking lad you see,
Turn a new leaf in your virgin page,
Quit your mamma and take lodgings with me.

WANDER, OH WANDER HERE.

I.

Wander, oh wander here
  Sweet is the sky-born fountain,
Bubbling soft, and lapsing clear,
  From old Saluda's mountain;
Fly from the city, fly!
  Pleasures will here delight thee;
Children of grove and sky
  With song and smile invite thee.

II.

Hither, away from the crowd!
  What can its tedious measure,
Mix'd of the selfish, the mean, the proud,
  Bring to thy heart of pleasure?
Hither, where Life will spring
  With a rosy blush to meet thee,
And Love delight to bring
  His tenderest song to greet thee!

III.

Never a cloud is here,
  Shrouding the morning splendor;
And the sun with a purple rare
  Crowns the sad dusk with the tender;
Here the fond song that greets
  Your ears with delight at even,
Morning with joy repeats,
  Even as she springs from heaven.

IV.

Sweetest, O sweetest, fly!
  Hither, where sun-loved Hours
Skim, 'neath a soft blue sky,
  Ever o'er beds of flowers.
Here will thy bosom glow,
  Here will thy bright eye glisten,
Love ever glad to vow,
  If Beauty but gladly listen.

AH! HAD I BUT YON SWALLOW'S WING.

Ah! had I but yon swallow's wing,
  I should not now thy loss deplore,
Nor with such sullen spirit cling
  A moment to this sterile shore:
But with a strong and fearless flight
  My form should wing its way to thee,
Nor aught of beautiful or bright,
  To stay its progress, seek or see!

Ah, happy, could the obedient clay,
  At summons of the longing heart,
To the dear region, far away,
  Even at a word, or wish, depart!
But with a will, and not a wing,
  The heart must gnaw its hope in vain,
And murmur, where it dare not sing,
  And weep, while other hearts complain.

TO THEE, WHEN MORN IS SHINING.

I.

To thee, when Morn is shining,
  My early homage tends;
To thee, when Day's declining,
  My evening song ascends:
When grief within me swelling,
  Leaves Hope no longer free,
I fly my lonely dwelling,
  To thee, my heart, to thee

II.

Come forth! thy step is lightest,
  I love that all should see;
Come forth, thine eye is brightest,
  My heart is proud of thee!
Come forth, where lips are parting
  In thoughts of eager glee,
And hopeful glances darting
  To thee, my soul, to thee!

III.

Oh! thou hast charms to brighten,
  When circles shine most gay,
 nd spells of grace to heighten
  The loveliest realm of play!
Would mine were worth, of splendor,
  To match with thine! Ah, me!
True heart and homage tender
  Are all I bring to thee!

OH, LOVELY WERE ONCE HER EYES.

I.

Oh, lovely were once her eyes, but grief
Their light hath now o'erclouded;
And her lips were sweet, like the budding leaf,
Though now their bloom be shrouded—
For in her heart a malady,
Like the canker worm in the rose,
Preys ever there, unceasingly,
And gives her no repose.

II.

It is sad to think, in a few short hours,
We shall look on her no longer,
For the glance gives sign of the failing powers,
And the pang grows hourly stronger;
We shall lose the balm of her budding breath,
We shall hear her voice no more;
We shall see those sweet eyes sealed in death,
That we once could so adore.

III.

Yet shall I not weep, though losing all,
For many long days, I so have loved;
The tear that from mine eyes would fall,
My thought has well reproved:
For hers has been a dooméd life,
And those who love her well, should pray
That she may quickly lose the strife,
Which has eaten her heart away.

BALLAD.—THE YOUNG HUNTER.

I.

Now lend me thy bow, young hunter, Love,
  And bring me thy cunning and crystal dart,
For I am bound for the gay green wood,
  This day to strike or to snare the hart.
The hart that runs in yon gay green wood,
  Is famed for a nimble and fearless foot;
He hath every shaft from my quiver stood,
  And baffled my arrows and best pursuit.

II.

But arm'd with thy bow, young hunter, Love,
  Thy wingéd arrow and crystal dart,
My hope is good, in the gay green wood,
  This day to snare or to strike the hart:
'Tis a wily hart, that hath strong allies,
  To keep his haunts from the hunter free;
And a subtle feeling of fear that flies,
  And a passionate pride in his liberty.

III.

He hath prudence, that watches the narrow way,
  And a sense so keen for the hostile foot,
That horse shall not bound, nor beagle bay,
  But he flies, and baffles the best pursuit;
But give me thy bow, young hunter, Love,
  Thy wingéd arrow and crystal dart;
And breathe but thy blessing upon my quest,
  And let me at once on the chase depart.

IV.

Thou hast tamed the master of many a wood,
The lion hath crouch'd in his strength to thee;
And the tiger fierce, at his feast of blood,
Thou hast brought to kneel, or made to flee.
Oh! give me thy weapons of magic, Love,
And breathe but thy blessing upon my quest,
And guide me in chase to the secret place
Where that wily hart takes his noonday rest.

V.

Oh! we hunt not the hart with a common art,
But with weapon charm'd, and a loving hate;
And we go to the chase with the desperate pace
Of one who deals with a mortal Fate!
And with spells of care we set the snare,
And hallow the charm with a vow of faith;
And we bait with a wile, of tear and smile,
And we lie in wait with a panting breath.

VI.

Oh! I know the game which shall make him tame!
I will sing in the forest a song of power,
And with tenderest tone, which shall win him on
To the laurel grove and the myrtle bower;
And, as not to win were a folly and sin,
I will peril myself by a sacrifice;
And bare my own breast, in the happy quest,
And make my own soul, if it needs, the price.

VII.

So lend me thy bow, young hunter, Love,
  And arm me with arrows and crystal dart;
And charm the bow with thy spell of power,
  And tip the shaft with thy subtle art;
And yield me the smile that suns the wood,
  And fill me with song to lull the air;
And warm my breast, to the loving quest,
  To will and to win, when I've laid it bare!

LONG I LIVED IN FANCIES.

Long I lived in fancies,
  Heart and mind at play;
Dream'd through bright romances,
  Night and day;
Loved too well the dreaming,
  Much to think of self;
Knew no arts of scheming
  After power or pelf.

Life was nought but loving
  Love the only true;
And, with fancies roving,
  Love was all I knew;
I had never a count or care
  Of the fleeting hours,
Since my wings, when not in air,
  Were among the flowers!

To be loved, was ever
  All my want and art;
To be held forever
  Close to one sweet heart!
Though on wing still roving,
  I had but one quest—
To find the mate for loving
  In a single nest.

Ah! the worldly fashion
  Ever mock'd at mine,
And my foolish passion
  Was not thine.
Seeking sway o'er many,
  Thou hast captured none;
And, unloved of any,
  We are both undone!

THE TAX-PAYER.—A FRAGMENT.

I HAVE nought worthy the assessor's eye;
  Poor is the homestead with its worn-out lands;
Hard is the labor, pitiless the case,
  And for the farm-house—see the way it stands!—
  I've built, as I may say, upon the sands!

Treasure I have, and precious beyond price:
  One lovely child that Providence had given
To cheer my days and comfort their decline;
  But she, thank God! hath been assessed by Heaven!
  I hope, one day, to meet her near the Seven!

DUSK, AND THE STAR.

The dusk was all about me, and my heart
Wore even a duskier aspect. Care had brought
A sense of gloom to shape the ungenial thought;
And shadows, sad or savage, seem'd to start
From the drear walls of vacancy. A chill
Settled on Fancy and the dreaming mood
That, whether it profits or not, in life is still
So precious to our forest solitude!
But while I brooded by the lattice, stealing—
As 'twere a spirit on meet service bent—
Sudden, the silent smiling of the moon
Made grateful all the shadows; and I leant
Forth, as if seeking to make sure the boon
And blessing that she brought me.
                                    There they lay,
The smiling gleams among the trees, revealing
All the fair aspects of the twilight's noon;
To every wingéd fancy straight appealing,
To every latent consciousness revealing
A miracle of soul—the soul ascending
Once more on wings of hope; while, with the ray,
The southern breeze that came at moments blending
Earth's echoes with music of seraphic spheres,
Awaken'd each delicious fount of feeling,
And made a treasure of my very tears!
  And, faith, I wept! I was alone with sorrow—
A sorrow given to memory! I felt
That angels were about me; and I knelt,
In hope from earnest prayer awhile to borrow
Sweet and more certain converse with the power,

Surely of love, that thus about me came,
My minister of peace in vexing hour!
  Ah! blessings on the fancies which thus melt
The rocks and chains of loneliness; which shame
The sinking spirit; which revive the past,
Only to soothe the present; and awake
The sleeping hopes and fancies of the heart,
To urge it to new purpose, and to take
The sting away that made its solitude,
Its horror. All the shadowy glooms depart
With love, and moonlight, and the breeze!—I brood,
And find the world sufficient—find it good!

BLOOD. (Impromptu.)

Blood's a most brave inheritance, but blood,
Without the brains, is little more than mud!
He who inherits name, inherits fame,
But must transmit it, or it shrinks to shame!
We are but heirs, in trust; and it requires
We leave to sons what we have got from sires,
With interest on the capital that's left;
Or we are bankrupt, with no power of gift.
The son, however high the name he claims,
Must make it higher, if he'd have it Fame's!
The blood, reputed for the race it runs,
Must never stagnate in the veins of sons;
Must swell with strength, well governed by the soul,
Or it's a puddle, in a filthy hole.

'TIS TRUE THAT LAST NIGHT I ADORED THEE.

'Tis true that last night I adored thee,
But 'twas moonlight, the song, and the wine;
The cool morning air has restored me,
And no longer I deem thee divine;
I confess thou art pretty and tender,
And when thou canst catch me again,
As last night, on a desperate *bender*,*
Once more I'll submit to thy chain.

The fact is, dear Fanny, I'm human,
Very weak, I may say, on a *spree*; †
And no matter of what sort the woman,
I'm her slave if she *cottons* ‡ to me.
But this cursèd sobriety ever
Undoes every chain of delight,
And my memory, by daylight, has never
Any sense of what takes place by night.

I'm a man of most regular habit
When daylight comes round, on my word;
And though loving, by night, as a rabbit,
With the sunrise I'm cool as a curd;
I'm quite willing in moonlight for capture,
But she's a bright woman whose skill,
Having spell'd the short hours with rapture,
With the daylight can fetter me still.

---

* Our Collegiate naturally uses what is supposed to be flash dialect. But, in truth, flash language, not to be guilty of a pun, is very often the language of the fancy. Here, the word *bender* is simply figurative; signifying the rather circuitous progress, snake fashion, which a young blood is apt to take, after the professors have all retired for the night.

† *Spree*, is simply an American contraction of the French word *esprit*, which, freely rendered in our idiom, means "on the wing."

‡ *Cottons*—clings closely; a figure drawn from the now general use of cotton wool in the manufacture of chemise and shirt.

HOPES WE HAVE NOURISH'D.

Hopes we have nourish'd,
If they be gone,
Joys that have flourish'd,
If they be flown;
Then welcome the winter that strikes at the root;
What matter the tree if it never bear fruit?
Let the storm make its moan—make its moan!

How rich was the pleasure,
How blessing the joy,
More than Rapture could measure,
Or Fate could destroy!
How lovely the visions that rose on our way,
How like to the meteors that shine to betray,
The footstep and faith of the boy—of the boy!

Raptures at meeting,
When heart grew to heart,
Bounding and beating,
As if life were to part!
Ah! hopeless our tears o'er the gleams that ye gave,
Like fairy bright eyes looking up through the wave,
That, even as we gaze, downward dart—downward dart!

Thou that hast won us,
Too precious deceit,
Thou hast undone us,
With raptures too fleet!
Yet our hearts may not grieve o'er the ills thou hast done,
Too precious the memory of joys that are flown,
And these shall be sweet—shall be evermore sweet!

STANZAS.—'TWAS MEANT FOR THEE.

I.

'Twas meant for thee, when all look'd dark,
And every friend my childhood knew
Shrunk from my slight and vent'rous bark,
As fearless o'er the waves it flew;
Unshaken still to keep thy faith,
And through each gloomy storm that came,
To shield me, in thy pray'rs, from scaith,
To keep me, in thy speech, from blame.

II.

When narrow fears beset the base,
And selfish hopes o'ercame the mean,
Thy love alone, with gentle face,
Look'd still unchanged through all the scene;
And, with the darkness of the hour,
Thy truth but more conspicuous shone,
As some sweet star, when clouds have power,
Looks proudly out from heaven, alone!

III.

Shall I not love thee, evermore,
Thou more than planet-guide to me,
Whose gentle light, on sea and shore,
Still spoke thy true heart's constancy?
Oh! be Time's changes what they will,
They can not change that sleepless thought,
That tells, that teaches of thee, still,
By thee, for evermore, still taught.

MEETING TO SEVER.

I.

Meeting to sever,
  Perchance to forget,
Would that we never,
  Oh, never, had met.
Better, unseeing,
  To come and depart,
Than linger in being,
  Divided in heart.

II.

In that first meeting,
  My heart revels now,
Every pulse beating,
  With rapture aglow:
But a moment, and terror
  Takes place of delight;
We awake to the error,
  And waking is blight!

III.

How can we sever
  From feeling and troth?
'Twere an agony ever
  In the future, for both!
Meeting in gladness,
  To rapture so rare,
That parting is madness,
  And Being despair!

HOMER. (Epigram.)

PARAPHRASED FROM SCHILLER.

They would tear the bright crown from old Homer,
The varlets and blockheads infernal;
They would prove it a monstrous misnomer,
To call *his* the Poem Eternal:
They would find it some thirty-six sires,
But in all their philistering and pother,
The boobies, whate'er their desires,
In thee, Nature, find the one mother.

ANDRÉ.—A BALLAD.

Oh! bright were the visions that bade him
The garb of the warrior assume;
And dear was the hand that array'd him
With the falchion, the helmet, and plume;
And fond was the voice that assured him,
And glorious the hope that allured him—
That promised a future in story,
Love's rose blent with laurels of glory;
Ah, hapless! to end but in doom!

Too blind, in the warmth of devotion,
To see the false image that led,
With brave armies he crosses the ocean,
Where an ocean of blood will be shed!

He stands in the land of the stranger,
A foeman, yet dreams not of danger;
And burning for Glory, he sought her
Through fields red with fire and slaughter,
  Nor shrunk from the horrors he spread!

Had he braved but the battle, how glorious,
  Had been his own trophies of fame;
Though the foeman had risen victorious,
  His shield had been free from the shame:
He had shown himself, spite of defeat,
The hero—the last to retreat;
Ever eager and fond in the sally,
Ever prompt for the desperate rally,
  The *cri de guerre* taking his name!

Alas for thee, child of Ambition!
  Not the glory thou won'st may atone
For the shame of that sad coalition,
  Which thy country herself must disown!
Not the grief of the land which deplores thee,
Nor the tears of that love who adores thee,
And who guilty will never believe thee—
None of these, hapless youth, can retrieve thee
  The whiteness of soul thou hast known!

And well, in thy dungeon of sorrow,
  In the night which to thee is the last,
May'st thou brood o'er that terrible morrow,
  Which must shame and discredit thy past.
Well, if dreaming of love, in glad bowers,
Thou canst woo back the rapturous hours,

When thy Delia* was fond, and thy vision
Still roving through regions elysian,
  Saw no single star overcast!

Ah! dearly thou pay'st for the error,
  And well, in that moment of gloom,
May'st thou shudder to gaze on the Terror,
  That links with dishonor thy doom!
To die, with each gallant hope baffled,
Were enough; but to die on the scaffold! †
What though Westminster Abbey enshrines thee, ‡
Yet the garland her tribute entwines thee,
  Hangs drooping with shame on thy tomb.

We blame thee that, worthy of glory,
  Thou forsook'st its fair shrine for a shade;
We weep thee, that, born but for story,
  Thou blott'st the fair record thou 'st made;
That, if seen 'mongst the names that men cherish,
Thine own were far fitter to perish;
Or, if rousing one other emotion,
It is grief, that such gallant devotion
  On so lowly an altar was laid.

---

* The reader will remember the pretty little song of André, beginning:

Return, enraptured hours,
  When Delia's heart was kind!"

Nor need he be reminded of Miss Seward's monody.

† André shuddered when he beheld the scaffold. He had hoped, to the last, that he would have been permitted, as he implored, to die the death of a soldier, that is, by shot. But his offense, according to the usage of nations, denied him the privilege.

‡ There is a monument to the memory of André in Westminster Abbey. England honored the offense which she could not justify.

SONNET.—DAYS VANISH.

DAYS vanish, and still other days arise,
  Like these to disappear: and still we crave
  From Time, indulgence—with a yawning Grave
Beneath us, that, with ceaseless utterance, cries:
"Ye ripen fast for me—the moment flies
  When ye should ripen for eternity;
Be diligent, if ye would take the prize
  Wrought for performance in humility;
In exercise of goodness, make ye wise;
  Each toiling in his station, as is meet:
  For still, however slow, the hours will fleet
Too fast for the most diligent! Your eyes
Will close on mightiest projects, still unwrought,
That were the favorite creatures of your thought."

TO THE SEA.

ON MY FIRST VOYAGE.

I.

I HEAR thee through thy voices, mighty Sea!
  I watch thee through thy billows, never stay'd;
Thine is the sleepless march of destiny,
  Thine is the might, in majesty array'd,
  That mocks the ambitious, makes the fond afraid;
Laughing alike at human strength and prayer;
  Rolling thy sullen waves o'er hearts that made
Their trust in thee to waft them to the dear,
Who still survey thy deeps in hopefulness and fear!

II.

The awe that is unbounded fills my soul,
  As I behold thee, limitless and lone;
Driving still onward, scorning all control;
  Keeping thy march, that never may be done,
  While man surveys thee, and the reverend sun
Directs thy course along the mighty deeps:
  Thou seek'st a goal that never may be won,
With race for aye renewing—seldom sleeps
Thy wing that never tires, thy form that never creep

III.

The frail barque bears me, bounding o'er thy breast,
  Yet am I not thy master! In my hand
I grasp no bridle which shall bid thee rest,
  No curb which may subdue thee to command,
  No scourge to make thee tremble and to stand;
Thou laugh'st at human conqueror—though thy mood,
  The mood of power in sport, at moments bland,
Moves thee to yield a pathway through thy flood,
To him who seeks for sway through darker seas of blood.

IV.

Upon thy shores he marshals his array,
  His soul exulting in his numerous bands;
He pants to give the signal for the fray—
  For conflicts, which shall redden all thy sands
  With human gore, and drain from distant lands
Their strength and beauty! A barbaric cry
  Begins the work of death; keen, clashing brands
Strike to the hearts of kindred; in the sky
Hurtles an iron storm from devilish enginery!

V.

Through the long day the work of death proceeds;
The terrors that once shook, familiar now,
The men of blood grow sportive in their deeds,
And rush where Rage, with grim and ghastly brow,
Shakes his red spear and aims his deadly blow!
With equal fury, a superior hate,
And better skill and strength, he meets a foe
Who stops him in his march! In scorn elate,
The conqueror strides o'er earth and does the work of fate!

VI.

Yet, Ocean, thou arisest on his path,
And half revengest all his deeds of wrong;
His navies vainly seek to fly thy wrath:
Thou hear'st no threat of pow'r, thou fear'st no thong,
Nor will thy rage permit the conflict long!
Thy trophies are oblivion! Thou dost set
Thy seal, in mountains, o'er the fierce and strong;
Vain are the toils of valor!—never yet
Hath force such force o'ercome—hath foe such foeman met!

VII.

Earth covers not her victims: man may slay,
But still the proofs of human crime remain—
No friendly hand to hide them from the day,
Conveys the bloody corses of the slain
To the veil'd realms of silence, from the plain
Late shaken by their thunders! But thy power
Needs no appeal for Heaven's benignant rain,
To cleanse from crimson sand, bruis'd leaf and flower,
And shuddering eyes of man the blood proofs of thy hour!

VIII.

The winds that gather on thy breast by night,
Bear to the distant cities all the tale
Thou deign'st them, of the forms which in their sight
Held hearts most precious! Thou hast heard the wail
That followed thy dread tidings, and thy gale
Has mock'd their griefs, and new aroused their fears
For others, like the lost ones, who make sail,
Trusting thy mercies! Many a watcher hears
Thy storms, that rise by night, with trembling and in tears!

IX.

The thin plank only keeps me from thy grasp;
The thin sail only lifts me o'er thy breast;
Thy mighty arms seem stretching out to clasp—
Thy mighty passions, in thy roar exprest,
Seem toiling now, and bounding to arrest
The flight of thy new victim!—madly glare
Thy vengeful eyes of terror!—thou would'st wrest
Thy prey, despite the mercy which would spare—
The mercy born of love, sole sovereign every where!

X.

Still mighty, though thy wilder mood be stay'd,
Thou mov'st not less my homage, that I feel
Thy billows baffled, and thy storms, that play'd
With wrecks, subdued to airs of May, that steal
Around me with a blessing, and reveal
Visions of gentlest climes; sweet streams that glide
Through groves and broad savannahs, where the seal
Has never shut the fountain—where the pride
That vexes human hope, is forc'd from Nature's side.

XI.

And peace is o'er the land, even as a veil
  That holds the freshening waters—as the dove,
Unharm'd and harmless, that descends the dale,
  And glides the social emblem of the grove,
  Whose inmates, in their attribute of love,
Acknowledge a superior law to ours;
  There still the sole communion helps to prove
The principle of promise for our bowers—
Love, which alone can charm the serpent from their flowers.

XII.

That love shall spell thy tempests, mighty Sea!
  Its voice of power is on thee, and confess'd,
Thy tossing limbs are fetter'd! Thou shalt be
  Subdued, even as an infant sunk to rest—
  Thou, that with giant limbs and heaving breast,
Strove 'gainst the heavens, and leagued with storm, arose
  Like one with fiendish enemies possessed:
Mad with unmeasured wrath, still prompt for blows,
Denied repose thyself, denying all repose!

XIII.

Roll on! roll on!—thy billows bear me far—
  And if my bones must whiten in the wave,
Beneath the influence of malignant star,
  I would not ask from fate a kinder grave,
  Nor offer up the homage which might save!
It might be longer life were longer wo;
  And he whom fortune still hath will'd to brave,
Might, safely rendered to his home below,
Find young affection's tear had long since ceased to flow.

RATTING. BY A YOUNG MOUSE, SIR.

When the old rats run from the falling house,
Show me the crevice shall shelter the mouse.
I am a mouse of the humblest pretensions,
Modest in appetite as in dimensions;
And when the house was in safest conditions,
Never sought any but humblest positions;
Kept in the cellar, or ranged in the garret,
Never once sought in the parlor to star it;
And now, when the prospect grows thorny and thicketty,
And the big rats run from the lodgings grown ricketty,
'Tis my just right, to be urged with propriety,
For some snug crevice in decent society.
I have my instincts, as well as my cousin,
And hate to be tumbled out just when I'm browsing;
I have a relish, like him, for good lodging,
And follow him closely when need is for dodging:
Never would quit a good fabric and feeding,
As long as 'twould shelter a rat of good breeding;
But when timbers are aching, and rafters are quaking,
And all the old house into flinders is shaking,
The maxim that then the old rats seem to mind most,
Be mine, and "the Devil, I say, take the hindmost!"
No doubt there is many a clever young mouse, sir,
Most anxious to find himself high in our house, sir;
Much too blind with ambition, to note its condition,
And see that 'tis far beyond help of physician;
But the wiser, who've lodged in it long, are more able
To judge if the fabric's sufficiently stable.
For my part, I follow the old rat, my cousin,
And will cheerfully yield up my place to a dozen.

Let them find out the truth for themselves when they've
pack'd up,
That the lodging was never the thing it was crack'd up;
But in its best seasons was never a house, sir,
Quite so properly built for the mouse as the *mouser*;
And fatal for rats of that blockhead fraternity,
Too soon from the apron strings freed of maternity.
But enough for us now! Oh! could I be shown a
Snug crevice which boasts of no absolute owner,
Into which I could slip, safe in cover and clover,
Till the old house is down and the rumpus blown over:
Where safe in my dignities, free from all dangers,
The public and I should henceforward be strangers.

NOW TELL ME.

Now tell me, now tell me, an hundred times o'er,
Dost love me, until thou canst love me no more?
Dost thou grieve when I'm gone, dost thou joy when I'm
near?
Dost sadden with sorrow until I appear?
Dost start when my name is but spoken, and then
Hark, blushing, in hope it be spoken again?—
Now tell me, now tell me, an hundred times o'er,
Dost love me, until thou canst love me no more?
Now tell me—oh, tell me!
Dost love me, until thou canst love me no more?

I've told thee, I've told thee, an hundred times
I love thee, until I can love thee no more!
I grieve when thou goest, and I grieve till I hear
Thy voice in the hall and thy foot on the stair.

I blush when they name thee, and till they repeat
The name that's so precious, my heart stops to beat.
Oh! I tell thee again, as I've told thee before,
I love thee, until I can love thee no more!
I've told thee, I've told thee,
A thousand before—I can love thee no more, I can love
thee no more!

LINGER AWHILE!

Linger awhile, awhile!
Too sweet's the hour to part,
While such raptures beguile
Each tenderly twining heart.
Linger awhile, awhile!
Oh! let thy fond lips rest,
Clinging, close clinging to mine;
Let me feel the warm beat of thy breast,
And thy arms about me twine!
Awhile, oh linger awhile!

Ah! the delirium! Hush
These tremors that shake thy soul!
Dear heart! I feel all the gush
Of thy life streams as they roll!
Linger awhile, awhile!
One moment! How keen is the sweet!
The parting hour so near!
Ah, me! is the mortal bliss complete,
Unless it be twinn'd with the tear?
Awhile, oh linger awhile!

STAR THAT WOO'ST ME!

I.

Star that woo'st me from yon height,
Could my erring steps pursue thee,
Sweeter were the sad delight,
With which now I view thee.
I behold thee sinking fast,
Soon to rise o'er Asian fountains,
Till my strain'd eye rests at last
On the dark blue mountains!

II.

Yet a pleasure warms my heart:
When thou mak'st those vales elysian,
Thou wilt equal bliss impart
To another's vision;
Sure, some young heart watching there,
Turns to yon opposing mountain,
Sad until thy beams appear,
Lighting up her fountain.

III.

Thou between that heart and mine
Shalt exchange the sweetest sorrow,
So when mutual souls repine,
Mutual bliss they borrow:
Oh! if that sad watcher there
Be some pale, sad, lonely maiden,
Then the missive thou shalt bear
Shall with love be laden.

BALLAD.—BENEDICT ARNOLD.

YES, long shall our country, recalling
  The deeds thou hast done, speak thy name,
And though from thy proud station falling,
  All shall not be lost in thy shame!
While she tells how thy crime had betray'd her
To the rage of the reckless invader,
Shall she also repeat the proud story,
Where thy gallantry led her to glory.

Yet, alas, even valor redeems not
  The life once deliver'd to shame;
The hero we love, it beseems not,
  That one shadow should darken his fame!
He must neither know falsehood, nor falter,
But as pure as the fire on the altar,
He must speed, in his garments of whiteness,
To the highest, from brightness to brightness!

Oh! the madness of soul, that, when holy,
  And proud, were the deeds thou had'st done,
Could win thee to worship so lowly,
  And lose thee the green laurels won!
Those left on thy brow do not grace thee,
They but show how thy treasons debase thee;
Yet thou might'st have gone down to the ages,
The glory, not shame, on our pages.

Ah! well shall it be for our nation,
  If but one of its bright lights be gone;
Stricken out from the height of its station,
  In the hour when most proudly it shone!

Thy fame, as thy shame, shall we cherish,
Since they teach us how glory may perish;
And our young shall be tutor'd to name thee,
While they loathe the foul deeds that beshame thee.

I BLAME YOU NOT.

I.

I BLAME you not!—I blame you not!
But, dearest love, why came you not?
  And such a night—
  A very moon and star delight,
  With pearly clouds so softly white;
  And, 'mong the trees,
  As 'twere a Love itself at ease,
  So frolic and so sweet a breeze!—
Ah! dearest love, I blame you not!
I sorrow—but why came you not?

II.

I blame you not!—I blame you not!
But prithee, sweet, why came you not?
  To loss of hours,
  Delicious, as if fed on flowers,
  Whose April tears are joys to ours!
  Ah! lost the eyes,
  Whose smile alone can make our skies,
  Who heeds, though moon and stars arise?
Ah! moon and stars could shame you not,
Why came you not? why came you not?

LOVE'S REQUIEM.—LIGHT OF HEARTS!

LIGHT of Hearts and Love,
  When mine eye first found thee,
How, in triumph, did'st thou move,
  Blisses beaming round thee;
Oh! the following worship there!
  Oh! the homage given;
Winter shed no snowy tear,
  In thy summer heaven!

I did homage then,
  With whole-heart devotion,
Nor from eyes of other men,
  Hid each wild emotion!
Would that hour we both had died,
  With no doubt to wring us,
Not a self-reproach to chide,
  No remorse to sting us!

We had then been blest—
  Naught of anguish knowing,
Save, in that one wild unrest,
  Souls with joy o'erflowing:
Lost in dreams of such delight,
  That increase of measure
Were but agony and blight,
  Not increase of pleasure!

So, perchance, it came
  That the sweet grew sadness:
And the pulsing blood of flame
  Rose at last to madness!

So it came, we fell apart;
  Eyes had no more seeing,
And that lake of fire, the heart,
  Swept away Love's being.

Never ours the crime
  Of crushing the rose in its blooming;
Never ours the guilt sublime
  The rapture at richest dooming!
They tore us apart, the powers,
  That had never a soul for heaven,
Smote the life of our heart's young flowers
  As with bolt of the fiery levin.

See'st thou the summer-time come,
  As of old, with its rosy fleetness;
And the buds—dost thou feel the bloom,
  As they strive with thy lip for sweetness?
Oh! what a mock was the dream,
  That told of all beautiful creatures;
Fair, floating free, with a golden gleam,
  And such wooing and winning features!

Yet vainer to weep those hours!
  As if tears could speak for the sorrow,
That followed that joyous night of ours,
  In the dawn of that terrible morrow!
Better laughter than tears—
  The maniac shriek of that demon wo,
Rising from deeps of a thousand years,
  As the worm, still gnawing, creeps to and fro.

JOY! JOY! FOR THE DAY-STAR!

I.

Joy! joy! for the Day-Star is breaking
  O'er all these wild forests and shores;
From a slumber of ages awaking,
  Her light again Liberty pours.
O'er the wastes of the New World ascending,
  Where but lately the red savage trod,
Young Freedom her war-song is blending
  With the anthem that rises to God!
The strong man starts up from his sleeping,
And the bright blade to sunlight is leaping!
    O clarion song! O glorious clarion song!
      Prevail above the hills—prevail! prevail!
    Make mountain echoes happy to prolong
      Thy choral burden, never more to fail!

II.

Oh! the young virgin land shall no longer
  By the despot's foul foot be debased;
The God in his own realm grows stronger,
  And his altars now rise undefaced.
From mountain, from river, from valley,
  The songs of the true heart ascend,
And the brave to the dread conflict rally,
  And the doom and the danger impend;
The blood of the free streams like water,
And the hills wear the garment of slaughter.
    O clarion song! awaken a new song—
      Proclaim how Freedom's battle must prevail!
    That Right shall trample down the hosts of Wrong,
      Till none be living left to tell the tale.

III.

'Tis the truth that hath made us victorious
  For what were our weapons of fight?
The boar-spear and bow are made glorious,
  'Gainst the legions all mailéd in might!
'Twas the virgin of Freedom that won us
  The fame and the spoils of the field;
And she flung her white mantle upon us,
  And this was our banner and shield;
And we build her an altar of ages,
Which shall mock all the enemy's rages.
    Pour, clarion, pour the ancient anthem out,
      So that new men, with former deeds elate,
    Shall face the glorious music with a shout,
      And front the spoiling foeman with a Fate!

LUTHER IN THE SHADES;

OR, THE DOCTORS OVER A DOUBTFUL SUBJECT.*

"Sore is my grief," cried Luther, with a frown;
  "My sorrow will not let me sleep nor sup,
Lest Johnny B——† should write me *down*,
  And Johnny B——‡ fail to write me *up!*"
"Pshaw!" muttered Calvin, "leave the dogs their bone;
  Rather rejoice in peace, my ghostly brother,
That you escape the *potions* of the one,
  And can not hear the *preachings* of the other!'

* Impromptu, on an interminable controversy in the newspapers touching the moral character of Martin Luther. The disputants were a Doctor of Medicine and a Doctor of Divinity.

† Three syllables here.

‡ Two syllables here. The Doctors, by a pretty coincidence, possess the same initials.

THE TEARS OF VALOR.

[It is mentioned in Moore's Life of Byron that the Polish officers in the army of Napoleon burst into tears when the name of Kosciusko was spoken in their hearing.]

I.

THEY wept to hear the Hero's name!—
  Ah! had they wept to emulate
His spirit's hope, his patriot aim,
Their tears were worthy of his fame,
  And they were worthy—of his fate!

But tears are toys—are mocks—unless
They rouse the soul which makes success;
Unless they rouse the patriot mood,
Oft baffled, never yet subdued,
  Which weeps not oft, but when in vain
  It strives to snap its country's chain,
And then—its tears are tears of blood!

These, from the deep soul's deepest source,
Give birth to Valor's mightiest force;
  Wake noble anger; sting the heart,
  Forgetful of its sacred part,
That long has slumber'd, to *Remorse:*
And this to stern *Resolve*—that braves
  A thousand deaths, of strife and pain,
Striving for honorable graves,
  But not to weep, or sleep, again!
Unlike that vainer *wo*, that cries,
  Still feels, but dare not seek in fight
Its fierce and fatal destinies,
  Though all its country bleeds in sight!

II.

They wept the Exile's fate and fame!—
Ah! could they but as proudly aim,
  His name would be a word to lead,
And they had sprung at Freedom's call
  To kindred fame, in equal deed,
And burst their own and nation's thrall!

III.

How vain the memory which would shed
  But tears o'er Kosciusko's name!
  Far better if they fell in shame
For country lost, and honor fled;
All but the cruel memory dead,
That in the past triumphant glows,
  On many a page of living fire,
When peerless Sobieski rose,
And with great soul and mighty blows
  Pluck'd Europe from the Moslem's ire!
Ah! sad reproach, such glorious tale,
For those who only wake to wail!

Call up these spirits! Let them be
His, first, who made all Europe free—
Great Sobieski! Next, the pure,
True soul these vacant souls deplore—
The man who strove, with countless odds,
For Poland's own domestic gods!
What think *they* of these men who weep,
Crawl, crouch, in foreign service creep,
And wake to wail, and wail to sleep?
Their spirits, if on earth, would crave
A future like the past to brave;

Not, craven-like, remain to boast
Existence, to their nation lost;
But in the fierce, unequal strife—
  The last sad struggle—still assert
That liberty, more dear than life,
  That makes the life's life of the heart!

The proper tears, by valor given,
  Are blood-drops wrung from Freedom's wo,
Pure, sacred, in the sight of Heaven,
  And blessing those for whom they flow!
Not woman's offering—weakness all—
That loathes—yet drinks—its cup of gall,
And downward, step by step, to save,
Sinks from the dastard to the slave;
Then, when the dregs of life are run,
  Through all its foul and base degrees,
  Drained to its vilest, bitterest lees,
Weeps for the deeds—it *might* have done!

EPIGRAM.—BOWS AND KNOTS.

EMMELINE boasts two strings to her bow—
  Might I teach her a wiser thing,
Then would the thoughtless damsel know,
  Better to carry two beaux to her string!
Sukey, with luckier judgment led,
  Wisely and silently shapes her lot,
And, never with idle delusions fed,
  Soon turns her one bow into a knot.

WHEN WE PART.

I.

When we part, shall the smile that now kindles thy cheek
  Give way to the tear of a longing regret?
Will thine eye tell the tale that thy tongue may not speak,
  Like the blue sky in April, the rain falling yet?
Will the heart that now tenderly throbs at my touch,
  With a thrill so delicious that rapture affrights,
Forget the rich joys that have bless'd us so much,
  All forgotten in newer delights?

II.

We part, and the long threatened shadows appear,
  To ruffle the sweet of our sky so serene;
But our sun shall shine out in its lustre more clear,
  And our landscape of love glow again in its green.
The true heart's own smile will in time clear the skies,
  And Love is a power of most wonderful art,
To conquer the barriers, however they rise,
  Between his desire and his heart.

III.

And my faith, ever fond, makes me brave in this hour:
  Well I know thou wilt weep for and wait my return,
Nor forget, in thy beauty's sure progress to power,
  The lessons thy heart found so grateful to learn.
I have faith in thy faith, though the ocean may part;
  Thou wilt nothing forget of the love thou wast taught;
For were not our lessons all gotten by heart,
  Love teaching both Memory and Thought?

AH! NO MORE OF YOUR ETHICS!

Ah! no more of your ethics and morals,
  They but pucker the sweetest of faces;
The muses that labor for laurels,
  Have never been famed for the graces:
Be a woman more loving than prudent,
  And be sure of more grateful successes;
Your chiding repels the young student,
  Who were won by your smiles and caresses.

Yet if ethics and stuff I must con over,
  'Tis something that you're the professor;
And if to your sect I am won over,
  'Twill be while you're mother confessor.
As our chaplain, your chance of succeeding
  Is better, a thousand times better,
Than such as we've had, of no breeding—
  Antiques, but not gems, in black letter.

Your eye beams with right inspiration,
  And teaches a pleasanter knowledge
Than any, misnamed Education,
  That but worries, not wins, through the college.
And that mouth, with its ripe recitation,
  Ah! wherefore thus torture its beauty
With such crudities, full of vexation,
  That but dull us with lessons of duty?

How different far the expression,
  When, lost in a fancy, the woman
Drops text, and dilates in digression,
  That shows us our tutor is human!

Such wisdom then beams in each feature,
  We grow wise through a glorious emotion;
Such divinity shines through the creature,
  That Jack Dunce is imbued with devotion.

With the priestess herself so angelic,
  Having lips so persuasive, 'twill hap ill,
Though she may not beguile to the relic,
  If she does not persuade to the chapel.
'Tis enough for my faith that you spell us,
  Through the witchery of wit, to be dutiful;
And though sometimes most wicked young fellows,
  We grow good through our love of the beautiful.

TOGETHER.

TOGETHER, dear friend, together,
    Thirty long years,
We have boated and galloped together;
    Shared the smiles, shared the tears,
    Of thirty long years,
        Together!

We've kept loving faith with each other,
    Thirty long years—
In the friend ever finding the brother!
    Had no fears, battling cares,
    Of thirty long years,
        Together!

And the march was made easy together,
Thirty long years;
As we strode o'er the height and the heather,
And with cheers met the fears
Of thirty long years,
Together!

Slept in one blanket together,
Oft in sad years;
In the woods, and in all sorts of weather;
Keeping faith through the fears
Of thirty long years,
Together!—

Had our gay humors together,
In youthful years,
When our hopes and our youth were in feather;
Snapt our fingers at cares,
For thirty long years,
Together!

From boyhood to manhood together;
Now, in late years,
When we're reaching the sunset together,
The memory still cheers,
Of our long loving years
Together!

How long we may still keep together,
In future years,
Matters not, if we sleep 'neath the heather,
In repose, at the close
Of the long journey together—
Thirty long years
Together! Together!

I DEFY THEE TO FORGET.

I.

They have torn us apart, but by those angel eyes,
And the sweet glance they gave when first we met;
By our first vow, so warm yet so unwise,
That still will cheer me when all hope hath set;
By my fond murmurs, by thy sweet replies,
Each precious memory fondly cherish'd yet,
Thy failing accents, and thy speaking sighs,
I dare thee—I defy thee to forget!

II.

By all we both must cherish of the past,
When thy dark eyes a darker fate had met;
That passionate kiss, the dearest as the last,
Whose sweetness on my lips is lingering yet:
By thy brave vow to brave with me the blast,
Nor in the world's scorn suffer one regret;
By all the love thou gav'st me, and still hast,
My heart defies thine ever to forget!

III.

Thou still must love me on through weal and wo,
Howe'er the wall between us hath been set;
They can not teach thy bosom not to know
How dear have been the raptures we regret;
Thou know'st I love thee, and thine eyes will flow,
To think how mine must evermore be wet:
By these I triumph—these defeat the blow!—
These dare thee—these defy thee to forget!

STANZAS.—WELL HAST THOU SAID.

I.

Well hast thou said, that mine was but a madness,
  The toys I sought, the pleasant hopes pursued;
Sweetly they seem'd to smile, and shapes of gladness
  Gather'd in fancy, won as soon as woo'd.
But soothly has the sage denounced the pleasure
  Thus quickly yielding to the grasp and lure;
How small its worth, how very brief its measure,
  How formed to cheat, how little to endure!

II.

There is nought sure but trial and transition,
  And best he wills, who to his task hath brought
The stern resolve to work in his condition,
  Nor to its profit, nor its loss, give thought.
The duty is not less assign'd to being,
  Though not a smile of fortune crowns the toil;
There is no refuge from the task in fleeing,
  And wisdom makes it happiness to moi

III.

Not from the bird or beast we take our moral—
  Man, only, hath the privilege to wear
His crown of thorns—far nobler than the laurel—
  And wins his immortality from care.
He forfeits his high destiny, imploring
  That freedom which is subject to him still;
The dog that sleeps, the bird that sings in soaring—
  These are but lowly vassals at his will.

THE MINIATURE.

There needs no painter's skill to trace
The lineaments of that dear face,
Or save, for memory's future tears,
The charms that fade in failing years.
Such portrait, too, as this, I fain
Would have thee feel as less than vain,
Since not, alone, were these the charms,
Dear Heart, that won me to thy arms.

Think'st thou that smile, though rich it be,
That eye so bright, those tresses free,
This little dimple, where the Loves
Sit smiling, as in sunny groves;
That cheek so rich, that neck so fair,
Each nameless grace, of glance and air—
Think'st thou that these, alone, could bind
In faith so fond, so wild a mind?

As soft a lip, perchance, as this,
Hath bless'd me oft with Fanny's kiss;
And Rosa hath an eye whose glow
Would plant a starlight in the snow!
Not these! Not these! But in thy breast
The lurking love that mine confess'd;
'Twas not, alone, for charms in thee,
But that thy heart was full of me!

Take back these lines, whose language weak
But tells that painting can not speak;
That, while it makes some beauties glow,
But mourns for those it can not show.

A portrait drawn with dearer art,
Lies perfect, sweet one, in my heart;
And truthful still, whene'er I gaze,
Thy love, as well as look, betrays.

OH! FRAILER THAN HOPE!

Oh! frailer than hope or than pleasure,
Than the tints of the bow fleeting fast,
Was the dear, but too vanishing treasure,
Our early loves won from the past.

Thou had'st beauty, and spells of a power,
Which the heart that has trembled like mine,
Can never forget, in the hour
That shows me the falsehood in thine.

Alas, for thyself! when the season
Of beauty is over, and years
Shall demand the calm office of reason,
And a love which, in faith, soothes its fears:

When thy beauty, so precious, is fading,
And thy heart, growing cheerless and lone,
In despair, its own falsehood upbraiding,
Seeks vainly the love which has flown!

When that hour, with its pang, is upon thee,
And thou look'st o'er the wreck of thy bliss,
Thou wilt feel 'tis thy guilt hath undone thee,
And that hour shall avenge me for this.

STANZAS AT SEA.—SHADOWS.

I.

The night is wild, but sweet to me
  The uncertain music that it brings;
And, o'er the darkly heaving sea,
  I hear the rushing might of wings:
That wailing wo that seems to brood
  Along the bosom of the deep,
Wakes in my soul a kindred mood,
  And I must watch, and may not sleep.

II.

Let me but muse—and with no sound,
  Save that which sleepless ocean bears,
To break the silence settling round,
  And vex my sense, and check my tears;
Be but this hour of gloom my own,
  Give but my bosom's mood its way,
And with my wayward thoughts alone,
  Let memory have her holy sway.

III.

A thousand shadows cross my sight,
  A thousand voices fill mine ears;
Eyes, perish'd now, that once were bright,
  Crowd, gathering round me, dim with tears!
Ghosts of a former day, they come,
  With thousand fancies dear as they;
They lift me high, they bear me home—
  I'm in the morning of the day!

IV.

The roaring of the sea is still,
  The wind is music, as when first,
By Ashley's wave and Cooper's hill,
  On childhood's eager ear it burst:
No more a wanderer on the deep,
  A homeless, hopeless child of care,
Eyes watch me now, with pride that weep,
  And sweetest lips proclaim me dear.

V.

A word has brought them all once more—
  The white-hair'd sire, the brother tall,
The gentle mother—she who bore,
  Yet bless'd the pang, the worst of all,
That none but mothers ever know!—
  The sturdy friend, as true as brave,
That stood between me and the foe,
  And pluck'd me from the greedy wave.

VI.

Sweet, holy phantoms!—how they rise!
  They pass, they smile, they wave their hands,
And beckon, blessing, to the skies,
  That open at their high commands!
Ah! wherefore seek the wizard's power,
  To bring us back the loved and lost,
When, by a prayer, and in an hour,
  We scale the heavens and hail the host!

VII.

The heart hath in itself a spell,
  More strong than wizard ever knew:
'Tis but to cherish memory well,
  And keep the faith forever true;

To cast the clamoring crowd aside,
  Yield the whole soul to thought and love,
And Heaven's blue portals open wide,
  And Pity watches from above.

VIII.

She watches, and her children come:
  White-wingéd Charity and Truth—
Hope, seraph of celestial bloom,
  As true as time and warm as youth;
They bear the boon the prisoner prays,
  God's first and fondest gift they bring—
Primeval love!—whose blesséd rays
  Send healing on affliction's wing.

IX.

Their light is on my heart: the weight
  That bore me down—the cold, cold gloom,
Are gone! The raging hell of hate,
  That vex'd my spirit, gives it room;
The sunlight warms my dungeon now,
  No more the sufferer sighs alone;
The fever passes from his brow,
  The sorrow and the night are gone.

X.

If now to die, when from the heart
  The hate and bitterness have fled—
When selfish hopes and fears depart,
  And love and truth remain instead:
'Twere now to join that happy train,
  That beckoning bless and upward fly;
To triumph in the past again,
  And win the future, in the sky!

CALM AT SEA.

I.

Calm o'er the deep! The heavy sail
Hangs flapping from the mast;
The sea, without a single gale,
Subsides in sleep at last;
And glaring through its depths, the sun
Looks down with fiercest light,
Till, far as eye can stretch, but one
Vast mirror hangs in sight.

II.

A world from all the world apart,
Chain'd idly on the sea,
How droops the eye, how sinks the heart,
Vain wishing to be free!
How dread the fear that fills the thought,
That winds may never rise,
To waft us from this weary spot,
Beneath these burning skies!

III.

The Pirate rears his bloody flag,
And leaves the Cuban shore: *
Blow, breezes, blow! for if ye lag,
We hail our homes no more!
And should our hapless fate be such,
We'll wrong not nature so,
To think that hearts who've sigh'd so much,
Will feel no touch of wo.

* This was written in 1824, and when Cuba was infested by piratical craft.

IV.

Ripple, ye waters, into smiles,
  This sun-spread bondage break,
While, far behind, Bahama's isles
  Shall vanish in our wake.
Nor will your dangers fright us more,
  Blow, tempests of the deep!
I better love old Ocean's roar,
  Than this his stagnant sleep!

BALLAD.—DORCHESTER.

Not with irreverent thought and feeling, I resign
The tree that was a chronicle in other days than mine;
Its mossy branches crown'd the grove, when, hastily array'd,
Came down the gallant partisan to battle in the shade;
It saw his fearless eye grow dark, it heard his trumpet cry,
When at its roots, the combat o'er, he laid him down to die;
The warm blood gushing from his heart hath stain'd the sod below—
That tree shall be my chronicle, for it hath seen it flow.

Sweet glide thy waters, Ashley, and pleasant on thy banks
The mossy oak and massy pine stand forth in solemn ranks;
They crown thee in a fitting guise, since, with a gentle play,
Through bending groves, and circling dells, thou tak'st thy lonely way:
Thine is the summer's loveliness—thy winter hath its charms,
Thus sheltered in thy mazy course, beneath their Druid arms;
And thine the recollection old, which honors thy decline,
When happy thousands saw thee rove, and Dorchester was thine.

But Dorchester is thine no more: its gallant pulse is still,
The wild-cat prowls among its graves, and screams the whip-
poor-will;
A mournful spell is on its homes, where solitude, supreme,
Still, couching in her tangled woods, dreams one unbroken
dream:
The cotter seeks a foreign home—the cottage roof is down,
The ivy clambers all uncheck'd above the steeple's crown;
And doubly gray, with grief and years, the old church tot-
tering stands—
Ah! how unlike that holy home not built with human hands!

These ruins have their story, and with a reverent fear
I glide beneath the broken arch and through the passage drear;
The hillock at my feet grows warm—beneath it beats a heart,
Whose pulses wake to utterance, whose accents make me start;
That heart hath beat in battle when the thunder cloud was high,
And death, in every form of fate, careering through the sky;
Beside it now another heart, to peace but lately known,
Beats with a kindred pulse but hath a story of its own.

Ah! sad the fate of maiden whose lover falls in fight,
Condemned to bear, in widowhood, the lonely length of light:
The days that come without a sun—the nights that bring no
sleep—
The long, long watch—the weariness—the same sad toil, to
weep!
Methinks the call is happiness, when sudden sounds the strain
That summons back the exiled heart of love to heaven again;
No trumpet tone of battle, but a soft note sweetly clear,
Like that which even now is heard when doves are cooing near.

1835.

MUTINEER'S SONG OF TAHITI.

[THE reader need not be reminded of the tragedy of Christian and his comrades, better known, perhaps, through the poem of Byron, than by the narrative of Captain Bligh.]

Now spread the sail for ocean's joys,
At last our souls are free—
Tahiti's charms are ours, my boys,
Tahiti soon will be:
Its women, glowing as the sun,
That wait us wild and warm,
With eyes and hearts already won,
Fond heart and blooming form.

The gem on ocean's breast, my boys,
Tahiti's balmy clime,
Persuades us far from Europe's noise,
Its tyranny and crime;
We fly to placid waters,
Fair fruits and sunny groves,
The young world's virgin daughters,
That look a thousand loves.

Ho! for that clime of tropic joys!
Tahiti's breeze blows fair,
And on its pinions fleet, my boys,
We soon shall revel there!
Done then shall be the toils of sea;
Unvex'd by tyrant powers,
We'll win a realm where love is free,
That island home of ours!

KING'S MOUNTAIN.—A BALLAD.

I.

Hark! 'tis the voice of the mountain,
 And it speaks to our heart in its pride,
As it tells of the bearing of heroes
 Who compassed its summit and died!
How they gathered to the strife as the eagles,
 When the foeman had clamber'd the height!
How, with scent keen and eager as beagles,
 They hunted him down for the fight!
 Hurrah!

II.

Hark! through the gorge of the valley!
 'Tis the bugle that tells of the foe;
Our own quickly sounds for the rally,
 And we snatch down the rifle and go!
As the hunter who hears of the panther,
 Each arms him and leaps to his steed,
Rides forth through the desolate antre,
 With his knife and his rifle at need.
 Hurrah!

III.

From a thousand deep gorges they gather—
 From the cot lowly perch'd by the rill,
The cabin half hid in the heather,
 'Neath the crag where the eagle keeps still.
Each lonely at first in his roaming,
 Till the vale on the sight opens fair,
And he sees the low cot through the gloaming,
 When his bugle gives tongue to the air.
 Hurrah!

IV.

Thus a thousand brave hunters assemble,
For the hunt of the insolent foe;
And soon shall his myrmidons tremble
'Neath the shock of the thunderbolt's blow.
Down the lone heights now wind they together,
As the mountain brooks flow to the vale,
And now, as they group on the heather,
The keen scout delivers his tale.
Hurrah!

V.

"The British—the Tories are on us,
And now is the moment to prove,
To the women whose virtues have won us,
That our virtues are worthy their love!
They have swept the vast valleys below us,
With fire, to the hills from the sea;
And here would they seek to o'erthrow us,
In a realm which our eagle makes free!
Hurrah!"

VI.

No war counsel suffer'd to trifle
With the hours devote to the deed,
Swift follow'd the grasp of the rifle,
Swift follow'd the bound to the steed;
And soon to the eyes of our yeomen,
All panting with rage at the sight,
Gleam'd the long wavy tents of the foeman,
As he lay in his camp on the height.
Hurrah!

VII.

Grim dash'd they away as they bounded,
  The hunters to hem in the prey,
And with Deckard's long rifles surrounded,
  Then the British rose fast to the fray;
And never with arms of more vigor
  Did their bayonets press through the strife,
Where, with every swift pull of the trigger,
  The sharp-shooters dashed out a life.
        Hurrah!

VIII.

'Twas the meeting of eagles and lions,
  'Twas the rushing of tempests and waves,
Insolent triumph 'gainst patriot defiance,
  Born freemen 'gainst sycophant slaves;
Scotch Ferguson sounding his whistle,
  As from danger to danger he flies,
Feels the moral that lies in Scotch thistle,
  With its "Touch me who dare!"—and he dies!
        Hurrah!

IX.

An hour, and the battle is over,
  The eagles are rending the prey;
The serpents* seek flight into cover,
  But the Terror still stands in the way:
More dreadful the doom that on treason
  Avenges the wrongs of the state;
And the oak tree for many a season
  Bears its fruit for the vultures of Fate! †
        Hurrah!

* The Tories.

† The Tory chiefs were hung after the battle.

SONNETS.—OH, FRIEND! 'TIS NOT MY CHEEK.

I.

Oh, friend! 'tis not my cheek that tells the tale—
My heart is wither'd in me; all is lost
Which I had striven to shelter from the frost—
My blossoms borne away upon the gale!
I've lived in vain; and now my spirits fail;
Hopeless of succor all, by fate denied;
Rebuked as well by fortune as by pride,
My powers at waste; the toils of thirty years
Fruitless; and they for whom alone I strove,
Scornful of all the tribute in my love,
And questioning the powers which even in tears
Have labored in their honor, for their fame!
And what is left me now, but nurse my cares
In the same solitude that hides my shame?

II.

You smile at my misgiving: see me move,
Still, calm, in this cold world, forgetting nought;
And ready, at each rising of the thought,
The ancient faculty to use and prove.
Yet am I withering fast. Even as the tree,
Which the worm gnaws within, and still must gnaw,
Looks green in the gay sunlight—with no flaw—
And wears a brow erect and aspect free!—
The doom is written—the proud tree shall fall,
Sudden, with all his green tops waving high!
You see my fate in his, and his in me—
And men who seldom know even what they see,
Wonder of what disease the tree should die,
That shone so late, the wonder of them all!

BALLAD.—WAKING, I GATHER.

Waking, I gather, from silence and night,
  The peace that I never could win from the day
The sad spirit, rather, retires from the light,
  Imploring forever the daylight away.
The soul which is bounded by bonds which it hates,
  Still flies to the lonely sad shades which are free;
The heart which is wounded by loss of its mates,
  To the night shadows only for refuge may flee.

And when softly the moonlight is streaming around,
  When curling the billow, and fresh from the sea
The night breeze takes flight, with a murmuring sound,
  Then from each cold pillow, ascending to me,
Sweet spirits of sadness keep watch o'er my heart;
  The dark Doubt is fleeting the moment they come;
The fear and the madness that vex'd me depart,
  And Faith and Hope meeting, bring peace to my home.

HEAR THE TALE OF A BOYISH HEART!

I.

Hear the tale of a boyish heart;
  Hear, and be wise, when you go to woo:
Ever with boldness play your part,
  Nor weakly sigh, nor timidly sue;
Hark to the tale of a boyish heart:

As I drew near to my lady's bower,
I sung her a song that might win a flower;
Song so gentle and sweet to hear,
It had suited well in a fairy's ear;
Lowly and soft at first it rose,
And touching the sigh at its dying close.

II.

It was the song of a boyish heart,
  Vainly I sang to my lady's ear:
A minstrel came, with a bolder art,
  And he carol'd in accent loud and clear—
But 'twas no tale of a boyish heart!

His spirit was high and his soul was proud,
His song was eager, and wild, and loud,
And oh! methought, how worse than vain,
Was the chorus strong and the wild refrain;
Song so stormy and wild to hear,
Will never suit for a maiden's ear

III

Such was the thought of a boyish heart!—
  But never you sing in your lady's ear,
As if your soul were about to part,
  And you stood on the edge of a mortal fear:
Tell her the tale of a manly heart!

A maid is a woman, and not a flower,
And she loves, in her lover, the proofs of power;
His soul should be ardent, his spirit high—
For her the soft note and the tender sigh;
She may be timid and tremulous still,
But he should be one who must have his will!

WEEP O'ER WILL!

AH! through what perverse translations
  Shape we Nature's sweetest tongue,
Dulling all her fine narrations,
  Making prose of what she sung!
Nay, with less than human feeling,
  From the gentle framing ill,
And while she is love revealing,
  Shaping out the evil still.
    Bird cry—Whip-poor-will!

From that cry of bird, incessant,
  Very pitiful and sad,
Mournful, tender, if not pleasant,
  We have only drawn the bad.
Let us find the true translation
  For a chaunt the saddest heard,
Changing all to fit relation
  By a little change of word.
    Bird cry—Whip-poor-will!

"Whip-poor-will's" the vulgar version,
  Drawing counsel, harsh and hard,
From a chaunt of matchless sorrow,
  The fond Bird above the Bard.
Let the Bard the bird decypher,
  Now, while fresh the burden springs—
Blending tone with proper feeling,
  "Weep-o'er-will!" is what she sings.
    Bird cry—Weep-o'er-will!

Ay, weep o'er Will, when in yon hillock
 The Bard lies sleeping, hearing nought,
Unless, perchance, the sad cry reaches
 The spirit heights of soul and thought.
Thou'lt weep, methinks, the last of any—
 Of all, the only faithful still;
And never heed the vulgar many,
 Who whipping long would whip him still.
 Thou'lt weep o'er Will!
 Bird cry—Weep-o'er-will!

NOTE.—The little conceit in this lyric was first framed into a sonnet, which follows. I have thrown it into the lyrical form, as above, in the notion that some grateful musical effects might be produced in singing, by a clever imitation of the bird cry, by the voice and instrument.

SONNET.—WEEP O'ER WILL.

How wretched is the vulgar world's translation
 Of the great poets. Here is one who sung
In the first dusky dawning of creation,
 And yet how much we misconceive his tongue.
His saddest of all elegies—a strain,
 Like Tennyson's "In Memoriam" o'er a brother,
Expressive only of an earnest pain,
 Pity and sorrowing, which he can not smother—
We turn, with little sense and less compunction,
 Despising all its sentiment and tone,
Into a brutal, tyrannous injunction
 To scourge the sufferer, spite of all his moan.
The wo that evermore hath whipt poor Will,
 Needs Love and Mercy, now, to "weep o'er Will."

SONNETS.—THERE IS A BABE OF BEAUTY.

I.

THERE is a Babe of Beauty in each breast,
  Which, if we nurse with a discretion wise,
  Will grow to perfect likeness of the skies,
With sunniest aspect, and a soul possess'd
Of heavenward hopes and fancies; eyes of blue,
  Large, dewy, bright, and blessing; lips that blow
  Like roses in the breast of Spring: a glow
Of cheeks like sunset, blending with the dew
Of starlight; from its lips shall breathe a song
  Of summer; while in every thought, a wing
  Shall bear it upward; as when birds that sing,
From passionate raptures, dart in flight along,
Through virgin forests, singing lullabies,
That make earth leap up to embrace the skies.

II.

Alas! how little care have we to nurse
  This love-babe Beauty! As in richest wood
  We find the reptile, innocent of good—
The frog, the toad, the loathsome—and, still worse,
The venomous, the serpent!—even while sing
Birds overhead, gay colors on each wing,
And the white rose and red, the jessamine,
  And thousand other flowers of rarest hue
  And fragrance, with delicious influence woo
Our steps to wander on through mazy twine
Of the deep forest: so within the heart
  Keep dark companions, nestling close beside
This babe of beauty; and with treacherous art
  They strangle, ere its eyes may open wide.

III.

Oh! Passions base of man, that ever prey
  On manhood's best possessions: Avarice,
  Gaunt even in gluttony; Lusts, that in a trice
Mock best resolves and virtues; Appetites,
That drench the soul in madness, and still sway
  To the worst overthrow of Good Intent—
  Why are ye Fates to this sweet Innocent,
This child of fond, immaculate delights,
This Babe of Beauty? Which, if ye would nurse,
Would save ye from the bondage and the curse;
Would bring ye to the beauty in the skies;
  The beauty blessing earth; the good, pure, brave
All that ye need, and all that Heaven denies
  To him who is of his own blood the slave!

EPIGRAM. (From the Spanish.)

To seek his wife, with little profit,
The Thracian Orpheus went to Tophet:
A realm of such a sad condition,
He could not seek, on sadder mission.
Grim Pluto, vex'd at quest so human,
In anger gave him up the woman;
Yet, as the bard's song overcome him,*
Grew softened, and back took her from him.

---

* Let not the Reverend Priscian storm or stammer,
Because to rhyme we sacrifice the grammar;
'Tis not, my Byron saith, the worst of crimes,
"Kings are not more imperative than rhymes!"

EPIGRAM.—TIBBATT'S PLAYED LONG.

Tibbatt's played long at fast and loose,
But lastly into matrimony run!
And thus—'tis pity for the goose!—
Though fetter'd fast in marriage noose,
He weeps to find himself *undone!*

BALLAD.—OH! NOT TO YON GROVE!

Oh! not to yon grove!
Oh! not by that tree!
These have been sacred to Love,
Sweet, and how sacred to me!
Lead me not there! Oh, lead me not there!
There, oh, there should I greet
Shadows of glories that fast,
As they were sweet—how sweet!—
Fled with the past—the past—
Fled when most beautiful—fled, leaving me desolate here.

Oh! never that song
Breathe again in mine ear;
For a sweet season 'twas long,
Ever the sweetest to hear:
Breathe it, I pray thee, no more! Oh, breathe it no more!
Would'st thou, cruel, recall
The horror, agony, blight,
That followed so terribly, all,
That last—delirious night,
When the song was hush'd in the shriek, and for me all the music was o'er?

Go, if thou wilt, to yon grove;
  Read, if thou wilt, on yon tree;
These are too sacred to love
  Not to be terrors to me—
The heart that is blighted forever reads never the record of blight.
Never again may these eyes
  The trophies of sorrow explore;
I know that the beautiful dies,
  Let me know nothing more!
Lead me not thither, I pray thee, it were a death to my sight!

BEAUTIES LATE THAT FED ME.

Beauties late that fed me,
  Wild, in wandering mood,
Wherefore have ye led me
  To the solitude?
Why, in nightly mirage,
  To mine eyes have given
Wooing glimpses of an image
  Like a form of heaven?
And I dream on, still dream, am forevermore dreaming
Of that form, dear form, too sweet for all mortal seeming,
Which, to woo me, ye show me,
  From morning to even.

Oh! as now ye see me,
  Wearied with the quest,
From the glamour free me,
  That disturbs my rest.

Let me, in these pages,
See no shape imploring,
Saving such as gravest sages
Find their wisdom's lore in.
Take from the leaf that face, that is evermore seeming—
Seeming to woo, with a smile from those eyes upward gleaming,
Which all adore—which one more
Will die in adoring.

WITCH OF ELLANO.

I.

Damsel wild of Ellano
Let them never idly tell,
That no more, on earth below,
Witchery works her spell!
In thine eyes
The fountain lies,
Of a magic far more deep,
Than, of old,
Subdued the bold,
Made the guardian dragon sleep;
Mischief play'd
With man and maid,
Making the one go rage, the other weep.

II.

Likeness of the forest land,
Where thy infant beauty grew,
Like a palm I see thee stand,
Beautiful to view.

Thou hast grown
In forest lone,
Near a stream of shaded grace;
And thy bloom
Cheers its gloom,
Makes all sweetness in the place:
Thou hast taught
A charm to Thought,
Till Thought grows one with Beauty in thy face!

III.

Beauty, the secret of thy power,
And it spells whatever sees;
In thy hair one virgin flower
Waves o'er mortal destinies.
And thy glance—
Indian lance
Never sped so sharp and well;
And thy brow,
Like his bow,
Makes each magic arrow tell:
Every smile
Hath its wile,
And all confess the witchery of thy spell!

ACROSTIC.—ALBUM.

A THING of glitter that's not gold;
Loose verse and thought and jingle old;
Big words, that sound a thousand fold;
Unfurnish'd chambers, dull and cold;
Meet (that's not meat) for misses bold

ECHO-DUETT.—HERE IN THIS VALLEY.

Here, in this valley of Aidenne,
  That sleeps in a peace of its own,
They tell of a beautiful maiden,
  Close captive in a bower of stone;
To the Giant of Rock that chains her,
  She pleads with a fruitless prayer,
Yet, in scorn of her pleading, he deigns her
  But a mock in the empty air!
There, dark, lies the hapless woman,
  Whom vainly we seek to see;
But hearken, I pray, while I summon
  Her voice, which shall speak to me!

O heart of stone,
  Which binds me;
    Oh, hear my moan,
      Oh, set me free,
        And let me flee
To any heart, to any heart,
  That finds me!
    Oh, set me free,
      And let me flee
To any heart,
  To any heart,
    That finds me!

Echo—O heart of stone,
  Which binds me;
    Oh, hear my moan,
      Oh, set me free,
        And let me flee
To any heart, to any heart
  That finds me!
    Oh, set me free,
      And let me flee
To any heart, to any heart,
  That finds me!
    Finds me!
      Me! me!

Thou weep'st at the piteous pleading,
  But the Being who dwells so lone,
Her own heart forever bleeding,
  Hath songs for a grief not her own.

'Twould seem that all sympathies human
  Should grow from one's sorrows at first,
And love never springs in the woman,
  Till her own soul is arid with thirst!
And now, if a heart of feeling
  But swells in that bosom of thine,
Hear the song of that maiden, revealing
  The passion that speaks for mine.

I pray to thee,
  Who binds me,
    Set me not free!
      Let me not flee
To any heart—to any heart
  That finds me!
    Thy heart alone,
      That hears my moan,
        My prison be!
Set me not free
  From thee—from thee!

Echo—I pray to thee,
  Who binds me,
    Set me not free!
      Let me not flee
To any heart—to any heart
  That finds me!
    Thy heart alone,
      That hears my moan,
        My prison be!
Set me not free
  From thee—from thee!
    From thee!
      Thee!
        Thee!

SURFACE VIRTUE.—EPIGRAM. (From Proverbs.)

She eats the fruit without alarm,
Then wipes her mouth, and—where the harm?

SWEETLY FALL THE DEWS.

I.

SWEETLY fall the dews of night,
Gently swells the evening air,
And the moon, with maiden bright,
Walks her dream-like sphere:
And the flow'r now folds her leaf,
And the bee hath ceased his hum;
Slumber stills the mourner's grief—
Rapture, too, is dumb.

II.

Not a murmur wakes the shore,
Fill'd with strife and sorrow long;
And, in place of ocean's roar,
There's a breath of song!
All's not grief that nature knows,
Skies are never all o'ercast,
And, from Heaven, a sweet repose,
Anguish wins at last.

III.

Wherefore battle with the cloud,
When the morrow's calm is nigh?
Even as we brood above the shroud,
Hark the lullaby!
For each joy that flies to-day,
One more bright the morrow brings;
For each dear bird flown away,
One to-morrow sings.

THE BRIDE OF CHRIST.

I.

Dusk, and its drooping banners!—the near cry
  Of the sad whip-poor-will—and now the gleam
Of the sweet star of evening, where the sky
  Still keeps soft flushes of the Day-God's beam—
  And Thought that broods, still doubting of her theme,
Sadd'ning with mysteries which she can not clear!—
  Shut up the ancient volume; for I dream
Of other realms—past seasons reappear,
Forms of the antique arise, and foreign tongues I hear.

II.

The hour and book have brought them. I have read
  Till the black letters faded from my sight;
And Thought and Memory, both by Fancy fed,
  Have conjured up fresh visions of delight!
  That star of dusk, so suddenly born bright,
Glows like some radiant vision of the Past;
  Finds fitting language in that Bird of Night,
And quires of deeds and seasons, that still cast
Their gleams athwart our sky, as meteors o'er the vast.

III.

Not the rude aspects of our forest land,
  These growing shadows, and this foreign place;
A stately grandeur rises on each hand;
  Great towers and columns, gathering in the space
  Of a most gloomy beauty, twinn'd with grace;
Speaking a genius whose majestic thought
  Declares the presence of superior race,
That, even in sport, with sword and sceptre wrought,
And, from a sovran will, its inspiration caught.

IV.

Most perfect the illusion!—art with nature
  Striving, and with such earnestness of aim,
So fondly, as to simulate each feature,
  And grow into another, yet the same!
  No doubtful likeness—coldly true, and tame—
But life in every lineament!—Warm hues;
  Rich, breathing flushes; strength, and grace of frame,
And glances, as when Passion's self imbues,
With speech, the quivering lips that else might speech refuse.

V.

The persons of the drama? Who shall paint
  The guise magnificent—the grand array
Of gold and purple?—brilliance, that makes faint
  The pomp of blazing altars, which o'er day
  Cast dimness, and but mock the sun's display!
What jewels flame! What plumes float rich in air!
  How gleams the glittering armor—and how gay;
The golden draperies flaunt from burnished spear,
And wave in blazon proud, when pours the trumpet's blare!

VI.

Princes and knights and nobles; stateliest dames,
  That sweep like swans of triumph through the crowd,
With necks gold-cinctured; bosoms bearing flames,
  Shrined in pale jewels; but with eyes more proud
  Of their soul-lifting lustre, which hath bow'd
The souls of mightiest sovereigns! Younger forms:
  Maids yet unconscious, but with charms allowed;
At glance of which the heart to rapture warms,
And Love, grown wild to win, wakes Passion up to storms.

VII.

A great cathedral minster, tall and grand
  With starry-pointed spires that seek the skies;
Great gothic wings, outstretched on either hand,
  With antique arches, on the sight arise,
  And wake strange thoughts, and wildering memories!
Here knights and princes knelt in holiest awe,
  While sacred priests, with grateful sacrifice,
Perform'd due rites, declared the inviolate law,
And call'd on God, himself, to bless the things he saw!

VIII.

Even as we gaze, the oaken doors unfold
  For solemn service; the harmonious strain
From glorious organ pipes is outward roll'd,
  A thousand voices rise in deep refrain;
  And far, the billowy thunders sweep the plain,
Swell upward to the heavens, and, echoing round,
  Roll back in choral burdens, that, again,
Catch wings from rising breezes, whose rebound
Floods the far groves and hills, till all the rocks resound.

IX.

There is a solemn service to be done,
  Worthy such glorious prelude. Gorgeous rites,
Such as might challenge tribute from the sun,
  Need fill the hungering soul with great delights;
  Need glorious strain of sounds, and pomp of sights,
And all that may to memory consecrate
  That sacrifice, where Passion yields all rights
To Love, and wedded to sublimer fate,
Renounces human joys, with all of human state.

X.

And all confess'd the action that inspired
  The group, the scene; with feeling all confess'd:
Some hearts perchance were trembling; others fired
  To ecstasy; and, swelling in each breast,
  The emotions, mix'd, too full to be repress'd,
Rose, self-forgetful, into cheek and eye;
  Sobs with the song declared the heart's unrest
In many; but the exultant strain swell'd high,
Shook the vast roof, and streamed, in incense, to the sky.

XI.

The enthusiasm of an elder time—
  The fiery zeal that harness'd thought in prayer;
The agony of penance felt for crime,
  To God, if not the kindred world, laid bare;
  The chastening rule of abstinence and care:
These, in this temple, found their world apart;
  Here were the Passions school'd to calm and fear;
Here was the realm of refuge, soothing smart,
To lift the struggling soul, and ease the bruiséd heart.

XII.

Such the fond promise, though the billowy strain
  Rose in a choral triumph! But the stream
Of mellowing sunset, through the pictured pane
  Stole sweetly soft, and soothing as the dream
  Of the pure heart in childhood; a mild gleam
Like that of a blest peace, that, hovering o'er,
  Calm'd every tumult; show'd the evening beam,
Delicious, shining down for sea and shore,
As teaching storm and strife Love's own subduing lore.

XIII.

All sights and sounds declared for harmonies,
Still nestling in the soul and free to grow,
With gentle nurture, into sympathies,
Blessing the fruitful heart with overflow,
Whose grateful incense up to heaven must go,
Winning new blessings, with new gifts of might;
Kindling fresh founts of feeling into glow,
And crowning, with new office of delight,
The power, that else abused, must only end in blight.

XIV.

Here, by Religion to due service won,
Had Art achieved her mission, to unfold
Each great ideal beauty of the sun;
To make affections sweet, and virtue bold;
Enliven thought, and rescue from the cold
Those delicate sentiments, that quickly die
In growth of hungry instincts; which take hold,
Like fiends, when Passion wins the mastery,
And wolve, if left unleash'd, on every virtue high!

XV.

Here, Art had caught her grandeur from the hills,
And from sky-vaulted forests; shapes of grace,
From grove and fountain; beauty from the rills
That music make in shady-haunted place—
While blossoms of sweet nurture crowd the space,
And innocent green of leaves, and shrubs of scent,
Delicious, languish in the wind's embrace;
And here, for spur of fancy, had she blent
Her wild and strange designs, compelling wonderment!

XVI.

Mingling in curious harmonies, the grand
  Grew twinn'd with the grotesque: the pillars, wrought,
Were twining serpents, and were made to stand
  Erect, and bear the rafters—that seemed brought—
  A natural forest—Art rejecting nought
Of spreading umbrage; stems and branches bore
  Their fruits; and gay vines wander'd off, untaught,
As seeking succor; giant birds hung o'er,
With wings outspread, and eyes great with miraculous lore.

XVII.

Shrine, rafters, columns, all—with strange device,
  Bore mystic meanings. Through fantastic pane
The sun stream'd broken—scarcely to suffice
  For light, though with soft beauty on each fane
  Conferring ritual virtues of great gain:
Like gleaming eyes of faery creep his rays,
  As crested serpents, jewelled; and remain,
So many broken rivulets, that, in maze,
Capricious flow and fleet beneath the admiring gaze!

XVIII.

Such was the scene, so grand and beautiful,
  All robed for ceremonial: Rites begun—
Music, alternate with deep roll and lull,
  And clouds of incense reddening with the sun,
  While, reeking up beneath the rafters dun,
Making the air grow heavy with the sweet,
  The sacred torches flamed: the altars won,
The white-robed priests the holy chaunts repeat,
While breathless hosts drew nigh with bared or sandall'd feet.

XIX.

Apart, a crowd of modest virgins stood,
  Veil'd and white garmented, who, haply blessed
With wisest foresight—free from vulgar mood—
  Had fled the mortal strife to cells of rest;
  Seeking, from storm, escape in sacred nest!
There, with the orphan of obscurest home,
  Stood one whose noble race wore ducal crest;
Yet all made happy in that sheltering dome,
Where peace broods, bless'd by prayer, and welcomes all who
    come.

XX.

And there were those whom Life had vex'd with wrong;
  Others with Love's denial; some who wept
O'er failing fortunes, suffering from the thong
  Of Poverty; and some who might have slept
  Long seasons with Remorse, and lately crept
To the white feet of Him who died to save:
  Here all might find fit refuge, and be kept
By Holy Love in safety; as the grave,
Fast, yet permitting still the unsatisfied heart to crave.

XXI.

There were, who might have mourn'd when first they came,
  Driven hither by the unweeting arm of power;
Others to save some noble House from shame,
  Or yield to better loved ones some fair dower!
  And sure 'twere grievous fortune, that the flower,
Born for the zephyr's kiss, and heaven's free sky,
  Should thus be torn from life in youth's fresh hour,
When all of earth is beauty to the eye,
And with devotion wrapt, while Love stands whispering nigh!

XXII.

Yet time had wrought due healing for the heart,
And prayer had soothed the spirit into peace;
The pang that follow'd the decree to part
From human joys—still promising increase—
Had taught the wildering Fancy soon to cease
The nurture of delusions, vague as vain,
That only vex; and, safe from man's caprice,
The eye forgot to weep, the soul complain,
And, in that sacred calm, all worldly loss was gain.

XXII

The storm that breaks upon the ambitious hills,
The snows that chill the voluptuous valley's breast,
The summer sun, that from the flower distils
The tainted breath, all nature to infest;
These never here disturb the holy rest
Of lives that knew not pride—of hearts that beat
With no unbounded passion to be bless'd;
Even Power's red arm, restrained by Reverence meet,
Dared never threat the peace of this most Holy Seat!

XXIV.

Thus sped the prolific seasons, yet the sun
Brought never change upon their calm domain;
Benignant rule, the submissive nature won;
The captive sigh'd not to go forth again;
The wounded spirit needed not complain:
Where had they found, in earth's unsheltered space,
So sure a home—so mild a realm and reign?
Sped the glad seasons in pacific chase,
Nor shook their blessings down upon a happier place.

XXV.

Such is the scene, and in that ancient hall,
 To Heaven's high worship and pure rites devote,
The fair indwellers are assembled all,
 To win one other sister to their lot:
 A fair young girl, with cheek as yet unsmote
By the world's scourges, at the altar knelt;
 And strange and nameless were the emotions wrote
On that young face!—Oh! had she never felt
One spell of mortal love, to make her purpose melt?

XXVI.

Never did lovelier being upon earth
 Descend from heaven; never did lovelier face,
Or form, from mortal mother spring to birth,
 Clad in immortal charms; with such a grace
 In glance and motion! In the sacred place—
The meek and beautiful, wedded—she appeared
 A thing of heavenly birth, and holier race
Than any child of mortal parents rear'd—
A special birth of light, that heavenly graces heir'd.

XXVII.

Yet she bends trembling; from her pale white brow
 The matron shears the golden locks away:
Locks that had long before won many a vow—
 In love's fond thought too precious for the prey
 Even of Religion! Doth one pang find sway,
As she resigns the treasure cherished long?
 Ah! see the tears in eyes so lately gay—
Tears, which she strives to check, misdeeming wrong,
Which force their way at last, for virgin will too strong

XXVIII.

One stifled sob—one faint but passionate sigh—
  Breaks from her struggling soul: declaring still
How sad the parting—what the agony
  Even of obedience to that better will,
  Adverse to youthful impulses, that thrill
With the sweet memory of the world she flies!
  One glance around her and the blue eyes fill:
'Tis the last look allow'd to those sweet eyes,
Of that bright beautiful world, to which, henceforth, she dies.

XXIX.

Oh! in that one quick tremulous look I see
  The passion that will never be denied;
There Love already wins idolatry,
  And vainly would Religion frown and chide—
  'Tis *her* religion; and grows deified,
Though to herself unconscious: in all hours
  Is felt, and, as a sovereign, sways in pride,
Bears the fond fancy back to banish'd bowers,
Usurps the altar's rites, and rules with mightiest powers!

XXX.

Even while she bows before the Holy Shrine,
  Amid the sacred service; while the rite
Seeks Heaven, and woos the presence most divine,
  To sanctify with blessing and with might,
  Her eye and mind, forgetful of their sight,
Range far, to one sweet solitude, well known,
  As scene of that delirious, first delight,
When in Love's dawn of being, grew to *one*,
Two hearts, that never thence went consciously alone!

XXXI.

Suddenly stopt in that sweet wandering:
  Made terribly to know the truth, that, hence,
The loving fancy never must take wing,
  The loving heart seek no more recompense,
  In that most precious mutual confidence—
Two souls made one by love—Love making bliss,
  Such as might serve—not wronging Innocence—
To make Heaven's own especial happiness,
To make a world, *for* Heaven, even of such a world as this!

XXXII.

Her soul grew chill'd as suddenly: then came
  A pang, as of an arrow through the heart;
One sharp convulsion, followed by a scream,
  And soul and body seem'd about to part:
  Then, from her knees uprising with a start,
She flung her hands in air: her dazéd eyes
  Glanced wildly round, as if they sought to dart
Through the great portals, seeking of the skies,
Succor from doom, that on her soul like horror lies!

XXXIII.

But the throng yields not; the great doors of oak
  Are fast: no wing, descending from above,
Stoops to embrace, and bear her from the yoke
  Which tears her from the sweeter ties of Love!
  No hope! no hope! The wing may never rove,
Again, in search of the denied delight:
  Prayer now, and solitude, must well reprove
The passionate Fancy, erring, though so bright;
And the pale lily droops, crush'd, prostrate in its blight.

XXXIV.

And o'er her head the awful veil is thrown
  That shuts her in forever from the crowd!
The great aisles echo with a single moan!—
  She hears it—she whose heart hath just been vow'd
  Away from earth—to Heaven's sole service bow'd!
She stifles not the answering moan, which cries
  For the Soul's liberty, in accents loud—
A wild, dread shriek!—but swift the anthems rise,
The organ rolls its waves, in billows, to the skies.

XXXV.

The mighty diapason sweeps away
  That wild heart outburst! A tumultuous thrill
Makes the great drooping banners outward sway;
  And the vast crowd, as by a sovereign will,
  Heaves with excited sympathies, that still
All doubts of the becoming sacrifice,
  Where the poor heart, with pang that well might kill,
Yields up, for severance, all its mortal ties,
Dying to each dear hope, ere yet to life it dies!

XXXVI.

Yet, 'midst the billowy roll of that great rush,
  That music tempest—breaking on the ear,
Like some great mountain torrent, from the hush
  Of mighty forest, suddenly waking fear
  In the surprised senses, as they hear—
The echo of that agonizing shriek
  Reverberates over all—not loud, but clear—
And woman faints; the powerful man feels weak,
And every heart grows chill, with awe that can not speak.

XXXVII.

They question of that music, in their hearts;
  The pomp, the pride; the virtue in that rite,
In ministry of which the spirit parts,
  As with the precious life and dear delight!
  The sunshine sudden dims upon the sight;
The altar smokes dispersed, ascend no more:
  Oh! these are omens that declare for blight!
Is it Religion thus that stabs the core—
Love, that from Life thus robs, the Love so dear before?

XXXVIII.

They dare not think—they must not feel—not brave
  The impious questioning of the Law Divine!—
Yet still they hear that cry above the wave;
  It broods, an awful Presence, o'er the shrine!
  So the strong swimmer, struggling in the brine,
Sinks in despairing weakness—one dread cry,
  As his soul yields, the conflict to resign,
Rises o'er raging sea, and stormy sky,
O'er all their wrath supreme, in its sharp agony!

XXXIX.

But the seas close above the drowning form,
  And the shriek's echo is dispersed in air;
The sorrows of the soul survive the storm,
  And though the cry is hush'd of that despair,
  The deadly desolation harbors there,
Still watching the heart's ruins, day and night:
  And memory comes, with melancholy care,
Watering her withered shrubs, whose hapless blight
No longer mocks the sense, no more offends the sight.

XL.

Perchance, in wisdom is the offering made;
  For earth is full of sorrow: he who dreams
With Fancy, is by Passion still betrayed;
  Pangs lurk in realms of rapture; brightest gleams
  Shoot from the serpent's eye; our noblest schemes,
Mock'd by denial, turn upon the heart,
  And prey like vultures; things that boyhood deems
His blessings, nestle, with insidious art,
And linger but to sting, nor while they sting, depart!

XLI.

These are the hourly, world-wide histories!
  How wise, if by rejection from the first,
We baffle such close-swarming enemies,
  And ere they wound us, see them at the worst;
  Conceive each snare; behold each bubble burst;
Anticipate the venom in its core,
  Ere yet its tortures make our lives accursed;
Deny the syren singing by the shore,
And from close-waxéd ears, shut out the treacherous lore!

XLII.

Secure in thoughts of holiness; in calm
  That never feels the gales of passion blow;
In prayer—that from austerity plucks balm,
  Superior, to the soul-relaxing flow
  Of fancies, too capricious in their glow—
The refuge grows the home; and, at the last,
  The heart, no longer vexed by mortal throe,
Learns, upward still, each yearning look to cast,
Fixes its hope on Heaven—the future, not the past!

XLIII.

The love which is eternal, pure as sweet,
  Takes empire o'er the mortal—in the place
Of those wild joys, that, perilously fleet,
  Were only joy's convulsions; leaving trace
  Of sorrow after pleasure; soul and face
Equally speaking for the illusive bliss:
  Unlike the rapture which hath birth in grace,
Compensative, for all we lose in this
Sad, weary world of toil, along life's precipice!

XLIV.

Yet may the virgin heart deplore awhile
  The loss of virgin fancies. Earth *is* fair;
And there's a glory in love's mortal smile,
  When first beheld, most exquisitely dear!—
  The child-heart longs to pluck the fruit so rare;
To gather up its flowers; bind heart and brow
  With blooms as yet unsunn'd—beyond compare—
And drink of nectarine dews, that seem to flow
From founts, that, even as they cool, make all the bosom glow.

XLV.

Ah! Love is but the mortal dream of Heaven—
  The earth's frail ideal of eternal love:
A faint and shadowy image, haply given
  The better to beguile the soul above;
  And happy she, whose loftier fancies move
To seek the substance ere the heart grows cold;
  For the cool temple, fly the passionate grove;
The Bride of Christ—no man of mortal mould—
Made sure in bliss 'yond all that mortal song hath told.

SERENADE.—GUIDE ME, OH GUIDE ME!

I.

Guide me, oh guide me, night of many stars,
  If love's young dream was ever dear to thee;
Guide me, while not a hostile murmur mars
  The music of the sweetly sounding sea;
While fearless up yon rocky steeps I clamber,
  Where hangs the beacon of my heart on high,
To where Bianca, in her latticed chamber,
  Sits silent, gazing in the silent sky!
Silent, so silent, gazing in the sky,
As if it had for her's an answering eye!
Oh! if young love be precious in thy sight,
Night of sweet silence, night of many stars,
        Guide me, sweet night!

II.

She knows my coming, waits me, gentle night!
  See where, half hidden by the lattice bars,
She looks abroad, still blessing the dear light,
  That makes love fruitful, of thy many stars.
Ah! dost thou hearken, as she murmurs now,
  Her prayer, that, guided by thy loving ray,
My feet may spring along the rocky brow,
  And safely reach her o'er the untrodden way?
Silent the prayer, but, gazing in the sky,
Thou see'st her very soul is in her eye!
Oh! if young love be precious in thy sight,
Mother of silence, night of many stars,
        Guide me, sweet night!

III.

Nor, when at last, within that chamber blest,
  Her beating bosom closely clings to mine,
Shall prayer of either heart be unexpress'd,
  Night of sweet stars, that thou hast bade them shine.
And when the summer evening hours are long,
  When 'neath the whispering groves of green we glide,
Our mutual souls shall follow thee with song,
  Fond as the loving light thou lend'st to guide!—
Oh! groves made holy, happy in our bliss,
Be each sweet night that hallows thee like this!
Mother of silence, night of many stars,
Oh! if young love be precious in thy sight,
        Guide us, sweet night!

SONNET.—AND MUST I SING OF BEAUTY?

AND must I sing of Beauty, and to thee—
  Thou in the precious sweetness of thy dawn?
  Sing of thy youth, when mine is almost gone?
Sing of thy charms, when not again for me
Such fruit may blossom on life's blighted tree?
Thy loveliness, when but a single glance
  Takes captive, binds, and never more sets free;
The whole soul fettered in a purple trance,
  Where Love himself, renouncing liberty,
Delights in bonds, nor asks deliverance:
Submissive gladly to the power whose sway,
  As heedless of the hunger of the slave,
  As greedy of his homage, still must crave,
Nor notes the victim dying, day by day!

TO A YOUNG GIRL.

I.

Oh! thou hast charmed me well,
Far more than tongue can tell;
Yet go, my sweet Gazelle,
  Go, singing free:
Happy and bright the skies,
That woo thy wing to rise,
Bright as Heaven's beams, those eyes,
  So bright to me.

II.

Go, lest the sunny grace
Of that sweet, smiling face,
Win me to mad embrace,
  In frenzies wild!
Better in peace depart!—
Even thou, with nought of art,
May'st rouse to fire my heart—
  Thou, but a child!

III.

Ah! 'twere for both a doom,
Did thy sweet, innocent bloom,
Within this breast relume
  That ancient fire—
Full of the madd'ning might,
Delirium, not delight,
Which brought the heart to blight,
  Bringing desire!

IV.

Better that thou should'st be
Still the dear child I see,
Laughing, and going free,
  Heedless of aught—
Save the glad song, the smile,
Child-play and childish wile,
As innocent of guile,
  As Love of thought.

V.

I would not have thee come,
Down, from thy native home,
Fresh with its matin bloom,
  To forfeit here
One smile of that dear face,
Laugh, motion, look of grace,
For which we cry out: "Place!—
  Bright ones appear!"

VI.

Alas! thou little know'st,
How, round thy steps, a host—
Passions of evil boast—
  Crowd to consume;
Armed each with cunning power,
Rifling, as birds the flower,
They sing thee, one short hour,
  Sing thee to doom!

VII.

Of all that thus pursue,
Seeming most fond, and woo—
How few are brave and true!
  Scarce shalt thou win
One young heart, free of blame,
With a fond, generous flame,
Untouch'd with self and shame,
  Unsmutcht with sin!

VIII.

The Love, which here they bring,
Himself's an earthy thing—
Crawls, creeps, without a wing,
  So—without heart:
Can make no sacrifice,
And, with a cunning nice,
Still polishes the vice,
  To the abuse of art.

IX.

Crawling about the bloom,
He robs the fresh perfume,
Cares naught, though bringing doom,
  And, like a thief,
Pursues his cruel toil,
Not to delight, but spoil,
And turns, with serpent guile,
  The joy to grief.

X.

Alas! the frequent tale!
Then thy young hope would fail—
Then thy young heart would ail,
  And, ere many days,
Over thy cheeks, the red
Of thy beauty would be spread,
With a pall, as of the dead,
  And with a dread amaze!

XI.

Then, no longer high,
Lifted to the sky,
Thy down-looking eye
  Would commune with blame;
Thy free step and grace
Fleet, and leave no trace,
And upon thy face
  Would be shame! Oh, shame!

XII.

And they'd have no care—
They who wrought the snare—
When, no longer fair,
  Thou hast felt the doom;
Of the crowd that knew,
Fawn'd and fondled too,
Scarcely one would strew
  Flow'rs upon thy tomb!

BALLAD.—THE ASPHODEL.

[With the Greeks, the Asphodel was the emblem of Death. It was held to be the favorite food of departed spirits. As a member of the lily family, haunting lonely tarns, gloomy waters shaded by the cypress, and, by its pure beauties, contrasting so spiritually with the localities in which we find it, there is a significance in this designation of the flower, reminding us forcibly of the malarious character of the regions which it seems to prefer.]

I.

Thou hast brought me a beautiful wreath,
But alas for us both, alas!
Thou hast gathered the asphodel,
Thou hast brought me the flower of death—
The beautiful flower of death!
Dost thou not feel its breath?—
The odor of the grave and the grass,
Of the swamp and the dark morass,
The perishing things that pass—
Of the clay that tell, and the hollow cell,
And the cypress that stoops to the gloom,
As if hung o'er the brow of doom?
Alas for us both, alas!
It is Death thou hast brought me—Death!

II.

And its odor's abroad in the air,
  Though the summer bloom be bright;
Though the jessamine hangs with a beauty rare,
  And woos through the shade to the light;
And there's never a breath in the sky,
  And never a sign of cloud;
And the woods and the waters are all so fair,
  And the purple blossoms are flaunting proud,

With starry centres of light, that gleam
Like large moist eyes looking love in a dream.
Oh! lovely and sweet beyond compare,
So wooing and blessing—so fair—so fair!

III.

So the serpent lies under the rose—
So, in hushes of noon and night,
The Tempest takes his repose,
At the dawning of day or its close;
And the sunset hush and the calm
Sink into our very souls like balm,
And we dream of a new delight!—
But the very hush is a fright,
And we feel there's a breath of blight;
And the conscious soul that has felt before,
With a shuddering sense that may sleep no more,
Feels that Death is abroad in the air!—
Though there be no cloud,
And the sky be fair,
Yet it knows that the shroud,
The shroud, is near:
That the Death is abroad—is abroad in the air!

IV.

Alas for us both, alas!
For what if but one shall fall—
We two, alone, who have dwelt as one—
If but one shall hear the call,
If but one of us twain shall fall!
What were Life then to thee or to me—
Life in its horror alone?
Could'st thou bear to behold me pass?—
Could I spread o'er thy limbs the pall?

What were left to either to feel or to see,
To think or to know when the one is gone—
The one who was ever the one o'er all,
The all that we've sought, or loved, or known,
The all that we've cared to meet or to moan?
Alas for us both, alas!
Alone! alone! alone!

V.

I know that the doom is near:
The fearful sign, it is mine, it is mine!
Yet to feel that the skies are so bright and clear;
And thou so bright, and both so dear!—
Yet where, thou ask'st, oh where?
In what is the portent of fear?
And how should so dread a sign
Thus lurk in a simple flow'r?
Alas for us both, alas!
When so simple a sign hath power
For the voice that speaks in the heart!
Oh speak with that voice of thine!
Speak, soothe me and stifle the fear,
That cries with such midnight tone,
So full of terror, so stark and so drear!
Alas for us both, alas!
It passes—the shadow—'twas meant to pass:
And hark, as it goes, it cries—it cries,
Hollowly, hollowly—groans and sighs:
"Depart! Depart! Depart!"
The doom is in every murmur of moan—
And the doom, it is mine, it is mine!
God be praised that 'tis only mine!
That it is not thine—that it is not thine,
Beloved! it is not thine!

VI.

Yet how dreary the prayer—how little fond—
As if life for either had aught beyond
The hour that shall see the one of us pass!
Alas for us both, alas!
What of thee when I am gone;
When my voice thou shalt hear no more;
When this loving breast, in its own deep rest,
Shall yield nor pillow nor rest to thine,
As in the long nights of yore?
Oh! the horror to think of thee—
Thou in thy widowhood lone,
Looking forth, but withouten moan,
But evermore looking forth lone!
Ah! then, when my agony's o'er,
And thou look'st for no love of mine,
Yet, at midnight thou callest for me—
Calling through slumbers that soothe no more—
Calling, how vainly, with what sad tone—
While the shadows pass o'er the misty glass,
And Day looks in with a glare through the pane,
Though the dawn brings with it the clouds and rain,
And thou feel'st that both are vain—
The night and the dawn!—
Oh! the horror to think of thee,
Thus, in thy widowhood lone—
How lone, how lone, but withouten moan,
Thou lone—how lone—and I gone! I gone!

SONNET.—TO W. PORCHER MILES.

O FRIEND! who satt'st beside me in the hour
  When Death was at my hearth; and in my home
  The mother's cry of wailing for that doom,
Long hovering, which, at last, with fatal power
Descended, like the vulture on his prey,
  And in his talons bore away our young!—
  Thou know'st how terribly this heart was wrung:
Thou cam'st with watch and soothing, night and day,
No brother more devoted! More than friend,
  Belovéd evermore—behold me thine!—
  Yet have I little worthy that is mine,
Save love, and this poor tribute; which must blend
With memories of thy watch, and of our pain,
And of those precious boys, we both have watched in vain!

BALLAD.—COME, LET US DISCOURSE.

I.

COME, let us discourse of our sorrow,
  The gloom, and the grave, and the night,
For what shall be our waking to-morrow,
  When the loved one no more lies in sight?
When he answers no more to the loving call,
  And pleads no more to the loving ear,
And stark and cold 'neath his desolate pall,
  Nor feels our groan, nor sees our tear?

II.

Oh, wail, wail!—nothing but wail!—
  Words are a mock, since prayer is vain;
The shriek and the moan must tell the tale
  Of our life-long wo, and his mortal pain!—
How, in his agony, panting, wild,
  Raging with thirst, yet still denied,
We watch'd the face of the dying child,
  With hearts death-stricken before he died!

III.

The boy of a thousand loving ways,
  So true, so innocent, fond and sweet,
What had he done, that his fair young days
  Should close so soon in the winding sheet?
What had he done, that the mortal pain
  Should fasten its fangs on his pure young life,
While the gasping cry, and the raving brain,
  Show'd the agony sharp of the deadly strife!

IV.

Oh, wail, wail!—nothing but wail,
  Can speak for the pangs of that mortal blow:
The shriek can but feebly tell the tale
  Of the pain he bore and the grief we know!
Vex us no more with the idle strain
  That bids us find solace in agonies o'er;
Teaches that prayer and care are vain,
  That the angel we've lost we shall see no more!

V.

Know we not this? And because we know,
  Is the groan, the moan, and the wailing cry;
It is not forbid that we feel the wo,
  And cry aloud to the far-off sky!

O child of our love! it is something won,
  To feel that thy innocent life on earth
Hath found thee a passport beyond the sun,
  In the blessèd sphere where thy soul had birth.

VI.

Yet, wo, my spirit! What else but wo
  At thy pangs, my boy, though they now be o'er?
'Tis something to soften the griefs we know,
  That thy fair young form shall have pain no more;
Yet, oh, the silence, so deep and drear,
  Dreadest of voices, that speak of doom,
And mournfully echo the cry: "Oh, where?"
  As wistful I wander from room to room.

BALLAD.—OH! MY BOYS!

Oh! my boys, my noble boys,
I am sitting 'midst your toys,
But I hear no pleasant noise;
  I shall hear no more
The sweet voices of your joys,
  Ever dear before.

It was only yesterday
Ye were by my side at play,
Bounding gleeful, all so gay,
  Happy, with such cheer,
That our hearts forgot to pray,
  Having no more fear.

Drum and trumpet, top and ball,
With such merry whoop and call,
Making racket in the hall,
  Deafening every ear:
Oh! that I could have them all—
  That I still could hear!

That I still could hear and see,
Shapes and noises of your glee—
My bright Syd—my Beverley!
  Oh, my noble boys,
Voice and form are lost to me,
  Sitting 'midst your toys.

PALO ALTO AND RESACA DE LA PALMA.*

I.

Now, while our cups are flowing
  With memories born to bloom,
And filial hands are throwing
  Their wreaths o'er valor's tomb;
While lips exulting shout the praise
  Of heroes of the past, that stood
Triumphant 'mid old Moultrie's blaze,
  And proud in Eutaw's field of blood—
Be not forgot the gallant train,
  That lifts our name in Mexic war:
One cup for Palo Alto drain,
  One cheer for Palma Resaca!

* This lyric was prepared for the Fourth of July celebration immediately succeeding the two battles above mentioned.

II.

For Taylor—"Rough and Ready,"
  True son of truest sires;
For May, who, swift and steady,
  Trod down La Vega's fires;
For all who in that day of strife
  Maintain'd in pride the stripes and stars,
The dead, who won immortal life,
  And they who live for other wars;
For those who, with their victory,
  New wreaths to grace our laurel bring—
A health that drains the goblet dry,
  A cheer that makes the welkin ring!

III.

Yet, though even now we falter,
  With thoughts of those who died,
And, at our festive altar,
  Grow silent in our pride—
Yet in the heart's most holy deep,
  Fond memory shrines the happy brave,
Who in the arms of battle sleep,
  By Palo's wood and Bravo's wave;
Nor in our future deeds forgot,
  Shall silent thought forbear to bring
Her tribute to that sacred spot,
  Where Ringgold's gallant soul took wing.

IV.

Fill to our country's glory,
  Where'er her flag is borne;
Nor, in her failing story,
  Let future ages mourn;

Nor let the envious foreign foe
  Rejoice that faction checks her speed,
Arrests her in the indignant blow,
  And saddens o'er the avenging deed!
Fill high, though from the crystal wave
  Your cup, and from the grape be mine
The marriage rites, that link the brave
  To fame, will turn each draught to wine.

OH, TELL ME NOT, DEAREST, THAT TIME.

I.

Oh, tell me not, dearest, that Time is still flying,
  Let him pour out the sands of his quizzical glass;
Be it mine, while the moments are darting and dying,
  To mark them with brightness and bloom as they pass.
I like not this creed, which, because I must perish,
  And in the last hour earth's raptures forego,
Denies me the charm of the present to cherish,
  And makes of the future a fate and a foe.

II.

No, never, while the bud is in beauty and blooming,
  Shall I pause ere I pluck lest I pluck it in vain;
While the zephyr comes laden with clouds of perfuming,
  Shall I shrink to inhale, lest I lose it again?
And because of the doubts that belong to existence,
  Forbear all its pleasures, till, school'd by my heart,
I seek them too late, and behold, in the distance,
  The last lovely train that had wooed me, depart?

III.

Believe me, my dear, this same cant of the college
 Is still with life's aims and its nature at strife;
To be happy, with me, is the soundest of knowledge,
 And wisdom the true art of living for life.
And searching for aye for our natural treasures,
 I heed not the speech of each bed-ridden sage;
I fly, like the honey-bee, laden with pleasures,
 To feed on in youth and to lay up in age.

IV.

I hear all your talk of the possible evil,
 You bid me forbear and you bid me reflect;
You tell me, the angel disguises the devil,
 And reason most gravely on cause and effect.
But tell me the object, my sweet one, of being,
 And if you can truly and certainly prove,
That with senses I must not be feeling or seeing,
 I will take up your logic, and give up my love.

V.

But when Joy, the young Hebe, stands by me, presenting
 Her goblet of soul; should a bubble appear,
The speck on its surface still idly lamenting,
 Shall I tremble and doubt, and the rapture forbear?
Such caution for him who with quick blood and passion
 Has never the spirit for venture and aim;
My heart has been school'd in more logical fashion—
 Its prudence is daring—its feeling is flame.
Then tell me not, dear, that old Time is flying,
 Let him pour out the sands of his mystic glass;
Be it mine, while the moments are darting and dying,
 To mark them with brightness and bloom as they pass.

BALLAD.—'TWAS ON A NIGHT LIKE THIS.

'Twas on a night like this, dear maid—
The memory serves us well—
With trembling hearts our footsteps strayed,
Adown this very dell;
The skies above, as now, were clear,
The moon as brightly shone;
Thine eye was bright, thy cheek was fair,
How could I but be won?

And not a murmur broke the charm
That night had woven then;
And thou, though touch'd with soft alarm,
Went with me down the glen;
The brooklet lapsed along in light,
Yet sang where no one sees;
And with its melody of night,
The zephyr swept the trees.

Oh! I remember all, as well
As if 'twere yesterday;
The same soft light, and breezy spell,
And magical array;
Thou wast the idol of the grove,
And yon the temple's shrine,
No wonder that I grew to love,
While haply waking thine:

And, all unconscious, straight poured forth
My passion's eloquence;
And felt, without a thought, the birth
Of bliss in every sense;

I know not what I look'd or spoke,
  In that delirium wild,
But well remember, ere I woke,
  Thy sweet eyes wept and smiled.

They wept and smiled with conscious power,
  And conscious joy, I ween,
And sacred did we feel the hour,
  That gave us such a scene;
And still we watch that maiden star,
  That shines for all who love—
Still feel the spells that won us far
  Adown this sacred grove!

THE NATURAL AIM OF A DECIDED SOUL.

The natural aim of a decided soul,
  Defrauded, is its death. The work denied,
By a false judgment, or the world's control,
  Which had declared the genius in its pride,
The whole heart sickens; from its day departs
  The star that shone for energy and strife!
This gone, so goes the impulse from our hearts,
  That else had glowed with a triumphant life.
Oh! wherefore gifts of God—the endowment rare—
  If not to proper service consecrate?—
If we deny the mission, and forswear
  The duty, making for ourselves a Fate,
Adversely to the Eternal!—to base fare
  Descending, when we might have dwelt in state?

CALHOUN.

[An address for a theatrical benefit in aid of the erection of the Calhoun monument.]

Nations themselves are but the monuments
Of deathless men, whom the Divine intents
Decree for mighty purposes.
They rise
Superior, by their mission from the skies,
To thoughts of self; and, in self-sacrifice,
Assert the race: guide, fashion, and inform,
Direct for conquest, gather from the storm,
And build in strength!

Their powerful arms maintain
The realm of Peace, and consecrate her reign
By Justice, Truth, Protection. They defend
The land that gave them being, and commend
Her virtues to the love of other climes,
That else had lapsed from weaknesses to crimes,
And so, to ruin! They foresee the fate,
And arm against the danger ere too late;
Meet the assailing foeman at the wall,
And nobly conquer, or as nobly fall.
Their lives, devote to patriot service, teach
How best to build the tower and man the breach;
Their hands, outstretch'd in blessing rites, have made
The nations safe and sacred in their shade!

We rear our humble column to the name
Of one who led our power and won us fame!
Whose wondrous genius, with Ithuriel spear,
Hath made the crouching fiend start up in fear;

Smote the foul reptile, even where he lay
Coiled round our altar, poisoning still his prey;
Expell'd the foe that threatened as a fate,
And saved from loss the sacred shield of state!

His lips spoke lightnings! His immaculate thought,
From seraph source, divinest fervors caught;
His fiery argument, with eagle rush,
Spell'd mightiest Senates into trembling hush;
While the great billowy thunders, echoing still,
With rolling surges round the Sacred Hill,
Strike with sharp terrors into nerveless awe
The insidious enemies of Right and Law!
Even to the last, still battling in the van,
For the great truths and natural rights of man,
He died in harness, in the thick of strife,
His very death a triumph—like his life!

The Great fall from us. We have need to fear,
When voice like his no longer thrills the ear!
When, in the Senate, owls and mousing things
Creep to high places which were made for wings,
'Tis need we should do homage, and implore
Great shoulders, such as his white mantle bore!
'Tis reverence brings the prophet. If we praise
The perish'd virtue, and its altar raise,
We may recall the genius, lost too soon,
And find, 'mong other sons, a new Calhoun!

LANDSCAPE.—SALUDA IN MIDSUMMER.

When to the city's crowded streets
The fiercer spells of summer come,
Then for thy calm and cool retreats,
Saluda, may the wanderer roam.

Then should he seek thy guardian haunts,
Thy rocky stream, thy shady tree,
And while the plain below him pants,
From all oppression find him free.

Above him towers thy giant form,
Rock-throned, and rising like a king;
Around him rides thy summer storm,
With cooling freshness on his wing.

Beside him, borne o'er craggy steeps,
From dells that never see the light,
Thy sun-bow'd cataract roars and leaps,
In joyous gush and headlong flight.

Below him—what a scene is there!
The hallowed, sweet repose of home,
The sheltered green, the waters clear,
The sylvan sway, the cottage dome.

Gathering above, the noonday clouds
The sun's intenser fires would chide,
His glories edging still their shrouds,
Palls not unmeet for princely pride.

And far in sight the streamlet goes,
  With ceaseless chaunt of grateful cheer,
Glad in escape from hungering foes,
  And singing but in friendly ear.

See where the hunter speeds his bark,
  Not as the Indian chief of old,
Bound on some errand, wild and dark,
  Whose legend still remains untold,

But bent to cross the foaming straits,
  And win the woods of yonder shore,
Where, hid in thicket, one awaits—
  She knows not why—yet feels the more!

How changed the strife for sweet repose;
  No more the red man scouts the wood;
The hunter through the thicket goes,
  Nor dreams of hostile hate and blood.

The wolf with mournful howl departs;
  The panther's spotty hide makes gay
The cot, where woman's gentler arts
  Woo young affections forth to play.

And safe within the cottage shade,
  The song birds, with a generous strain,
Teach Nature's music to the maid,
  Who pays them back with song again.

The prowler hawk no more infests
  Their home; and o'er the sacred place,
They pour from glad and grateful breasts,
  Their raptures for the guardian race:

Crown home with grace, make lonely cot,
  For humble hearts, a home of joy;
Such as makes sweet the lowliest lot,
  And glads the dream of man and boy.

Oh! not alone a dream, while here
  The Nature well achieves her part,
And in her colors, bright and clear,
  Prepares the holier dawn of art.

Hence, to the city, well transferr'd,
  Our poet-painter bears the scene:
We see the landscape, hear its bird,
  Dance with its groups, and feel its green;

Joy in the gush of living streams,
  That bound from prison forth to light,
And feel, all quivering through our dreams,
  The music which they make in flight;

And hear, with reverent awe, the roar,
  From gathering winds, through many a dell;
Of heights we may not oft explore,
  That rush, a wondrous tale to tell.

Oh! but to dream beneath the rocks,
  And hear that song so wondrous sweet,
While Fancy every door unlocks,
  And brings us, Nature, to thy feet!

OH! MINGLE NOT!

I.

Oh! mingle not, in future hours,
  When I no more thy smiles may share,
To dim thy sky, to chill thy flowers,
  With feeling's thought, the feeling tear.
The grief that's felt for him who knew
  But rapture when thy smile was won,
Were to the precious past untrue,
  'Twould pain his heart, 'twould wrong thine.

II.

Whate'er thy mood, whate'er his wo,
  'Twas never once allow'd to rise,
To cloud the sweet, benignant glow
  Of beauty in thy gentle eyes;
To vex thy soul with aught of care,
  Or chide the bliss that, when he came,
Thy heart was ever glad to share
  With one who brought an equal flame.

III.

True, thou surviv'st! Thou hail'st the moon,
  As bright as then—no beauty dim
In all that sky whose placid noon
  Thou'st watch'd, nor heeded hours, with him!
And he no longer shares with thee
  That vigil of the sky and night,
Torn from his best felicity
  While youth was love, and life delight.

IV.

But, even as then, he seeks thee now,
  And would not have a cloud arise
To dim that eye, to cloud that brow,
  In which he ever sought his skies;
There for him still, as when, at first,
  In hours of pleasant calm like this,
Thou taught'st how virtue might be nurst,
  On Love's own breast, by Beauty's kiss.

SONNET.—LADY, WHEN O'ER MY HEART.

Lady, when o'er my heart thy smile was cast,
  Like moonlight o'er the waters, thou didst wake
A strain of song within me which must last,
  Less for its own frail worth than thy dear sake.
The Muse thus hallows low devotion's prayer,
  Though lowly; lifts the worshipper on high,
To mounts of song in the olympian air,
  And makes earth lovely with divinity!
Love thus, itself, converts to excellence
  Clay that was lowly; purges it of dross;
Lights the dull eye with sweet intelligence,
  And makes a gain to good of evil's loss.
Thus hath that smile of thine uplifted me—
How can my heart be ill, thus full of thee?

CONTRERAS.—DID THEY FALTER?

I.

Did they falter or fail at the summons,
  The sons whom to battle we sent,
When the bugle rang out for the rally,
  And the bright steel for charging was bent;
When wild rose the shriek of the dying,
  And wilder the shout of the foe,
And our own gallant soldiers replying,
  Sprang eagerly forth to the blow?

II.

Contreras shall speak for that meeting,
  When the blood of our sons flow'd as free
As the streams that leap down from our mountains
  To a joyful embrace with the sea;
Not the shout nor the shot could appall them,
  Nor the shock of a conflict so new;
Thus taught that, whate'er might befall them,
  They must still to their fathers be true!

III.

Oh! gallant and faithful as ever,
  We joy in a race that has still,
From the first of our fortunes and conquests,
  Proved the worth of its virtues and will;
Ever true to the flag floating o'er them,
  To the courage that came from the past—
They died!—but how can we deplore them,
  Thus conquering and true to the last?

ODE.—WELCOME, THRICE WELCOME.*

I.

Welcome, thrice welcome, men of the Palmetto!
Your country rings out welcome from the steeples,
Our cannon speaks your welcome, with our voices,
And our full hearts.

II.

We look with pride upon your little squadron,
With pride that weeps while voicing your full triumphs;
Our tears flow freely for your perish'd numbers,
The brave who fell!

III.

Green be their honors in our proudest annals,
Green be your trophies in all changing seasons,
Freshen'd by Love, that still records your valor,
Among our first.

IV.

We watch your first fell passage with the foeman—
When your light legions, through the Mexic lances,
First bore the gay green banner of our people,
At Vera Cruz.

V.

We follow with sad eyes your weary marching
O'er plains of sand, to conquer Alvarado,
While the dread sun still shooting fellest arrows,
Troubled your host;

* This ode was written to welcome the return of the remnant of the Palmetto Regiment from Mexico.

VI.

Your painful term of weariness and waiting,
Madden'd to hear the strife at Cerro Gordo,
While ye were sunk with sickness, slow recruiting,
Eager, but weak.

VII.

Then do we see ye marching on Puebla—
It yields—it gives no trophy to your valor,
Taxing your patience only, your forbearance,
And not your strength.

VIII.

But soon the signal called ye to Contreras—
Then do we see ye smiting, darting onward,
Wherever foeman waited, or trump summon'd
Your souls to strife.

IX.

How swept ye to the fight at Churubusco,
How mow'd ye down the legions of Valencia,
How drove, and crush'd, and captured the foul traitors
That joined our foe.

X.

There saw ye sink our Butler—there, another,
The gallant Dickinson, too quickly followed,
Both, at the head of your advancing columns,
Slain 'neath your eyes.

XI.

Ye wept, but quailed not; saddened, ye were strengthened,
Fiercely to take sweet vengeance on the legions
From whose dread ranks the fatal missiles issued,
That struck your brave!

XII.

Oh! not unworthy of the bright example,
Was the fierce lead of Gladden, when ye darted,
Among the first, o'er walls of that strong castle,
Chapultepec!

XIII.

Then followed the last strife at La Garita,
The gates of the proud city of the Aztec,
When, pressing through the aqueducts' great arches,
Ye won the prize.

XIV.

First, o'er the city walls your banner waving,
First, o'er the trampled foe your warriors rushing,
First, with your shout of triumph in the battle,
First in our hearts.

XV.

Welcome, thrice welcome, men of the Palmetto,
Well have ye borne our banner with the bravest,
And long, and proudly, shall our Country honor
Your deeds of fame.

CAROLINIANS, WHO INHERIT.*

CAROLINIANS, who inherit
  Rights your sires have bought with blood,
Seek ye now an equal merit,
  By an equal hardihood;
With a name renown'd in story,
  'Tis for you, where all are brave,
Still to seek the heights of glory,
  Though they only yield a grave.

Hark ye, as ye hear the clarion—
  In the furrow leave the plow:
Sons of Sumter and of Marion,
  Speed ye to the battle now;
Ye have fields of fame before ye,
  Such as joy'd your sires of old;
Ye can write as proud a story,
  With a stroke as sharp and bold.

Hear the cry of Louisiana:
  "Lo! *our* sons at Monterey!"
Tennessee, too, waves her banner,
  Joyous in her deeds that day;
Shall they shame us, Carolinians,
  While a past so proud as ours
Waves us on, with eagle pinions,
  To a proof of eagle powers!

---

* This song was written when the Palmetto Regiment was in course of organization.

Never!—Be the spirit written,
  In each eager soul and glance;
We who braved the steel of Britain,
  Will not heed the Mexic lance:
To the field where glory beckons,
  Soaring high o'er Aztec towers!—
He, who of the danger reckons,
  In the fight, is none of ours!

THE SPIRIT OF THE LAND.

I.

The spirit of the land,
  The mighty cry hath heard;
The trumpet of command,
  The forest deeps hath stirr'd;
A voice is on the hills,
  And a voice is in the vale,
With a sound that nothing stills:
  "Do not fail! Do not fail!"

II.

But it needs no voice to wake
  The fierce spirit of the land:
It has wild revenge to take,
  And it stirs with bolt and brand;
Not in sudden wrath it comes,
  Like the rising of the gale
That in summer noontide hums,
  Soon to fail! Soon to fail!

17

III.

But with souls that long have striven,
With a rising, rousing strength,
To whom mighty thoughts are given,
Being mighty deeds at length;
Ye behold them on their path,
And ye may not doubt the tale,
That a people right in wrath,
Never fail! Never fail!

NOW WAVE THE GREEN PALMETTO!*

I.

Now wave the green Palmetto,
And cheer the glorious sign,
That tells of many a victory,
Your fathers won and mine;
They strove and struck together
And we will strive as they,
While an arm can wield a weapon,
Or a foeman fills the way!
So wave the green Palmetto,
Our Carolinian tree;
Our fathers bore it through the fight,
And so, my boys, shall we!

---

* Written for the Palmetto Regiment while at its rendezvous near Charleston, before the departure for Mexico.

II.

Good limbs of Apalachian,
  If they'll but wait the strife,
We'll show these mongrel Mexicans,
  Though battling to the knife;
Good blood that, coursing freely,
  For twice two hundred years,
Has given two mighty nations
  To sway both hemispheres!
A keen wing to the rifle,
  A fleet spur to the steed,
A shout to make the welkin ring,
  And we have done the deed!

III.

Now wave the green Palmetto,
  And when the fight is worst,
We'll bear it on, through strife and storm,
  'Mong charging lines the first;
We'll think of ancient valor,
  When fields at home were won,
When Marion made the foeman skulk,
  And Sumter made him run!—
We'll think of friends and brothers,
  Whose hearts with triumph burn—
And gentle maids, that look with tears,
  To welcome our return.

NOW FLOWS THE BANNER.

I.

Now flows the banner to the breeze,
Now sounds the trump that bids us go;
The barque is ready on the seas,
And we must speed to seek the foe;
And never hearts more proudly yet
Went forth at Freedom's trumpet cry:
But ties we can not well forget,
Bring tears to many a manly eye.

II.

We do not weep with human fears,
With sense of danger, dark and dread;
The foe shall never see the tears
That fall upon a sister's head;
Behind the cottage door where Love
Stands waiting for the parting kiss—
'Tis there the deepest pang we prove,
Where first we found the sweetest bliss.

III.

Ah! thither—when in fields of strife,
Our hearts in fancy still shall fly,
There still, when struggling wild for life,
Shall cling each fondest memory;
Perchance, even then, some earnest prayer
Shall crown with peace our parting breath,
And still the sigh of heart most dear,
Shall bless the spirit freed by death.

THE MARCH TO ALVARADO.*

I.

Weary the march o'er hot and stifling plains,
  Droops the green banner in the silent air;
No cooling spring to soothe our burning pains,
  No sudden breeze the languid heart to cheer;
The fever swells and courses in our veins,
  Our comrade faints, who never yet knew fear;
Still we press onward, while no lip complains—
  Oh! for the strife, the strife, to calm this deep despair!

II.

Better the battle with uncounted foes
  Than this oppressive sickness, this dread weight;
Oh! grief, to perish thus, without repose,
  Sinking along the way side, 'neath a fate
That makes an obscure death the worst of woes,
  And the poor dying heart thrice desolate;
Denied on field of strife the eye to close,
  Where pride and hope may still the pangs of death abate.

* In this march, which was rendered unnecessary by a gallant achievement of the Navy, the sufferings of the Palmetto Regiment were very great. To this has been traced the terrible mortality which followed it, and which lamentably thinned their ranks before going into battle.

OUR PLACE WITHIN THE PICTURE.*

I.

"'Our place within the picture"—such place as oft of yore,
The sires, whose names we cherish still, in forward manhood
bore.
A thousand hearts of hope we bear, that leap to win a fame
As bright as that they left to us, which hallows still their name.
Give us our share of canvas, too, that when our children see,
They'll say, as we have felt and said: "Behold! such sires
had we!"
Our valor their inheritance—our deeds a guide for their's,
Framed in our nation's pictured life, and brightening still with
years!

II.

Our place within the picture that shows our nation's powers;
Our numbers few, a little space is all we ask for ours;
But doubt not we shall fill it well, nor faintly show through
shade,
Crouch'd in the background basely still in doubtful light dis-
play'd;
Our flag among the first to rise when fierce the battle goes—
Our shout of battle first to shake the hearts of gathering foes;
True to the name our fathers gave, shall be our pride as sons,
With a bright place in the picture, "near the flashing of the
guns."

* These were the words of Colonel Butler, in a letter to General Worth, imploring active service for the Palmetto Regiment. It had been their misfortune to lose the opportunity at Cerro Gordo, that battle having been fought while they were on their march to Alvarado, or recruiting at Vera Cruz.

WE'VE A RIGHT FROM ANCIENT VALOR.*

"We've a right from ancient valor,"
To the chief, our hero said—
To be first in ranks of danger
When the fiery bolt is sped;
Our soldiers pant for battle,
As the war-steed when he hears
The shrill summons of the trumpet,
And the cannon, at his ears!

The youth of my green banner
Are no serviles bought with gold;
They'd not lose the precious season
For the India's spoil untold;
Still they murmur, gathering round me:
"Who is he that danger shuns?
Let us seek the foe's strong places,
Near the flashing of his guns!"

"They have rights from ancient valor,"
And will make those rights their own;
They are children of the noblest
To our forest country known;
And the humblest of our people,
Still remembering whence he came,
Will fight on, as if his valor
Were for Carolina's fame!

* It was the urgent entreaty of Lieutenant-Colonel Dickinson, embodied in the letter of Colonel Butler to General Worth, to "be near the flashing of the guns." South Carolina might well claim "the right from ancient valor."

OH! SHARPER THE STING IN THE GRIEFS.

I.

OH! sharper the sting in the griefs that deplore him,
That he fell not in battle where fame might be won,
With the shouts of his comrades exultingly o'er him,
And the voice of his country proclaiming her son;
That with spirit as eager as any for glory,
No bugle sang wild in his ears as he died—
No drum beat the conquest, o'er fields black and gory,
Cheering life, as it fleets, with a promise of pride!

II.

But silent and sad, with each image of sorrow,
In the glooms of the camp, with disease at his heart,
Still vainly he sighs for the glorious to-morrow,
Which shall see his brave comrades to battle depart;
They will rush to the van when the storm-cloud is rising,
They will thrust the red steel to the heart of the foe,
Clamber up his high places, his cannon despising,
And pluck the bright honors of fame with each blow.

III.

While he, on his lone couch still destined to languish,
'Neath a struggle that pleases not pride to endure,
Still moans o'er the thought, full of bitterest anguish,
That tells him even death can no triumph secure;
No impulse of fight the death agony smothers,
No friends may exult while they weep o'er his name,
And the country that shouts o'er the deeds of his brothers,
Still forgets the poor victim that died without fame.

"THREE CHEERS FOR SOUTH CAROLINA!"

[As the Palmetto Regiment was filing past General Scott, on its way to the battle field of Churubusco, the veteran General raised his hat and cried to his Staff: "Gentlemen, three cheers for South Carolina!"]

"THREE cheers for Carolina!"—
The gallant band that hears,
Well knows the mighty chief that speaks
Will never shame those cheers;
They know the iron storm that waits
Their eager march across the plain,
But they will brave the worst of fates,
To hear that hero's voice again,
In cheers for Carolina!

II.

"Three cheers for Carolina!"—
What tale it tells, that cry,
Of valor proved in other fields
And names of chiefs that can not die!—
Of blood too often tried of yore,
To leave a doubt that these will seek
Worse fields than valor knew before,
That Fame shall still as proudly speak,
In cheers for Carolina!

THE WIDOW OF THE WARRIOR.

I.

They parted in tears, but the sorrow
  That spoke in that tender farewell,
Was tinged with a hope that still brighten'd
  The hues of each drop as it fell;
For how could love dream of such meeting,
  Or that one who so lately was blest,
Should lie coldly nor speak to her anguish,
  With her cheek pressing, pale, on his breast!

II.

She knew not one image of sorrow,
  When, at the first summons to strife,
She saw him go forth in his beauty,
  The model of manhood and life;
Ah! little the confident passion,
  That worshipp'd his beauty and grace,
Ever dreamed of that manhood in marble,
  That coldly receives her embrace

III.

She clings to the bier, nor will listen—
  While gazing on features so dear—
To the counsel that chides her entreaty,
  To the sense that can never more hear;
Though her kindred around her are weeping,
  Her love, still unwilling to part
With the dear one again in her keeping,
  Still fancies a pulse in his heart.

AND WHAT, WHEN HIS COUNTRY?

I.

And what, when his country is loud in his glory,
And the song of the minstrel is pour'd in his praise,
When the chronicle gives up its page to his story,
And eloquence glows with his deeds into blaze;
What voice of the heart shall enliven her sorrows,
Who sits by the lonely hearth brooding the past,
When hope had its tale of a thousand to-morrows,
Each happier than true love had render'd the last?

II.

Yes, pride shall be hers, that the heart whose devotion
Brought love's sweetest solace to share with her own,
Had a courage as firm in the battle's commotion,
And a life which she shared with his country alone;
She will glow with the voice that is loud in his honor,
She will feel that its praises are dear to his fame;
And the country whose need flung these sad weeds upon her,
Shall atone by the tribute it brings to his name!

III.

But vainly the song of the minstrel, deploring,
Shall teach that forgetfulness needed o'er all;
And vainly the cry of our eagle upsoaring
Shall soothe the deep sorrows that keep her in thrall;
E'en the voice that repeats of his deeds the proud story,
Must enliven the griefs it can never remove;
And the very same plaudit that rings with his glory,
Shall teach but too truly his loss to her love!

THE DEATH OF BUTLER.

I.

When Butler heard the signal
That show'd the battle nigh,
Though feeble on his couch he lay,
His spirit mounted high;
He buckled on his armor,
He mounted his good steed;
"Ho!" said he, "Carolinians,
I'm here with you at need."

II.

The signal rang for battle—
The voice of Shields arose:
"Look, men of the Palmetto,
Our foemen round us close;
The common laws of danger
Would teach us now to fly,
But we've a better lesson,
To break through them or die!"

III.

"We're ready now!" cried Butler,
"Our boys are few but true;
Upon them, Carolinians,
We've but to dare and do!"
Then rang the fearful volley,
Then came the fearful rush,
Then rose the shout of triumph,
And then the awful hush!

IV.

He fell—the steed of Butler—
His master rose again;
He fell—the gallant chief himself,
But not among the slain.
Once more he waved his banner,
And led his column on,
Then died, upon the glorious ground
His people's valor won!

"TELL ME," CRIED THE YOUTH.*

I.

"Tell me," cried the youth when dying,
"Tell me that I do not shame
That dear land that gave me being,
And my father's honor'd name;
Say, my General, that, in falling,
I was seeking still the strife,
Through the tempest unappalling,
For their honor staking life."

II.

Then the gallant chieftain, weeping,
O'er the dying youth, replied:
"By these eyes that speak my sorrow,
I shall speak your deeds with pride;

* Young Brooks of the Edgefield Company, when dying of his wounds, appealed to General Shields for his testimony in favor of his conduct, that it might be conveyed to his father and his country. It was with tears that Shield answered the entreaty, grieving bitterly that a youth so truly noble should be cut off in the very hour of his victory.

With the bravest, you have ever
   Been where raged the battle most;
In your fate, your country never
   Braver heart or champion lost."

III.

"Ah! the sting from death is taken,"
   Then the dying youth replied;
"Heart of youth might well be shaken,
   Dying thus in strength and pride;
But, in death, I do not perish,
   With this sweet assurance won,
That my sire and country cherish
   Proudest memories of their son!"

OH! STERN WAS THE VOICE.*

I.

Oh! stern was the voice of that anguish that bade him,
   The gray-headed sire, look forth for his son,
And welcome the form, on his shield where they laid him,
   For whom his old heart had its welcome alone;
Yet no voice answered fond to the cry of that feeling,
The pride of the past, and its dream both revealing,
That still to the ear of the dead one appealing,
   Declared, in the triumph, the hope that was gone!

* In writing this little poem, I had in my mind's eye the particular cases of my old and excellent friends Whitfield Brooks and General Cantey, both losers of young and promising sons in the battle fields of Mexico.

II.

How proud was that hope in the hour of their parting,
  When the young hero drew the sword flashing for fame!
No doubt in his soul, that the tears sudden starting,
  Could mingle the thought of that moment with blame!
Such pride, in the strength of his manhood, displaying,
As with sword and with sash his fine person arraying,
His young soul in arms, not a moment delaying,
  To rush to the battle field seeking a name!

III.

To fears of the foe and the combat a stranger,
  His race had been thus from their earliest hours—
Fearful only of shame and exulting in danger,
  As the mother of deeds and the nurse of their powers;
Alas! but too fondly the conquest pursuing,
He rush'd up the heights where the storm cloud was brewing;
But though stricken down by the red bolt of ruin,
  His hand waved his flag o'er the enemy's towers.

IV.

In his triumph he fell, in a strife that was glorious,
  The first on the ramparts where conquest was won;
He knew, ere he died, that his flag was victorious,
  And his dying shout cheer'd his brave followers on;
And his old sire glows with the glowing narration,
And his kindling eye gleams with the praise of the nation,
But, with night, he forgets all the glorious ovation,
  And in dreams he is calling: "My son! Oh! my son!"

THE HEAD OF THE FORLORN HOPE.*

I.

Do not forget, when loud the cannon pealing,
  Exults in dangers past and victories won,
How forth he sprang, when death around was dealing
  His fearful shafts, your own unhonored son!—
The humble name, the undistinguished station,
  Unsashed, unplumed, declare no hope of fame;
Death might secure a moment's approbation,
  But where the laurels for that lowly name?

II.

Yet, with the single motive of a spirit
  To whom the sight of danger hath its charms—
With active impulse, thoughtless of the merit,
  He hears with joy the combat's fierce alarms;
Hears but to answer, when, as sacrifices,
  To seek and brave the danger, came the call
For the adventurous few, to make the crisis,
  And, with forlornest hope, to die for all!

III.

Honor'd for aye, the heart so well devoted,
  Though lowly be the simple name he bears;
Still be his memory in our annals noted,
  Though cypress be the mournful wreath he wears;

---

* Something more is due to the leader of a Forlorn Hope, than he generally receives from posterity. Ordinarily, he perishes. It is in the full conviction that he is dedicated to fate, that he stands forth and offers himself a sacrifice. Yet how seldom is he remembered—his name, perhaps, not even given, and all the glory for which he has deliberately yielded himself to death, for the safety of the rest, merged in the single great name that commands the army.

Death found him first the angry torrent heading,
  Careering o'er the summits of the foe—
Hopeless himself, the way for others leading,
  For whom the column soars, the laurels blow.

THE RETURN OF THE PALMETTOS.

I.

Where move the gay Palmettos,
  That late went forth in pride,
Glorious in strength and stature,
  Brave soul'd and eagle-eyed?
Lo! wan and few returning,
  The relics of that band,
That bore our gay green banner
  In gladness through the land!

II.

How are their mighty fallen,
  On loftiest places slain,
As bearing up that ensign bright
  They never bear again!
They won their crowns of laurel
  Thrice dyed in bloody strife,
A wreath of bloom unfading—
  But paid for it with life!

III.

Their country's joy is shadow'd,
  As they who won the field,
Hear nought of our rejoicing,
  Each silent on his shield;

Above the noise of shouting,
  Lo! woman's wail is heard,
Each, in her home of mourning,
  Above the form preferr'd.

IV.

The wife of Kershaw sorrows,
  The widow o'er her slain;
And maids of Edgefield languish
  For youth beloved in vain;
While Barnwell's matron bending
  Above the cottage loom,
Still stains the woof with weeping
  Her first born's early doom!

THE DIRGE OF THE PALMETTO.

I.

Oh! mournfully—oh! very mournfully,
  Sound the returning bugles; we have won,
But in the shout that tells our victory
  Rings the sharp death-shriek of each gallant son;
It rises o'er the tumult of the field—
  It stays the shout of triumph; we deplore,
That, to the God of Battles, we must yield
  The brave, who to the fight shall go no more!
Mournfully still, oh! very mournfully,
The clarion's sudden plaint, the bugle's faint reply!

II.

They were among our noblest—with the fire
  Of generous youth still bounding in each heart;
We saw them hurry forth with keen desire,
  Burning for glory, eager to depart;
They bore aloft the ensign of our name,
  The flag made famous by our sires of yore,
And, as they vow'd, they freshen'd it with fame,
  Though to the battle they shall go no more!
Mournfully still—oh! very mournfully,
The music that declares their death in victory!

A WELCOME TO OUR BROTHER.

I.

A WELCOME to our brother,
  Home-returning from the strife,
He hath nobly won his laurels,
  In the fields that perill'd life;
He hath sought the front of battle,
  He hath borne him as became
A true son of Carolina,
  And our people's ancient fame.

CHORUS.

Thrice welcome to our brother,
  With a shout of three times three—
Hurrah, hurrah, hurrah, hurrah, hurrah, hurrah!
      Hurrah, hurrah!

II.

We have welcomes for our brother,
  From the depth of hearts that feel,
That his own, in peace or conflict,
  Hath been ever true as steel!
By his truth and love he won us,
  Till we gave him spear and shield,
And he brings them undishonor'd,
  With new trophies, from the field.

III.

O'er the plains of Churubusco,
  We behold him as he goes,
With our gallant young Palmettos,
  O'er the heads of humbled foes;
At Chapultepec's grim castle,
  At Contreras, and as well
Through the throes at *La Garita*,
  When the Aztec city fell!

IV.

Thrice welcome to our brother,
  Thus in peace and battle tried;
He hath crowned our name with honor,
  And we speak his name with pride;
Though in fields of foreign danger,
  Through long seasons he may roam,
In our hearts, no more a stranger,
  He shall still find "welcome home!"

SONNET.—SIT THEE BESIDE ME.

Sit thee beside me for awhile, and rest,
On the green marges of the slope, and hear,
As yon shy brooklet sends up to the ear
Its chaunt of murmurs, like a strain repress'd
By sobbings of the heart that pours it out!—
I mind me, dear one, it is now about
Some thirteen summers, since I laid me down
Beside this little streamlet, as I left,
Grieving, with boyhood's heart, my native town!
To this I now return—of youth bereft,
And thorns about my head in place of crown.
Then all was, "lo! the triumph!" in my breast,
My thought, heart, eye, on one achievement set!—
Now! all is changed save this poor rivulet.

SONNET.—I SAW IT IN MY DREAM.

I saw it in my dream! Oh! could I task
My sense again to slumber, nor awake
So long as the dear vision were in sight!
I will not do it so much wrong to make
My rude words show the picture thou dost ask:
Behold it in my passion!—a delight
Trembles through all my utterance! Oh! I feel,
In the devoted beatings of my heart,
That I should look enjoyment, nor appeal
To vain resource of language to impart
This vision of a most rare happiness,
That rapture, it would madden to reveal;—
Which song itself would render spiritless;
It was such sweet, such sad, heart-touching tenderness.

SONNET.—I WILL BREATHE MUSIC.

I WILL breathe music in the little bell
  That cups this flower, until it takes a tone
  For every feeling human heart hath known:
Though hearts their secrets do not often tell,
Mine shall be charms to win them. I will wake
  Strains which, though new to men, shall never fail
  To make them tremulous, tearful; an old tale
Shall clothe itself with newness for your sake.
Love will I win from friendship. The old lure
Will I make fresh, and all the new insure.
Beauty shall be no serpent to beguile,
  Nor faith a hollow mock; nor love a lie;
And there shall be no treachery in a smile,
  And on a sweet kiss hence shall no man die!

SONNET.—HERE ON THIS BANK.

HERE, on this bank of wooing violets,
  That the crush'd odor comes from, lay thee down,
  And listen to the Silence, and leaves blown,
Until thy overtask'd, sad heart forgets
  The sleepless struggle of yon busy town!
There, every passion sickens ere 'tis spent,
  Here, others follow ere the first are done,
Each, like its fellow, meetly innocent,
  Soul-sweetening, and most easy to be won!
And woman!—thou shalt see her as at first,
  When, on a bank like this, in Eden sleeping,
On sight of its lone habitant she burst,
  Suddenly bright, as heavenly rainbow leaping,
From the retiring cloud where it was nurst.

SONNET.—DELPHI.

Voiceless! No more the sacred oracle
Declares the will of fate! The iron tongue
Grew silent, when it could not speak her own,
And, with Parnassus, in dumb sympathy,
Cover'd her head with weeds! But these have wrung
A voice from out the silence which must spell
The children of the ages—and the Unknown,
Redressing the great Past, shall gather nigh—
A stranger, yet a worshipper—and tell
How fresh the echoes still, that once among
These gray rocks, rose to thunders—how the tone
That lost itself in these proud solitudes,
Took wing, and found new temples where it broods,
A God in exile, true, but not without a throne.

SONNET.—THESE ARE GOD'S.

These are God's blesséd ministers, methinks,
  These breezes whispering to the heart subdued,
So winningly, that still the sad ear drinks
  Their messages of mercy; and the mood
Grows chaste and unresentful—while the blight
  Passes from off the spirit that, but late,
Gloom'd with the gloomy progress of the night,
  And spoke defiance to the will of fate.
Comfort they bring with the submissive thought
  That teaches Sorrow still is the best friend,
And moves to bless the chastener, that has brought
  The heart to tremble and the knees to bend—
Counselling the better hope, that, born of fears,
Is nursed in trembling and baptized in tears.

SONNET.—THE SPIRITS THAT DO DRESS.

The spirits that do dress the flow'rs with dew,
And trip it on the green sward, by the moon,
And play fantastic tricks both late and soon,
When March with blossoms promises the Spring—
Have been about me in the merriest ring:
Methought among their forms were some I knew;
They came with hushing laughter—for I slept
Beneath our willows—slyly round me crept,
And prankt my brow with blossoms—in mine ear
Whispered the wildest dreams of elfin land,
Then, in a circle, dancing hand in hand,
Sang me a ditty from the Moon's own sphere!
Starting from slumber, in the dear delight
Of such a vision, it was gone from sight.

SONNET.—LOVE!—(Imitated from Old English.)

If Love had not an understanding eye,
If Love's eye had not comprehensive speech,
If Love were not a thing of memory,
Or if to aught but Love, Love aught could teach;
How much, sweet heart, have I said fruitlessly,
How much fond speech were thrown away on thee;
How much have both remember'd bootlessly,
How much have others seen who should not see;
How profligate our hearts of moments wasted;
How vain the fond expectancies that led;
How wild the dreams whose raptures sleep untasted;
How sad the sweet delusions which have fed;
The heart's whole being from this danger shrinks—
Yet Love is no such profligate, methinks!

SONNET.—THERE IS A MOOD.

THERE is a mood that sometimes makes us cry,
  In very weariness of soul: " 'Twere well,
Methinks, if I could lay me down and die!—
  There is no terror in the solemn knell
That ushers to the grave, which gently opes
  Its peaceful arms, and promises repose
From vexing strifes and still deceiving hopes,
  Friends failing, and the sleepless herd of foes."
And then we find similitude in things
  Beneath us, the poor leaf and flow'r which dread
The blight of winter, and the recoiling springs
  That shiver as the wind sweeps overhead!—
Thus fevering, till awakes the manlier mood,
When we go forth and conquer in warm blood.

SONNET.—OH! WHAT IS THERE OF MAGIC?

OH! what is there of magic in thy name,
  That thus my heart should tremble, though long years
Have fled since, following a delusive flame,
  I learn'd how little profit came from tears;
How great the shame of weakness; what the scorn
  Of Power at meek Devotion; and how vain,
  When Pride finds pleasure in inflicting pain,
To hope that nobler feelings may be born
In the tyrannic bosom? Shall it be
  That, from the Passion which has brought me shame,
  The sacrifice of hope and peace and fame,
The Fates deny me ever to go free?
Ah! wherefore love if thus? But Love reproves
The question, since he lives alone who loves!

SONNET.—BENEATH MY CHAMBER WINDOW.

Beneath my chamber window I recline,
  And all is still around me. Nature lies,
With her poor children sleeping. All, save mine,
  Are closed, the easily persuaded eyes!
  Sweet visions pass before them, such as rise
On childhood's innocent slumbers; *they* can sleep!
  Alas! why is it that we would be wise,
And in hard study and conclusions deep,
  Learn only of the precious gifts we lose,
  The sweet affections that we never use,
When we might live in them, and through their smiles
  Feel the sad Night pass o'er us with her dews,
As if, assuming all our lowlier toils,
  She held herself, alone, the privilege to weep.

SONNET.—ALAS! AND THIS IS ALL.

Alas! and this is all! and thus we toil
  In spirit, while the sweet repose of night
Gives respite to the happier crowds who moil
  While day yields labor its twelve hours of light—
Sweet rest to us denied—through worlds remote,
  Still piercing ever with the dreamer's flight,
  In nature's mockery oft, in reason's spite,
Wooing the vague creations of our thought—
Shaping out shrines for worship—realms of dream,
  That glitter on our wreck—receive our prayer
  To fling it back in echoes on our ear,
Such as the fiends, grown wild in hellish scheme,
  Delight to mingle with our songs of cheer,
  Startling the soul's best raptures with a sneer!

THY PAGE IS PURE AS YET.—[In an Album, 1826.]

Thy page is pure as yet—so be thy life;
And through the storms of time may they remain,
Thus pure; thy book unsullied with a stain,
Thyself still free from passion's madd'ning strife!
Yet if the hope thus breath'd for thee be vain,
If life's young barque must find a stormy sea,
Tost on the waves of doubt and grief and pain,
Fear at the prow, and wreck its destiny—
May the sweet hope, that softens sorrow's power,
Cheer thee and strengthen; be the comforter,
Beside thee, in the dark and perilous hour;
Teach thee that surer pathway to prefer,
Which storms invade not, where wild waters cease,
And skies are calm for aye, 'neath smiles of hallowing peace.

SONNET.—GOD GIVE ME STRENGTH!

God give me strength to struggle for the truth!
Truth is not easy in a world like this,
Where all is bias—whether curse or kiss;
And one is warp'd even in his tend'rest youth,
To a false cognizance, till all's amiss!
Where the heart's full of tenderness, then ruth,
Shrinks from stern justice, and we seek to soothe,
When we should ruffle! If there be a pride,
Goading ambition to achievement rare,
We tremble, lest the sneer of man should hiss,
And strive to please, when better 'twere to chide;
We think too much of men, and too much care
For the world's judgments! Help me, God, in this—
To be the thing I should be, though left bare!

SONNET.—THE RECORD SHOULD BE MADE.

The record should be made of each brave deed,
That brings us pride and freedom as its fruits;
So that, while tending on the vigorous shoots,
Our children may perpetuate the seed:
And, naught forgetting of the glorious past,
Lay good foundation in the future's womb,
So, when the hardy sire succumbs at last,
The emulous son shall still defend his tomb.
Thus chronicled, the mighty deed begets
Still mightier; and the column soaring high
Speaks histories the good son ne'er forgets!
He too will conquer; will not fear to die;
Heading the storm, will man the breach and prove
His valor not unworthy of his love.

SONNET.—THE OPEN SEA BEFORE ME.

The open sea before me bathed in light,
As if it knew no tempest; the near shore
Crown'd with its fortresses, all green and bright,
As if 'twere safe from carnage ever more;
And woman on the ramparts; while below
Girlhood, and thoughtless children bound and play
As if their hearts, in one long holiday,
Had sweet assurance 'gainst to-morrow's wo:
Afar, the queenly city, with her spires,
Articulate in the moonlight. Far above
The pale sad Hecate with still virgin fires,
Moans the lone state that never asks for love:
The hooded stars grow envious; while the seas
Roll up their tribute hymn of billow and breeze!

SONNET.—ANOTHER YET, AND YET ANOTHER.

Another yet, and yet another height,
  And still the last most wearisome! But, hark!
  Comes not, like blesséd starlight through the dark,
Hope's confident whisper, that, with sudden bright,
  Makes glad the landscape; cheers the spirit still;
  Mocks at small toil, o'er rocky plain or hill,
And sings a sweet assurance of the joy
  That waits and beckons at the cottage door?
How little then appears the day's annoy,
  And Bliss rewards us when the toil is o'er!
And if in arms that love us, we should tell
  Of the day's labor, wearisome and sad,
'Twill be in thanks and blessings, that so well
  It ended, in a night so bright and glad.

SONNET.—THIS FAERY VISION GLADDENS US.

This faery vision gladdens us no more,
  As in our days of childhood. It is gone—
The glory which in fancy's eye it wore,
  The crown of spiritual semblance it put on,
The lustre, and the holy tenderness,
And the weird music of its mystic lore,
  Appealing, as it were, to ancient ties
  With some past being, which we love not less,
Because beyond our memory's reach it lies.
And yet this soft and most capricious light,
  That sad and sinking star, these solemn woods,
And gushes of strange sounds within their shade,
Lift to fond thoughts and most superior moods,
While Oread glimpses beckon down the glade.

THERE IS A PALE AND SOLITARY STAR.

THERE is a pale and solitary star,
That, with a sudden but a sweet surprise,
Nightly, with little heed of bolt or bar,
Peeps in upon my couch and opes mine eyes.
The office of so pure a visitor
Must be for healing. Lovely was the thought
That, in the dreams of old astrologer,
The fate of star and man together wrought.
Nor, though this presence robs me of my rest,
And makes me sad with sleepless memories,
Shall it be curtain'd from my weary eyes:
As my twin-angel, blessing still and bless'd,
I welcome it, and still lament the night,
When storm or cloud denies it to my sight.

SONNET.—WE ARE A PART OF ALL.

WE are a part of all things that we see,
Share in a common nature, and are taught
By what they suffer; with their feelings fraught,
Are bound by their captivity; or free,
When they are wanton. Earth and sea and air
Master us through our sympathies. We share
The elements around us, till we flee
From our own nature to a converse strange
With other natures; find in rock and tree
Mute friends that teach, and never disagree;
Rebuke not, yet exhort; and so we range
Capricious as the winds that stir the sea,
Constant in nothing save the love of change.

SONNET.—SPIRIT THAT DWELLEST.

Spirit that dwellest in the opening flower,
And bathest in the morning's earliest dew,
Thou that hast wings to hurry on the hour,
And makest that lovely which were else but true ;
Yielding fresh odor to the hungering sense,
Making the thought from common things to spring,
So that the zephyr grows to eloquence,
And, when alighting on capricious wing,
Bringing rare song and homage to the rose,
Thou giv'st such ravishing sweetness to his tone,
That the cold fountain in the wood o'erflows,
And falling leaves make music like his own ;
With a new soul the inanimate nature glows,
And the fond thought forgets that love had ever foes.

NOT BLIND TO MINE OWN WEAKNESS.

Not blind to mine own weakness, which lacks power
To save, though things most precious in mine eye
Sink, needing help, and vainly to me cry,
I cry to thee, O God! in this dark hour!
Spare us in mercy! Let thy chastening blows
Fall lightly on the bruised and suffering heart,
Already desolate! I have seen depart
All my life's dear ones; and a herd of woes
Have wolved on mine affections, till I move
Almost alone i' the forest. To my years
Be merciful; and to the woman's tears
Accord the one dear life that's left her love!
Spare it to us, even while thou mak'st it thine—
For the poor mother's sake, if not for mine!

SONNET.—I DO REMEMBER ONE.

I do remember one, a noble youth,
  Of wondrous faculty; a genius rare;
  Enthusiasms of the upper air,
And soul forever struggling for the truth.
We went together in our school-boy days,
  Loving and wondering; he with highest aim,
  Already having a vague dream of fame,
And winning, as he went, a voice of praise.
For him the noblest height had been decreed,
  Were he left free for conflict. But in vain!
  They bound him, a born eagle, in a chain
Of miserable custom; bade him feed
At common stalls. Thus lived he, day by day,
Till at the last he grew imbruted even as they.

THOU HAST ENAMORED ME.

Thou hast enamored me of woodland life,
  Good shepherd, for thou showest me, in thy faith,
  More than thy argument, how free of scaith
Thy cottage—how secure against the strife
That beats on prouder dwellings. So I glean
  Thy secret from thee, of true happiness,
  Inbred content, and quiet humbleness,
That striving only at the golden mean,
Can never be o'erthrown by soaring high,
And vexeth not the glare of envious eye.
Thy blessings are of that serener kind,
  Which, as they rouse no passions up, must be
  Liked to that breeze benign that strokes the sea
From rages into murmurs. No rude wind
Disturbs thy placid waters, and deforms
The glory of thy peace, with its unreckoning storms.